MISSION COLLEGE
LEARNING RESOURCE SERVICES

Indexed in
General Lit

19**75**-

D0699709

E   Studies in Italian
184   American social
.18   history : essays in
S82   honor of Leonard
        Covello.

3 1215 00010 9956

MISSION COLLEGE
LEARNING RESOURCE SERVICES

STUDIES IN ITALIAN AMERICAN SOCIAL HISTORY

Essays in Honor of
LEONARD COVELLO

Leonard Covello in Sicily, late Spring, 1975

STUDIES IN ITALIAN AMERICAN SOCIAL HISTORY

Essays in Honor of
LEONARD COVELLO

EDITED BY
FRANCESCO CORDASCO

ROWMAN AND LITTLEFIELD
Totowa, New Jersey

Published 1975 by Rowman and Littlefield

COPYRIGHT 1975 BY FRANCESCO CORDASCO

All rights reserved. No part of this book may be reproduced or translated in any form, by print, photoprint, microfilm or any other means without written permission from the publisher.

Library of Congress Cataloging in Publication Data

Cordasco, Francesco, 1920–   **ed.**

Main entry under title:

Studies in Italian American social history.

"Handlist of selected writings by Leonard Covello": p.
Bibliography: p.
Includes index.
CONTENTS: Cordasco, F. Leonard Covello and the Casa Italiana Educational Bureau: a note on the beginnings of systematic Italian-American studies.—D'Antonio, W. V. Ethnicity and assimilation: a reconsideration. [etc.] 1. Italian Americans—Addresses, essays, lectures. 2. Italian Americans—Social conditions—Addresses, essays, lectures. 3. Italian Americans—Social life and customs—Addresses, essays, lectures. 4. Covello, Leonard. I. Covello, Leonard. II. Cordasco, Francesco, 1920–
E184.I8S82   301.45′15′1073   75–14462
ISBN 0–87471–705–1

Mass emigration to the Americas, which brought hundreds and thousands of Italian immigrants into the United States, changed all previous concepts of Italians, as far as Americans were concerned. It was indeed difficult to associate the incoming Italian immigrants of the period between 1880 and 1910 with the glories of the Renaissance or what may be conveniently called Italian culture. To Americans, watching southern Italian immigrants as they disembarked by the thousands at ports of entry, or observing them at work or in their every-day activities, there was nothing about them that would make the previous concepts of Italy and Italians applicable to them. This contrast between the previously held concepts of Italians and the appearance of an unexpectedly strange group of people resulted in a reaction of antagonism toward them. Conflicts, which were unavoidable at the first contact, grew in intensity and in frequency, as interaction between Italian immigrants and the American environment increased.

Leonard Covello, *The Social Background of
the Italo-American School Child* (1944)

Table of Contents

Preface

In this period of heightened attention to the Italian-American experience (with the concomitant study of the Italian past in the United States, itself part of the rediscovery of ethnic identity in America), it is singularly appropriate that a *festschrift* honor Leonard Covello (1887–   ) who has a special place in the annals of Italian-American historiography. It was Leonard Covello who more than anyone else understood the need for the study of the Italian experience in the United States; and it was he who strove for decades to direct the energies of the Italian community to critical assessments of its needs and prospects in an American society essentially indifferent and hostile to Italian immigrant aspirations. If Leonard Covello's greatest contribution was a half-century of educational service in urban schools (with the creation of a successful community oriented school in the Italian ghetto of East Harlem, New York City), he was equally a social historian (as his massive *Social Background of the Italo-American School Child* affirms), and a social reform activist in the traditions of the pre-World War II melioristic progressivism whose dynamics animated both hope and evolving promise. Above all, Leonard Covello is a protean figure whose long life and multiplicity of identities with the changing fortunes of the Italian-American community make him both a witness to, and a surrogate for, the Italian-American past.

This *festschrift* is long overdue. When I initially proposed it over a decade ago, a host of forces precluded its assembly: academic contexts were inhospitable to Italian-American studies (at best, American ethnic historiography, unsystematic in form, did not encourage the study of the Italian-American past); Italian-American academicians were rarely encountered in the colleges and universities (a phenomenon not unanticipated and largely due to the doleful exclusion of minority peoples);[1] and the

---

[1] An interesting commentary on the continuing discrimination is *Status of Italian-Americans in the City University of New York* (New York: Association of Italian-American Faculty of the City University of New York, 1974). "This report will statistically demonstrate that the Italian-American has been subjected to *de facto* discrimination in the City University system. Despite the historical length of time that the Italian-Americans have been a major contributing group in the New York City community and despite their status as the second largest minority group, their progress in and through CUNY has been slow and disproportionate." (*loc. cit.*, p. 1)

pejorative connotations of the past treatment of Italians in American society largely dissuaded Italian-Americans from a study of their antecedent conditions and experiences.[2] That it has been assembled now is due, no doubt, to the attenuation of some of the forces noted above; but it would be presumptuous to draw from this the conclusions that Italian-American studies will prosper in the colleges (or for that matter, ethnic studies generally), and that Italian-Americans will eagerly support the study of their past and present conditions: these matters remain very complex and are related to the intricate set of dynamics which animate ethnicity within the socio-political *milieu* of the modern state.[3]

It is hardly necessary, here, to recite an account of Leonard Covello's life; this he has done himself in a sensitively poignant autobiography, itself a richly detailed portrait of Italian immigrant life in the New York City East Harlem ghetto.[4] But some biographical data are appropriate. Leonard Covello was born on November 26, 1887 in Avigliano (Potenza), Italy, and brought to the United States by his emigrating parents in 1895 who settled in East Harlem. Leonard Covello's life (and the forces which influenced it) are inextricably linked to East Harlem, an immigrant enclave located in the northeast sector of Manhattan Island, New York City (the 1930 census indicated a total of 89,000 Italians of first and second generation living in East Harlem).[5] It was here that he went to school (P.S.

[2] As late as 1938/1943, the Yale University Institute of Human Relations sponsored studies of Italian-Americans *vis à vis* their intractability as an unassimilable group, and their special needs as a foreign group. See Irvin L. Child, *Italian or American? The Second Generation in Conflict* (New Haven: Published for the Institute of Human Relations by Yale University Press, 1943. Reissued with an introduction by F. Cordasco, New York: Russell & Russell, 1970); Phyllis H. Williams, *South Italian Folkways in Europe and America: A Handbook for Social Workers, Visiting Nurses, School Teachers, and Physicians* (New Haven: Published for the Institute of Human Relations by Yale University Press, 1938. Reissued with an introductory note by F. Cordasco, New York: Russell & Russell, 1969). Protestants assembled a major ministry to Italian immigrants who were considered "a negative force in American life as long as they adhered to the Catholic faith." See, Salvatore Mondello, "Baptist Churches and Italian Americans," *Foundations: A Baptist Journal of History and Theology*, vol. 16 (July/September, 1973), pp. 222-238.

[3] See, generally, Nathan Glazer and Daniel P. Moynihan, "Why Ethnicity?" *Commentary*, vol. 58 (October, 1974), pp. 33-39; and Nathan Glazer, "Ethnicity and the Schools," *Ibid.*, vol. 58 (September, 1974), pp. 55-59. See also, Rudolph Vecoli, "The Italian Americans," *The Center Magazine* (July/August, 1974), pp. 31-43.

[4] Leonard Covello [with Guido D'Agostino], *The Heart Is the Teacher* (New York: McGraw-Hill, 1958). Reissued with an introduction by F. Cordasco (Totowa, N.J.: Littlefield, Adams, 1970). [*Teacher in the Urban Community: A Half Century in City Schools*] An essentially biographical study is Robert Peebles, *Leonard Covello: An Immigrant's Contribution to New York City* (Unpublished Ph.D. dissertation, New York University, 1967).

[5] For East Harlem, see F. Cordasco and R. Galattioto, "Ethnic Displacement in the Interstitial Community: The East Harlem [New York City] Experience," *Phylon: The Atlanta University Review of Race & Culture*, vol. 31 (Fall, 1970), pp. 302-312.

No. 83 and Morris High School), and here that he was to spend a near quarter-century (1934–1956) as principal of Benjamin Franklin High School. Following graduation from Columbia College (B.S., 1911), Leonard Covello served as a teacher of French and Spanish at De Witt Clinton High School (his teaching began as early as 1913), and from 1926–1934, he served at De Witt Clinton as Chairman of the Department of Italian. It was from De Witt Clinton in 1934 that he went on to the principalship of Benjamin Franklin High School. As early as 1930 he had matriculated for the Ph.D. at New York University, and he achieved the degree in 1944 (Educational Sociology), depositing as his thesis, *The Social Background of the Italo-American School Child*, the massive socio-cultural chronicle which had taken over a decade to write.[6] Between 1929 and 1942, Dr. Covello taught as an adjunct professor at New York University where his course "The Social Background and Educational Problems of the Italian Family in America" represented the earliest systematic enquiry (at the university level) of Italian family mores in the United States.[7]

Leonard Covello touched the life of the Italian community in New York City in a multiplicity of ways: there was virtually no activity organized by Italians in which Dr. Covello did not participate. As early as 1910, he (with John Shedd) organized the Lincoln Club of Little Italy in East Harlem. At De Witt Clinton High School, a *Circolo Italiano* was established as early as 1914 under Dr. Covello's sponsorship; and he participated in the work of the Italian League for Social Service (organized in 1915), and the Young Men's Italian Educational League (organized, 1916), energetically ambitious early efforts to improve the lot of Italian-Americans. From its inception in 1912, Dr. Covello served as vice-president of the Italian Teachers Association [New York City], a major force in stimulating Italian language study; and he was the guiding force behind the Italian Parents Association (organized, 1927) which afforded a bridge between the schools and the Italian community. It was Dr. Covello's strategic deployment of the influence of the Order Sons of Italy which helped lead in 1922 to the New York City Board of Education granting parity to Italian with other modern languages in the city schools. And there were continuing involvements and participations: in the work of the Italian Educational League; the Italy-America Society; the Casa Italiana Educa-

---

[6] The work was finally published in 1967 and reissued in 1972. Leonard Covello, *The Social Background of the Italo-American School Child: A Study of the Southern Italian Family Mores and Their Effect on the School Situation in Italy and America.* Edited and with an Introduction by F. Cordasco (Leiden, The Netherlands, E. J. Brill, 1967; Totowa, N.J.: Rowman and Littlefield, 1972).

[7] See Appendix I, *infra.*

tional Bureau; and the Istituto di Cultura Italiana (later, the Casa Italiana of Columbia University); and it was Dr. Covello who provided the major impetus for the founding of the American Italian Historical Association in the mid-1960's (whose operating expenses he assumed for several years in a lonely vigil passed in an East Harlem brownstone, as though awaiting the Italian community, long since gone, to be reborn).[8]

The essence of all of these experiences is distilled in Dr. Covello's remarks following his acceptance of the Meritorious Award of the State Department of the State of New York. In speaking of his long tenure at De Witt Clinton High School, he observed:

The Italian Department at the De Witt Clinton High School began with one class in 1920 and by 1928, had a register of 1,000 students with a full four year course, and two 4th year classes. Cooperating with the Italian Teachers Association, parity for the Italian language was established in 1922 after a ten year campaign. For during that period school authorities felt that having Italian students study the Italian language would segregate them from other students and retard their "Americanization"—an old and often repeated story—an idea with which we very definitely took issue.

The Italian Department was not only concerned with the study of the Italian language and with the appreciation of the culture of Italy, but also, through its club activities, sponsored many Italian programs in the Italo-American communities of the city. It put on performances of Italian plays, music and folk dances in settlement houses, churches, schools and Italian Society centers. At these performances the students assumed the important role of speaking to the parents, urging them to keep their children in school to achieve at least a high school diploma, and stressing the importance of having their children study the Italian language. Some of these students were trained to *teach English* to Italian immigrants and to help them obtain their American citizenship papers in centers in East Harlem and on the lower East Side of the city.

The alumni and senior students of the Department established *Help Classes* for the younger students who were having a difficult time maintaining themselves in High School. Home visiting was also carried on by older students and teachers.

In 1929 the Department of Italian created the first Italian Parent Teachers Association at De Witt Clinton even before the high school itself had a Parent Teachers Association.

A Department and Club magazine *Il Foro* was launched and students were given the opportunity to carry on this very valuable activity.

The purpose of all these varied activities was to stimulate the young Italo-American student not only to *aspire* and to *achieve* for his own personal advancement, but also to give him an opportunity to *serve*.

In the course of these activities, we all gained a great deal of insight into the problems that Italo-Americans were facing in our city—in the *"Little Italies"* of

---

[8] Dr. Covello, over the years, collected reports, papers, correspondence, and memorabilia which touch on (and in some instances chronicle) the history of these groups and organizations. The *Covello Papers*, which are in my possession, will be deposited in an appropriate archives devoted to the study of the Italian-American experience.

that period. So that when Benjamin Franklin High School was organized, there was already the conviction that for this school to carry out an effective educational program, it had to involve itself in the life of the community. So we attempted to create a Community-Oriented—a Community-Centered School.[9]

In a somewhat belated tribute, Columbia University conferred its "Medal for Distinguished Service" on Dr. Covello. Although the laconic commendation studiously avoided the use of words like "immigrant" or "Italian," the tenor of its message was clear—the university was honoring a distinguished alumnus whose professional life had been spent in the service of the immigrant poor: "Declared by generations of his professional peers to be one of New York City's greatest educators, having demonstrated a quarter of a century ago that a large urban high school can serve its whole community; a man who throughout his career as teacher, principal and consultant has demonstrated the vitality of our great ideal of equal, excellent, integrated education for people of all races, creeds and conditions: For your tireless and continuing efforts to bring schools and communities together in the service of all children and youth, Teachers College [Columbia University] confers upon you its Medal for Distinguished Service."[10]

I deeply appreciate the contributions which distinguished academicians have made to this volume. When invited, each was quick to respond, affirming the high esteem in which Dr. Leonard Covello was held; and Professor Jerre Mangione's letter of acceptance contains a tribute to Dr. Covello whose sentiment is universally entertained: "He personifies all the fine qualities that are ideally found in a man: a strong sense of humanitarianism and social responsibility, which can only come from love of mankind, as well as the ability and willingness to express that sense in concrete terms."

This volume is a collection of original essays on the multifaceted Italian experience in the United States; and the papers are as diverse as this experience has been: included are papers on conflict, acculturation and assimilation; on Italian immigrants in Louisiana's sugar parishes; on anti-Fascist reactions in the United States; on the Italian language press; on the Italian immigrant woman; on early Italian political refugees; on Philadelphia's Italian community; and on the contemporary patterns of Italian emigration. I have contributed an overview of Leonard Covello's early efforts at systematic study of the Italian-American experience in his Casa Italiana Educational Bureau. Included also are Dr. Covello's detailed

---

[9] The text of Dr. Covello's remarks was entered into the *Congressional Record* by the late Senator Robert F. Kennedy. (*Congressional Record*, 90th Congress, First Session, May 16, 1967)

[10] [Leonard Covello] Teachers College, Columbia University. Medal for Distinguished Service. June 2, 1970.

syllabus for his New York University seminar on "The Social Background and Educational Problems of the Italian Family in America" [1929], and his "Outline for Study of Cultural Change in an Italian Community" [*circa* 1934], both of which are invaluable conspectuses. I have added, too, a handlist of Dr. Covello's major writings, and a general bibliography which serves (beyond the documentation in the papers) as an introduction to the vast resources which the Italian-American experience has generated.

In 1972, Leonard Covello accepted an invitation from Danilo Dolci, the Sicilian social reformer, to serve as a consultant to Dolci's Center for Study and Action in western Sicily where the Center is waging a militant crusade against disease, unemployment, hunger, illiteracy, and violence. In his frequent letters to me, Dr. Covello talks of the wondrous excitement and challenge of his work in Sicily (*e.g.*, [September 5, 1974] "I have been in Ispica twice to help create a Geriatric Center, a *first* in southern Italy. Once this has been going for a year, we plan a service for migrants and their families.") These Sicilian years are, for Leonard Covello, the fulfillment of a life's grand design spent in the service of humanity.

FRANCESCO CORDASCO
West New York, N.J.
November, 1974

Contributors

FRANCESCO CORDASCO is Professor of Educational Sociology at Montclair
State College, and has taught at City University of New York, the
University of Puerto Rico, and New York University. Professor Cordasco has published numerous reviews and articles in professional
journals, and is the author of books on ethnicity and social class
stratification in American education; on educational sociology; and
on urban education, and the immigrant child. Among his books, those
dealing with Italians include *Italians in the United States: A Bibliog-
raphy*; *The Italians: Social Backgrounds of an American Group*;
*The Italian-American Experience: An Annotated and Classified
Bibliographical Guide*; and (editor), *The Italian Community and Its
Language in the United States*. Dr. Cordasco served as Advisory
Editor, *The Italian-American Experience*, 39 vols. (Arno Press/New
York Times, 1975).

WILLIAM V. D'ANTONIO is Professor of Sociology, and Chairman, Department of Sociology, University of Connecticut. He has taught at
the University of Notre Dame, and the University of Michigan, and
is serving as Executive Secretary, Society for the Scientific Study of
Religion. His publications include (co-editor), *Power and Democracy
in America*; *Religion, Revolution and Reform: New Forces for Change
in Latin America*; (co-author), *Influentials in Two Border Cities*;
Sociology: Human Society; and *Female and Male: Dimensions of
Human Sexuality*.

FRANCIS A. J. IANNI is Professor of Education and Director of the Horace
Mann-Lincoln Institute of the Teachers College at Columbia Uni-
versity. Dr. Ianni has served as Associate Commissioner for Research
and Director of Educational Research for the United States Office of
Education. His books include *A Family Business: Kinship and Social
Control in Organized Crime*; and *Black Mafia*.

JERRE MANGIONE is Professor of English Literature at the University of
Pennsylvania, and director of the University's creative writing program. He has taught at Bryn Mawr College, and served as visiting
professor at the Rome Campus of Trinity College. His many books

include *Mount Allegro*; *The Ship and the Flame*; *Reunion in Sicily*; *Night Search*; *Life Sentences for Everybody*; *A Passion for Sicilians: The World Around Danilo Dolci*; *America Is Also Italian*; and *The Dream and the Deal: The Federal Writers' Project, 1935–1943* which was nominated for the National Book Award in History.

PELLEGRINO NAZZARO is Professor of History, and Chairman, Department of History, Rochester Institute of Technology. The author of many scholarly articles, Dr. Nazzaro's *The History of Fascism and Anti-Fascism in America: 1922–1945* is scheduled for early publication.

HUMBERT S. NELLI is Associate Professor of History at the University of Kentucky. His publications include *Italians in Chicago, 1880–1930: A Study in Ethnic Mobility*, and many articles in scholarly journals. Dr. Nelli served as a member of the Editorial Board for *The Italian-American Experience*, 39 vols. (Arno Press/New York Times, 1975).

MICHAEL PARENTI is Associate Professor of Political Science at the State University of New York (Albany). The author of books and articles on ethnic politics, American public policy and foreign policy, Dr. Parenti's most recent book is *Democracy for the Few*, a critical study of the American political process.

JOANNE PELLEGRINO is an historian for the National Park Service, Department of the Interior, in New York City. Miss Pellegrino is a member of the Executive Council of the American Italian Historical Association, and is an active member of the America-Italy Society, and the Istituto per la Storia del Risorgimento Italiano.

ANDREW ROLLE is Cleland Professor of History at Occidental College (Los Angeles). In 1970 and 1971, Dr. Rolle was a Resident Scholar at the Rockefeller Foundation Research Center at Bellagio, Italy. His many books include *The Road to Virginia City*; *California: A History*; *The Lost Cause: Confederate Exiles in Mexico*; *The Immigrant Upraised: Italian Adventurers and Colonists in an Expanding America*; and *The American Italians: Their History and Culture*.

REV. NICHOLAS JOHN RUSSO is Professor of Sociology and Anthropology at Cathedral College (New York), and [Brooklyn] Diocesan Coordinator of the Apostolate for Italian Immigrants. He has served as editor of *Il Crociato*, a bilingual Catholic weekly. Dr. Russo is serving as Director of the Italian Board of Guardians of Brooklyn, and as Director of the Ferrini Welfare League of Queens, charitable organizations which administer to social needs of Italian families and their children.

JEAN ANNE SCARPACI is Associate Professor of History at Towson State College (Baltimore), and a member of the Executive Council of the American Italian Historical Association. Dr. Scarpaci is the author of scholarly articles on the Italian immigrant experience, and is currently engaged in a project on "Oral History: Baltimore's Ethnic Communities."

CLEMENT L. VALLETTA is Associate Professor of English, and Chairman, Department of English, King's College (Wilkes-Barre, Pa.). A member of the American Studies Association, Dr. Valletta is the author of articles on American social history. Currently, he is Director of a project funded under the Ethnic Heritage Act, *i.e.*, "A Study of Ethnic Minorities in Northeast Pennsylvania." Professor Valletta is readying for publication *A Study of Americanization in Carneta: Italian American Identity Through Three Generations*.

RICHARD A. VARBERO is Assistant Professor of History, State University of New York (New Paltz). A specialist in social, urban, and immigration history, Dr. Varbero has published a wide range of scholarly articles. His *Urbanization and Assimilation: A Study of Philadelphia's Italians, 1918–1932* is scheduled for early publication.

JOSEPH VELIKONJA is Associate Professor of Geography at the University of Washington. Dr. Velikonja has written widely on the demography of the Italian immigrant in the United States, and on the patterns of Italian migration. Professor Velikonja is author of *Italians in the United States*, a pioneer bibliography on the Italian-American experience.

VALENTINE ROSSILLI WINSEY is Associate Professor of Psychology at City University of New York (John Jay College), and has served as a consultant to the Institute of Educational Development, New York City Board of Education. Dr. Winsey has taught at Pace University, New School for Social Research, and Seton Hall University, and is the author of a wide range of articles in scholarly journals.

STUDIES IN
ITALIAN AMERICAN
SOCIAL HISTORY

Essays in Honor of
LEONARD COVELLO

FRANCESCO CORDASCO

Leonard Covello and the Casa Italiana Educational Bureau

A Note on the Beginnings of
Systematic Italian-American Studies

The vigorous study of the Italian-American experience in the last decade is unusual in one respect: it is virtually a new phenomenon as a systematic scholarly enquiry, without those antecedents which would have been expected for an immigrant community so long resident in the United States. That the 1960's should have witnessed so energetic an attention to the Italian-American presence and its history is not unrelated to the new ethnic consciousness which accompanied the turbulent events of the 1960's, to the Civil Rights movement, to the "minority" statuses defined by HEW (which excluded the descendants of white European immigrants), and to the complex reactions to a concatenation of events compressed within so restricted a time frame.[1]

If Italian-Americans were unaware of their history in the United States, the 1960's compelled its attention, and the new ethnic consciousness enveloped Italian-Americans as it did other ethnic communities; at best, the *risorgimento* of an American *Italianità* is a very complicated phenomenon to understand. If the ethnic resurgence of the 1960's is in part an explanation, the improvement of the condition of the Italian community (both its proletarianization and its embourgeoisment) in the post World War II period made practicable the study of the antecedents of an Italian-American presence: put another way, Italian-Americans, until very recently, lacked the resources (the leisure and the inclination), the security, and an American-born professoriat which would prompt the study of their past. Certainly no systematic investigations of the Italian-American past were undertaken in that period from the beginnings of great migrations (*circa* 1890) to the near mid-20th century.[2] Against this background, the short-lived Casa Italiana Educational Bureau, launched by Leonard Covello in the early 1930's, has a special significance.

The Casa Italiana of Columbia University was formally opened in 1927 as "a center of Italian culture in America under the auspices of Columbia University." It had largely been built with money raised in the Italian

1

community (with generous support from the Paterno and Campagna families).[3] Between 1930 and 1940, Casa's director was Giuseppe Prezzolini (an expatriate northern Italian), Professor of Italian at the University, and largely without any meaningful awareness of the life of the impoverished Italian community of the City.

It was not unexpected that Leonard Covello should have regarded the Casa Italiana as the appropriate auspices under which an Educational Bureau (whose formation he had proposed in the early 1930's) should function. But the University's Casa had other more traditionally academic interests. At best, the Casa offered Leonard Covello modest facilities to house his proposed Bureau; Giuseppe Prezzolini consented to be named one of the Bureau's directors: but neither the Casa Italiana nor Prezzolini participated (or, for that matter, encouraged) the work of the Bureau. It could not have been otherwise. An Italian professoriat (largely engaged in language instruction) had appropriated the Casa Italiana for their own interests: separated by social class and origins from the teeming Italian masses of the City, these erstwhile Italian expatriate academicians (and non-Italians associated with the Casa) would not have understood what Leonard Covello proposed for the work of his Bureau, and had they understood, their reaction would have been one of disinterest and disinclination, if not disapproval.

Leonard Covello organized the Casa Italiana Educational Bureau in May, 1932. Housed in two small rooms at the Casa Italiana, its financial support derived from the Federal Writers' Project which had been set up by the United States Government as part of the Works Progress Administration: as such it was a small part of that chapter in American sociopolitical history which saw needy writers, actors, artists and musicians put to work as WPA head Harry Hopkins remarked, "because they've got to eat just like other people."[4] The CIEB was, of course, a very small part of the WPA and its Federal Writers' Project; additional support came from the Italian government which contributed $3000, and a benefit held on the transatlantic liner, Rex, raised another $6000. In all, very modest support for what Leonard Covello planned. If financial support from the Italian-American community was expected to be small (the economic depression and the plight of Italian-Americans in the 1930's explain this), an unanticipated difficulty arose in the hostility in academic communities to the Casa Italiana, which was considered to be under Fascist domination. (Covello notes: "There was hesitation in assigning personnel to the Casa because it was considered a Fascist stronghold.")[5] Leonard Covello, nonetheless, proceeded undaunted.

In late 1933 (with the work of CIEB underway for a year and a half), Covello prepared a brief descriptive bulletin which outlined the purposes and programs of the Bureau. At the outset, he noted that "where the Italian immigrant is concerned, the assimilative process has been retarded partly because of lack of intelligent handling on the part of the larger American community and partly by the Italian community itself." He further observed:

> The American community could not, or would not, see the problems that were being created. It is also reasonable to conclude that the Italian, because he considered himself a transient, failed to become conscious of his broader social responsibilities. There was no real development of an immigrant community— it was rather an agglomeration of numerous disjointed groupings. The genius for leadership, which the Italian has exercised thru the ages was given little chance to express itself. Wholesome social forces within the groups were never integrated to a common program of ministering to the varied needs of an immigrant people.
>
> The need for unification and coordination of all kinds of educational work in Italian-American communities is therefore a pressing matter. The policy of drifting and of short-sighted opportunism has been all too dominant in shaping the direction of Italian-American community life. The urgent need for some central educational organization has been felt, recognized, discussed, wished for, and longed for on the part of a great many social-minded individuals of Italian origin and others who have understood the significance of the question. In this report on the need for and purpose of the Bureau, we cannot treat this matter as fully as it deserves to be treated. We shall return to this argument in subsequent bulletins because we feel not enough intelligent public discussion has taken place on this very vital subject.

The purposes of the CIEB were very ambitiously proposed:

> The purposes of the Bureau may be listed under three categories:
> 1. The Bureau will be a *fact finding* organization. Its purpose is to gather and present social and educational facts for all agencies and individuals to whom such information may be of interest and value.
> 2. The Bureau will serve as a medium for *centralization of efforts* directed toward social and cultural advancement of the Italian-American.
> 3. The Bureau will formulate and initiate a *promotional* program of educational and social activities. To this end it will concern itself with the establishment and guidance of similar organizations throughout the United States.[6]

Almost from its initiation, the CIEB undertook a number of projects "in laying a sound foundation for the larger aspects of its work." It began a campaign "for the diffusion of the Italian language by utilizing the educational elements in the Italian communities, as well as those elements in American life that show a desire to cooperate in this movement." It defined a number of reference and research areas and began the accumulation of data: (a) a study of the Italian population in New York City; (b) a study of the disintegrative and disruptive forces in the Italian-American communities of New York City (*e.g.*, retardation, truancy, and juvenile delinquency); (c) a study of the Italian language press in the

United States; and (d) "a comprehensive list of reference material as well as a bibliography on immigration and problems created by the immigrant in America with special reference to the Italian group." And it organized a speakers' group which "will concern itself with Italian-American educational problems and will be at the service of any cultural or educational organization."[7]

Beyond the problem of continuing financial support for the CIEB (and the related encouragement necessary for success from the Italian community and the larger American community), Covello needed staff for the Bureau's ambitious projects. For the most part this staff was recruited from the WPA bureaucracy (technically, from the Emergency Work Bureau and the Works Division of the Department of Public Welfare, New York City), and Covello acknowledged to me that "I got the workers assigned to the Bureau because of my close friend Walter Pettit who trusted me." Pettit, who was an assistant director of the New School of Social Work, evidently exercised some considerable influence in the City WPA structure, and he served nominally as a consultant to the CIEB.

There was, of course, no Italian-American professoriat of any size to whom Covello could have turned. The consultants who served the CIEB were largely non-Italian: they included, among others, Florence G. Cassidy (National Institute of Immigrant Welfare), Robert E. Chaddock (Columbia University), Frederick E. Croxton (Columbia University), George W. Kirchwey (New School of Social Work), Walter W. Pettit (New School of Social Work), Sophia M. Robison (Welfare Council), Frederic M. Thrasher (New York University), and Bessie B. Wessel (Connecticut College for Women). With the exception of Dr. Pettit and Professor Thrasher,[8] it would appear that their consultancies were largely honorific: itself understandable and not unusual given the period of time (the early 1930's), and the absence of Italian academic cadres from which Covello could have drawn. As to working staff and contributors, Covello was most fortunate: among them were included indefatigable investigators, *e.g.*, Jay Beck, John D'Alesandre, Marie A. Lipari, Isadore S. Meyer, Genoeffa Nizzardini, and William B. Shedd.

In July, 1934, Covello reiterated the aims of the CIEB: by this time the Bureau had published a number of *Bulletins*; it had begun the accumulation of a vast depository of clippings from newspapers, magazines, and ephemera which came to it from Italian-American communities all over the United States; and (in conjunction with the Italian Teachers Association)[9] it was compiling a universal retrospective bibliographical register on the Italian immigrant, on the Italian-American communities, and on Italy, generally. In an ambitious schema on a sociological research program of Italian-American communities, Covello observed:

Before any plan can be worked out intelligently certain fundamentals are absolutely necessary. There is needed the indispensable fact-finding concerning the Italian American and the Italian American community. This process of gathering authentic information must be scientific and objective. The efforts to obtain this information must be centralized to avoid duplication. For this there should be a competent organization, interested primarily in an unbiased approach to the problems that it plans to tackle. It must then enlist the aid and cooperation of all the experts who are interested in the problems of the Italian American and of all the educational and social institutions in New York City, elsewhere in the United States, and in Italy. What is more—in offering its services—educational, fact-finding, promoting Italian language and culture, facilitating the adjustment of the Italian American to his life in this country—it must interest Italian American students, particularly those pursuing graduate work, in the much needed studies of these problems and of their solution.

In being authentic, objective and scientific, the approach to these problems must also consider the attitude and viewpoint of the Italian American. Probably he alone can approach the problem with a keen and sympathetic understanding; feel more immediately the urgent necessity of such a study; sense most intimately the perplexities that confront his own people—for he, himself, is undergoing or has undergone the processes of adjustment to the American scene.

This function the Casa Italiana Educational Bureau intends to fulfill by endeavoring to give direction to wholesome social and educational forces for the Italian American community.

Surprising as it may seem, the fact is that there has been no such organization. Since there is no organized and unified Italian community in this country, how can we speak authoritatively as being a centralizing factor in the development of such a community?

Our answer is that we fully realize that only upon the basis of the results of our work will such recognition be accorded us. We feel that these results will justify and gain the recognition, support and cooperation of the Italian American people. Already through the auspices of this Bureau—for the first time in the history of the Italian colony of New York—over 250 independent societies, lodges and affiliations of national organizations in New York City and vicinity were brought together during the past season to support a definite educational program which resulted, among other things, in the establishment of a permanent fund for scholarships for American students of Italian origin.

Our immediate efforts are focussed on the problems in New York City and its environs, where there is the greatest concentration of Italian immigrant population in the United States. With the proper backing, and if its endeavors prove to be worthwhile here, the Bureau will willingly cooperate with and offer its services to all Italian American communities in a consulting capacity.

This brings us to another point—our function in a consulting capacity. It was in this capacity that we realized the dearth of real knowledge and the need for such knowledge. During our very brief existence we have been consulted time and again by various organizations and individuals, Italian and non-Italian, for data concerning the Italian population. Educators, teachers and students have secured material and references from us to facilitate their programs for intergroup relations between various immigrant groups and the native population. We have been asked for data concerning the Italian contributions to

Western civilization in general and to America in particular. We have supplied information to students of the problems that directly affect the Italian American groups and individuals. We have made available to them the sources of information relating to these problems.

Competent students should be interested in such problems as:

1. The Italian American background—social, political, economic.

2. The history of Italian migrations and in particular Italian immigration to the United States.

3. The adjustment of the Italian to American life and the problems involved; causes of maladjustment; attempted solutions; processes of Americanization at work in the Italian American community.

Of course, all these studies are broad and general in nature. We indicate here, in brief outline, specific studies, some of which we have been working on, and some of which are merely projected.[10]

This comprehensive program was never implemented. Although the CIEB was involved in a multiplicity of efforts which touched the Italian communities of New York City and its environs in many ways (*e.g.*, involvement of Italians in the work of the Folk Festival Council of New York City), its main objectives were not achieved. In all, it published 13 *Bulletins* (between 1932–1935) which were of uneven quality, but each of which was significant in attesting a seriousness of purpose:

[Bulletin #1] Mario E. Cosenza. *Eleventh Annual Report*. Italian Teachers Association. [1931-1932].

[Bulletin #2] Peter M. Riccio. *Why English Speaking People Should Study Italian.*

[Bulletin #3] Rachel Davis-DuBois. *Some Contributions of Italy and Her Sons to Civilization and American Life.*

[Bulletin #4] Leonard Covello. *The Casa Italiana Educational Bureau—Its Purpose and Program.*

[Bulletin #5] Henry Grattan Doyle. *The Importance of the Study of the Italian Language.*

[Bulletin #6] Leonard Covello. *The Italians in America. A Brief Survey of a Sociological Research Program of Italo-American Communities with Population Maps and Tables.*

[Bulletin #7] William B. Shedd. *Italian Population in New York City.*

[Bulletin #8] John D'Alesandre. *Occupational Trends of Italians in New York City, 1916-1931.*

[Bulletin #9] Giuseppe Prezzolini. *A Program of Cultural Activities for Italian Clubs or Societies.*

[Bulletin #10] Marie Lipari. *The Padrone System: An Aspect of American Economic History.*

[Bulletin #11] Leonard Covello. *Language Usage in Italian Families.*

[Bulletin #12] Genoeffa Nizzardini. *Infant Mortality for Manhattan, Brooklyn, Bronx.*

[Bulletin #13] Genoeffa Nizzardini. *Health Among Italians in New York City.*

The *Bulletins* were not all published under the imprint of the CIEB; straitened financial circumstances forced the publication of a number of them in the *Italy-America Monthly* and in *Atlantica*: those published under the Bureau's imprint were done in short print runs, and are very rare in their original form.[11]

The support which Covello had hoped for from Italian communities never materialized. He sadly noted: "The Italian communities, I regret to say, never understood educational programs of this character. Their allegiance and their interest and involvement were with the political leaders and such things as educational research and educational programs even for the propaganda for the Italian language never had any financial support." For Covello, this absence of support was not unanticipated; he had been involved over the years in a number of organizations whose objectives encompassed strengthening Italian-American communities, encouraging Italian language instruction, improving the education of Italian children, and generally enhancing the position of Italian-Americans in American society: all of these efforts had, at best, limited success. They included the Italian Teachers Association (convened as early as 1912), in which Covello served as vice-president; the Italian Parents Association (organized in 1927); the Order Sons of Italy, whose New York Chapter formed a Committee on Education for which Covello served as secretary; the Italian Educational League (organized in 1909); and the Italy-America Society established during World War I. In 1925, Covello joined in an effort to coordinate the activities of the different Italian societies, organizations, and associations. This Coordinated Program of Italian Educational Activities faltered for lack of financial support. The CIEB was, in many ways, the culmination of all of these prior efforts, attesting both Covello's continuing hope and recognition of need.

When the WPA program terminated, the CIEB came to an end; with no staff, and the support of the Casa Italiana (if only for modest facilities) wavering, the Bureau could not have continued. Covello did not give up at first. He rented a store front on 108th Street in East Harlem, created an Italian-American Educational Bureau (and an Hispanic, *i.e.*, Puerto Rican, Educational Bureau), and carried the files of the CIEB along with him. In 1942, he rented a whole floor over the National City Bank at 1st Avenue and 116th Street in East Harlem for what he called the East Harlem Educational and Research Bureau, "paid for rent, personnel, etc., for two years and then simply had to quit. The collection went to the Sanitation Department for old paper." The collection included 54 transfer files of carefully catalogued materials—an irretrievable loss: in Covello's words, "It was hard for me to give up what I thought was the record of the strivings of our people to make their way in the new world—but financial support never materialized."

The CIEB was a unique undertaking; it proposed a number of functions, but it primarily sought to provide Italian-American communities with help in understanding and meeting needs (and at a time when these communities were most vulnerable): the Bureau's other purposes were subordinated to this role. With the dispersal of Italians and the disappearance of the Italian-American urban ghettoes of the 1930's, the CIEB (as Covello visualized it) would have little meaning today. However, in a very real sense, the Bureau initiated the socio-historical study of the Italian-American experience on a systematic basis, and, despite its limited success, its pioneering efforts remain important. More to the point, there is no evidence that the socio-historical investigations which Covello proposed are being systematically pursued elsewhere under any auspices; and the archives/collections of materials which chronicle the Italian-American experience are only now being assembled. Leonard Covello's Bureau was, ostensibly, related to its time; yet much of what it proposed has still to be achieved. And the CIEB's true significance may be recognition of that fact.

NOTES

1. See F. Cordasco, "The Children of Columbus: Recent Works on the Italian-American Experience," *Phylon: The Atlanta University Review of Race and Culture*, vol. 4 (September, 1973), pp. 295-298; also, Rudolph J. Vecoli, "European Americans: From Immigrants to Ethnics," *International Migration Review*, vol. 6 (Winter, 1972), pp. 403-434. For Italian-American bibliography, see F. Cordasco, *Italians in the United States: A Bibliography of Reports, Texts, Critical Studies and Related Materials* (New York: Oriole Editions, 1972), and F. Cordasco, *The Italian-American Experience: An Annotated and Classified Bibliographical Guide* . . . (New York: Burt Franklin, 1974).

2. Although the work of the Sicilian journalist, Giovanni E. Schiavo, merits special attention and has a neglected importance, it was not systematic: certainly, Giovanni Schiavo (and his Vigo Press) were the most energetic forces in Italian-American studies for decades, and it is beside the point to denigrate his work by calling it filiopietistic.

3. See generally, *Casa Italiana, Columbia University: Thirty-Fifth Anniversary Souvenir* [The Casa Italiana, 1962]. The Casa was never hospitable to the Italian immigrant community or its history.

4. For the Federal Writers' Project, see the invaluable history by Jerry Mangione, *The Dream and the Deal: The Federal Writers' Project, 1935-1943* (Boston: Little Brown, 1974). Covello's Bureau was a subsidiary beneficiary of the federal largesse. For a detailed notice of the New York City Federal Writers' Project (outside of whose orbit Covello functioned), see

Mangione, *passim.* (The New York Project did publish *The Italians of New York* [also in Italian as *Gli Italiani di New York*] in 1938.)

5. For allegations of Fascism at the Casa Italiana and the controversy which surrounded it, see "Fascism at Columbia University: The Casa Italiana and the Italian Department," *Nation*, vol. 139 (November 7, 1934), pp. 523-524; 530-531; discussion, vol. 139, pp. 550-552; 565; 590 (November 14-21, 1934); vol. 140, pp. 117, 129-130, 377-378, 388 (January 30; April 3, 1935); *School and Society*, vol. 40 (November 24, 1934), pp. 695-698.

6. Leonard Covello, *The Casa Italiana Educational Bureau: Its Purpose and Program.* Bulletin #4. New York: Columbia University, Casa Italiana Educational Bureau [c. 1933], p. 3.

7. *Ibid.*, pp. 4-5.

8. Thrasher was the author of a major study on juvenile delinquency, *The Gang: A Study of 1313 Gangs in Chicago*, 2nd ed. (Chicago: University of Chicago Press, 1936). At New York University, Thrasher headed a research project on youth activity in East Harlem. Covello played an important part in the study; and Thrasher became a close friend of Covello, serving later as a member of the sponsoring committee for Covello's doctoral dissertation on the social background of the Italo-American school child. On the East Harlem study, see Frederic M. Thrasher, "The Boys' Club Study," *Journal of Educational Sociology* (December, 1932).

9. For the Italian Teachers Association, see F. Cordasco, ed., *The Italian Community and Its Language in the United States: The Annual Reports of the Italian Teachers Association* (Totowa, N.J.: Rowman and Littlefield, 1975).

10. Leonard Covello, *The Italians in America: A Brief Survey of A Sociological Research Program of Italo-American Communities* [With Two Population Maps and a Table]. Bulletin #6. New York: Columbia University, Casa Italiana Educational Bureau [1934]. Pages are unnumbered.

11. Numbers 1, 2, 5 are reprinted in F. Cordasco, *The Italian Community and Its Language in the United States*; Numbers 4, 6, 7, 8 are reprinted in F. Cordasco, *The Italian-American Experience: An Annotated and Classified Bibliographical Guide*; Number 10 appeared in *Italy-America Monthly* (April, 1935); Number 11 was published in *Atlantica* (October, November, 1934); Number 12, in *Italy-America Monthly* (May, 1935); and Number 13, in *Atlantica* (December, 1934).

WILLIAM V. D'ANTONIO

Ethnicity and Assimilation

A Reconsideration

In this paper I propose to review the process by which I have come to join the rising chorus of scholars and activists who are calling for a re-evaluation of assimilation—both as theory and as ideology. This is more or less an autobiographical statement—perhaps confession—of a third generation Italian-America, born and brought up in New Haven, Connecticut during the 1930's and forties. More than that, this paper represents the attempt of a sociologist-activist to learn to live comfortably with the fact of his ethnicity, to understand its meaning for himself and for his family, and to use this understanding toward the development of a new theory of intergroup relations. Finally, this paper represents an effort to explore again the relationship between ideology and theory. In this latter case, I would hope that the paper would go beyond the problems of ethnicity and assimilation to the broader question of the interrelationship of theory and ideology in the social sciences.

Growing Up in New Haven: The Formative Years. My grandparents on both sides came from Italy in the 1880's and '90's from villages in Casserta and Benevento. They settled along with most of their relatives in New Haven, Conn., where both my parents were born in 1899, in Italian neighborhoods. My father graduated from New Haven Hillhouse High School and my mother from night school with a degree in practical nursing. Both parents valued education and pushed us hard (I am one of four sons) to achieve in school. My father's entire job career was in the United States Postal System, the last decades as superintendent of the Yale University Postal Station—a not-unimportant influence on my life. I did not appreciate the fact at the time, in fact, not until 1962 or so, when Professor A. B. Hollingshead of Yale pointed it out to me, but my family was among the early arrivals from Italy, and we were in the vanguard of third generation Italian-Americans.

Family Life. As I remember my youth, we lived within an extended family, Italian-American style. My paternal grandfather owned the three storey house we lived in, and occupied the first floor with my grandmother and unmarried aunts and uncles. An aunt and uncle with four cousins lived on the second floor and we lived on the third floor. All of my grandfather's married children lived within walking distance; indeed, so did most of my mother's family. Seeing and being with relatives was a daily experience which was heightened on weekends, and reached a crescendo during the big holidays. On Easter and Christmas especially, we could expect to see all of the paternal relatives, and because of my mother's position as oldest child in her family, her family also gravitated toward our house.

No one had struck it rich, but there was also little of poverty. An extraordinary number of my father's relatives worked for one or another branch of the government, mostly for the Post Office. This fact took on new shades of meaning for me, first as I sought extra money at Christmas time, and later as I came to appreciate the struggle for control of the New Haven Postal System between the entrenched Irish-Americans and the increasingly aggressive paisani.

My paternal grandfather was in charge of the family, and we all accepted the fact that he could and did give us orders, and could and did punish us. Nor do I recall my father ever raising his voice to his father; the lines of authority were clearly demarked. My grandfather believed in hard work, saved his money, but was very cautious in how he invested it. He knew many of the city's Irish leaders and was deferential to them. And he was unusual among his peers in that he was a pillar of his parish church. He was one of those ascetic Italians who went to church all the time. From all I have been able to gather, he was self-employed just about his entire working life in the United States, as a vendor of fruits and vegetables. He valued education for its practical effects in improving one's job prospects. The ethic was to work hard, pay your debts, don't take any risks, be careful, don't trust people outside the family. Too much recreation was looked at askance, and the world was generally seen as a "vale of tears." Most of the family was—and remains—solidly Democratic, but there were and are some notable exceptions, mostly through marriage.

Neighborhood.   We lived in a fringe neighborhood, working and lower middle class, mostly two and three story houses that were privately owned and frequently painted. The immediate neighborhood was overwhelmingly Italian, with a few Irish and one or two Polish families scattered within. The neighborhood was near the areas that have long been associated with the heart of Italian family life in New Haven (Wooster Square and Grand Avenue), but our daily living patterns gradually took us away from those areas. For the neighborhood was also near Polish and German neighborhoods and also allowed us to interact in the solidly middle and upper middle class neighborhoods that were then peopled largely by third and fourth generation Irish-Americans. It seemed to us at the time a comfortable neighborhood to grow up in—lots of friends and relatives to play with, and, as long as we stayed within our boundaries, little trouble with out-siders.

The family barber was Fred Guida, then also the City Sheriff and one of the first Italians to gain a place on the Democratic ticket. His son Bart is currently the Mayor of New Haven and continues to live in the same neighborhood in which he grew up, which during the 1930's and 40's was much more fashionable and primarily Irish-American. The remnants of my paternal family live just across the street. So there are still strong family ties to the past, even though the entire area comprising the larger neighborhood has changed greatly—the original neighborhood on East St. was largely wiped out by the construction of I-91.

Part of my growing up was to learn that there were Italians and Italians, that only Neapolitans could be trusted, that "i siciliani no sono cristiani," "i calabresi sono capodosti" and all northerners were stuck-ups. We had to watch out for the Jews, don't mix with the Poles, and recognize that the Irish were in control of things—but we would have our turn some day. The blacks must not have been a factor in the early days; I never heard anything about them. They lived in their neighborhood along Dixwell Ave-nue, at least until the expansion pressures during and after World War II.

As I reflect on those days, I find that ethnic differences were highly refined, were accepted as natural, that is, as part of the nature of things, and were passed along as guidelines as to how we were to orient ourselves to those others if we wanted to get on well. These were things you had to know in order to protect yourself. People were prejudiced, but like Archie Bunker of Television fame, they seldom if ever did more than talk. Dis-crimination was something else. No one was then in a position to discrimi-nate in employment, and I can't recall much movement in or out of the neighborhood during my youth. It was a stable neighborhood of striving Italians; the Irish who remained were well-entrenched, and looked upon as models. The prejudices passed on to us were simply the maps designed to guide us through the encounters we were likely to have as we grew up.

Religion. We were Catholic, but not fanatics. So, we were not sent to parochial schools. My mother must have had some bad times with the Irish nuns who dominated the system; she didn't say much but she was not about to let us come under their control, at least not more than necessary. We were about as Catholic as anyone in the neighborhood, in fact more so than most of the other Italian families. That is, we went to Mass and Sunday School regularly. In this regard, we behaved more like the Irish around us. The fringe nature of the neighborhood led to some strange church patterns. Many of the people went to St. Patrick's on Grand Ave., once the pride of the Irish, but now taken over in numbers by the Italians, except that the clergy and nuns were Irish. My paternal grandparents went to St. Donato's, a small Italian parish, almost a mission parish in Fair Haven (also controlled by Irish clergy). My father also went to St. Donato's, and we went there for occasional novenas, bazaar's, bingos and the like. My father was a leader in the Holy Name Society. But just before we began grammar school, my mother switched us to St. Joseph's Church, a predominantly Irish, middle and upper middle class church, one of the wealthiest in the city. St. Joseph's was notable also because it did not have a parochial school, but was located next to one of the oldest public schools in New Haven which was still functioning. And to which we were assigned in the city school districting.

It was never clear to me why the children went to St. Joseph's, but I don't recall that my father objected. Thus, my father went to church either by himself or with members of his family, while my mother and her sons went to St. Joseph's. With time, more and more members of the family switched to St. Joseph's, and several members still go there. Perhaps one problem with St. Donato's was that while the parish was predominantly Italian, the clergy were Irish, and spoke an Italian not too dissimilar from the Spanish spoken by anglo priests in Puerto-Rican and Mexican-American parishes today. Except that clerical attitudes seem to have changed. The Irish clergy had a mission to Catholicize pagan Italians, an attitude that was resented by many younger family members. Or perhaps there was a clear-cut difference in status between the parishes which was recognized but not stated. Gradually, St. Joseph came to mean to us a more refined form of Catholicism; a brother and I joined the choir and learned to sing Gregorian Chant; we appeared on radio, and even were invited to sing at special ceremonies at Yale's new Thomas More Center. Fr. J. Ralph Kelly, a shy, scholarly priest, had a great impact on some among us, although he was not well-liked by most of the parishioners who considered him effete and intellectual. Fr. Kelly introduced us to the liturgy and to some literature about the liturgy and the church, and I have always felt that he was as much a factor in giving me an identity as a Catholic with which I could live and adapt as anyone within the family. He seemed at home intellectually with non-Catholics, and in introducing us to the larger scene, helped to foster the assimilationist ideology. Again, I must say that my experiences at St. Joseph were such as to strengthen my identification with the larger community. The Irish may have been in control but I was not aware of ways in which this might have affected my own chances to get ahead or to see religion in any but a positive light. At the same time St. Joseph provided me with my first look at upper middle class life, and that was unsettling at times. We were able to glimpse the comforts of such a life sufficiently to want it for ourselves. The Church and the school supported it, and urged us further along the path of achievement and assimilation. Could a parish really make that much difference?

School.   We went to Edward St. School, the same school my father had gone to, and in kindergarten and first grade we had the same teachers he had had. The school was old, but the teachers were good, all but one were single, and most were Protestants. In fact, one of my vivid memories about primary school was my parents' warning that when we said the Lord's Prayer at the beginning of school each morning, we should be sure and stop at the Catholic ending and not say the Protestant part, and we should not let the teacher try to make us learn to say THAT PART. (For those unschooled in such niceties, the so-called Protestant Part is "For Thine is the Kingdom, the power and the glory, Forever and ever, Amen.")

For those who were in a position to benefit therefrom, the school was a good avenue for mobility. We were being taught by people who exemplified the middle class Protestant values of American society and they did their job well. They felt a missionary zeal to Americanize us and were proud of their achievements.

An interesting example of the process at work which I can recall occurred in the sixth grade. I was asked to recite a poem by William Daly entitled "Leetala Georgio Washington," written in broken English. The poem tells of an Italian immigrant who relates the legend of George Washington, and ends by assuring the youngster that, if he works hard, studies hard and does not tell a lie, he too can grow up to be President of the United States.—I wonder if Blacks, Chicanos and Puerto Rican children have yet heard a similar message, to say nothing of women.—

High School Was a Mixed Bag.   Our parents were urging us to think in terms of college and we signed up for the pre-college program. At that time, Hillhouse High School had a reputation for academic excellence, despite the rapidly changing nature of the student population. The largest grouping of students were Jewish, with an equal admixture of Italians and Irish, a scattering of other ethnics, and a few WASPS; most of the WASPS were attending New England's prestigious private schools.

High School seemed to do several things:

a—Highlight Ethnicity—We had ethnic oriented fraternities and sororities—dating was ethnic oriented, and cross-ethnic dating was a matter of family and peer discussion and censure. The WASPS had originated the system with their exclusive fraternities and sororities. The ethnics simply followed suit and established their own. In 1943 we broke new ground in Intergroup Relations by sponsoring a dance jointly between an Italian and a Jewish fraternity.

*b—*Made me keenly aware of status, power and class differentials, along with religious and ethnic differences. These differences were evident in our dating, in our high school politics; in what we learned about the other groups that came from other parts of the city; and they were increasingly evident in what we were learning about the larger community of New Haven. The question of race did not enter as a factor in our lives in 1943.

c—Fostered the assimilationist ethic at the same time it fostered an ethnocentric pluralism. The message was clear: school was available to all those who wanted to get ahead. The teachers were there to help us on the way—as long as we followed their rules. They were believers in the system!! And so were we!!

d—Tended to obscure class and status divisions by the focus on ethnicity. Thus, for example, the members of the fraternity I belonged to came from families with income levels ranging from just above poverty to upper class. In this setting, the ethnic tie was more important than the class tie, and this carried over into the dating patterns.

e—Most important, Hillhouse High School made Yale University possible. Actually, my parents never talked about any place other than Yale, and my older bother and I both succeeded in winning scholarships to Yale. In looking back at the identity of those who won scholarships to Yale that year from New Haven, I find four of Irish background, five Jewish and four Italian among fifteen scholarships awarded. In some ways we were the blacks and Puerto Ricans of that day.

On the Road to Assimilation. During the decade between 1943 and 1953 I found myself increasingly absorbed into the mainstream of American life, embracing wholeheartedly the ideology of Assimilation and individual achievement, and abashed by and ashamed of the ethnic struggles that seemed to absorb the energies of my elders. I was probably a typical example of the third generation American who fulfilled the dreams of the parents on the one hand, but caused them anguish by disavowing their ethnic ways.

The Yale Experience. My freshman year at Yale was a near disaster, socially and academically. I was unprepared for the level of work expected, mostly because I was not ready to cut myself off from the neighborhood gang, and the high school fraternity gang. In their midst I was important, had achieved something and my marginal status was like that of most others. At Yale I felt out of place and of course the fault was clearly mine. I didn't know how to dress, or act, or how to study. And while just about everyone else lived in one of those magnificent Yale buildings, I was a townie.

One interesting and in retrospect somewhat amusing attempt to compensate for the social insecurity was to join the Italian Junior League, a club composed of high school graduates, the poor people's imitation of the prestigious New Haven Junior League. While they had their own private club to meet in, we met in the "Y." The IJL did provide an opportunity for social life with high school graduates, and for some of us it did provide an opportunity for leadership training; we weren't ready for the big time, but we did run an organization, and we could pride ourselves on the success of our dances and big parties.

A two year stint in the U.S. Navy intervened to alter my life experiences, to gradually wean me away from ethnic ties, and to provide me with a much broader perspective on the world. Religion and class began to replace ethnicity as central concerns. My concerns focused more and more on the troubling question of trying to reconcile religious beliefs with secular knowledge, and problems of peace and economic exploitation. And the race question began to emerge as important to my life processes.

On my return to Yale I studied Italian, but as a student of language not as one concerned to rekindle his ethnicity. Most of the students in the class had spent time in Italy, and talked knowingly about Firenze and the Ponte Vecchio. In some ways I was probably quite visibly ethnic, a New Haven Italian with a Neapolitan accent who knew practically nothing about Italy, Italian Opera or the like. In fact, I couldn't even speak Italian well, so tuned to American ways had family life become.

A number of significant events occurred during my post war years at Yale. We moved to a comfortable English tudor style home outside New Haven near the Yale Bowl. We were finally free of my grandfather and the ethnic neighborhood. But not of family ties. My parents celebrated their move by frequent family picnics. For years our home was the center for extended family gatherings.

Meanwhile, Italian power had finally come to New Haven, first with the election of William Celentano on the Republican ticket, ending a fifty year reign for the Irish. And that was followed shortly by the election to Congress of Albert Cretella, also on the Republican ticket. Italians were deserting the Democratic Party in large numbers to assert their desire for top political office. The major patronage result of these changes in fortune for my family was control of the New Haven Post Office. I found myself upset at the openness of the power play and the knowledge that key appointments would go to Italians, regardless of achievement, competitive examinations and the like. And I found my father upset at me for the silly notions I had about how the system was supposed to work.

The main source of family discontent centered around a Sociology course I decided to take, my first one, on Race and Nationality Relations. It was taught by Raymond Kennedy, one of the most popular lecturers at Yale. He had a reputation for tearing apart the foibles of the white ethnics and brazenly defending the cause of the Negroes. I found the course stimulating and exciting, and began to preach the cause of total assimilation and integration, which meant of course racial intermarriage. I reminded my family that there wouldn't be any Negro race in two hundred years because we would all become one great admixture. I assumed of course that this was what blacks also wanted. And while I cheered on the cause of the blacks, I chided my family about the statistics showing Italians with higher rates of violence and rape than blacks.

Ethnic clubs like Sons of Italy and Amici became very distasteful to me, as did the reality of ethnic politics. We should be assimilating, treating everyone as equals. Instead we seemed to continue what were clearly now un-American patterns of behavior. I focused my attention increasingly on Latin American Studies and Spanish, and on trying to develop a reasonable understanding of myself as a Catholic American, trying to prove I was as good an American as anyone else.

The Loomis School: Completion of the Assimilation Process.   Through a series of fortuitous circumstances (upon graduation from Yale), I was offered a position as teacher of Spanish at the Loomis School in Windsor, Ct. Loomis was and is one of New England's Prestigious Prep Schools. If I was the token Italian at Loomis, that fact went pretty much unnoted. It was the religious factor that mattered. Loomis had a distinctly Unitarian orientation, and I found myself in regular conversation about Catholicism. While there were several other Catholics on the faculty, they didn't discuss religion. Since I was eager to, and felt increasingly comfortable in the discussions, I found a wide range of Protestant and Agnostic faculty wanting to probe my Catholicism.

In many ways Loomis was the culmination of the assimilation process for me. After a bumpy first year, I found myself increasingly at home there, and impressed by the emphasis on self-discipline, internal democracy and the like. The gospel of American democracy and the American dream was preached with great enthusiasm. To strive to achieve was the key. The school even had a regular guest speaker's program entitled "Loomis Learns from Leaders."

In 1950 I married a third generation Italian whose father had achieved notable success as a small businessman, in New Haven. In fact, he offered us a wedding reception at the New Haven Lawn Club. With some concern about whether our relatives would be "comfortable" in the New Haven Club, we went ahead and had a very delightful if somewhat non-ethnic wedding with the wedding mass in St. Joseph's and the reception at the New Haven Lawn Club, thus presumably completing the assimilation process.

On to Sociology.   In 1954 I began work on my Ph.D. at Michigan State University, in Sociology and Anthropology. Throughout my years as a graduate student, and until the mid-1960's, the most pressing ideological question I faced was how I could possibly be a sociologist and a practicing Catholic at the same time. On a theoretical level, I was taught to be value free, and that the proper model of society was built on concepts like integration, assimilation, equilibrium, order and functionalism.

For 16 years I worked on and off along the U.S.-Mexican border, studying influentials, elites, business and politics, and the images which leaders had of each other. I was early on aware of the plight of the Mexican-Americans, but I understood their situation within an assimilation framework. Along with Julian Samora, the first Mexican-American to earn a Ph.D. in Sociology, I looked for evidence of the assimilation process at work; in 1962 we published an article on Ethnic Stratification in the Southwest, but our message was that through such vehicles as the Catholic Hospital, Mexican-Americans were slowly but surely finding their place in American society.[1] Indeed, we found that their progress compared favorably with that of Italian-Americans in New Haven, measured in terms of achievement in professional medical occupations. I was aware of the prejudice and discrimination from which Mexican-Americans suffered in the Southwest, but felt certain that the assimilation process, which I thought had worked so well for the ethnics of the north, would surely be at work in places like El Paso.

As I moved away from social psychological to more strictly sociological concerns, I began to become aware of the differences that organizational strength made in the chances of individuals and groups. The anglos were well organized, the Mexican-Americans were not. I began to wonder if ethnic clubs were really all that bad. The Democratic Political Party was weak in El Paso, there were no strong labor unions, and ethnic clubs were lacking. Without organization, people had little political or other clout, and were not likely to improve their class and status positions.[2] The word *chicano* was not in use then; the brown power movement had not yet begun.

By 1962 I was rethinking deTocqueville on the importance of voluntary associations in American society, and Durkheim about the importance of intermediary structures between the individual and society. Meanwhile, community power studies were in vogue, and a lively debate developed among those involved about the nature of the power structures we were finding in El Paso, New Haven and elsewhere.[3] Dahl and his colleagues argued that ethnic politics was being replaced by a new coalition of business and political leaders, a party oriented pluralism that blurred the traditional lines. At best the pluralism seemed to some of us truncated, with groups like the Mexican-Americans not getting their fair share of the pie. But again, it was assumed that it would be only a matter of time before the situation would be corrected; perhaps New Haven under Dick Lee was a model for the nation.

The Critical Years: 1963–68. Within the Catholic Church Vatican II was bringing new hope; I was now a member of the Notre Dame faculty and an increasing number of non-believing colleagues in the midwest universities grudgingly conceded that perhaps I could be a Catholic and a sociologist after all. The birth control issue and population growth in Latin America occupied an increasing part of my time. So also did Civil Rights and the Great Society. Along with so many other white liberals I joined the march for the civil rights of blacks.

The Civil Rights issue was and remains a complex one, that I'm not sure I fully understand to this day. In 1965 I was full of energy to help bring about both integration and the great society. By 1967 like many others I was discouraged—and by 1969 I was ready to ask what went wrong?

Can we attribute failure just to the loss of key leaders like Robert Kennedy and Martin Luther King? I think not—although their loss was a crushing blow to their movements, revealing how dependent the organizations were upon their charisma.

Had we run up again against the old adage that "Stateways cannot change folkways?" In part, yes, and in part no. The Supreme Court decision of 1954 in the Brown-Kansas education case did change folkways. Just as the Civil Rights Act of 1965 gave voting power to blacks in the South for the first time (in 1974 blacks now hold some 1200 major electoral offices in the south alone, from less than 100 in 1965). But neighborhood integration was another matter.

In part, white liberals were preaching—we were preaching integration of the races, as if the melting pot had done its job on the white ethnic groups. We fostered the myth that whites were one big happy family, a great affluent middle class, and now all we had to do was add the blacks to the family.

And we were preaching with a vengeance: we were telling white Catholic ethnics in the North that they could only be Christians if they accepted the blacks as brothers and sisters and living in the house next door.

We were mixing religion, class and ethnic factors—to our own downfall, and focusing primarily on prejudice as if personal prejudice were the chief cause of discrimination in society.

We became very unsociological, those of us who were sociologists and pro-integrationists; we believed our own rhetoric about assimilation, consensus, equilibrium, the end of ideology and the like. We no longer saw white ethnics as we saw blacks, or Puerto Ricans and chicanos. How could we? We believed that all whites had made it, or were about to. At least all the whites who wanted to make it and were willing to work.[4]

But white ethnics hadn't made it out of their ghettoes. And their ghettoes were still meaningful communities to them. We discounted the values of that community life, and the knowledge we should have had about the strength of their solidarity. We didn't get the point of Glazer and Moynihan's book *Beyond the Melting Pot*.[5]

In part also, the move to integration denied to blacks the possibility of a liberated black culture with its own values, its own apartness, organized black power and the like. Had we succeeded in integrating the blacks in the 1960's it would have been on white terms, a goal desired by whites, and to a great extent it implied that as blacks took on white dominant group ways they became better persons. Just as I had been taught to think that about my own integration years earlier.

The above factors were all exacerbated by the failure in Vietnam, the failure to be able to produce both guns and butter, the failure of urban renewal to help blacks, or ethnics in general, the failure of the peace corps, and the failure of the anti-poverty programs. We came to perceive all these events as failures—as if we had some right to expect that we should succeed whether the matter were guns or butter.

I spent the summer of 1968 teaching in Innsbruck and traveling throughout Europe. I was impressed with the regional (ethnic) prejudices that were still so strong in Italy, Austria and other places. I concluded that comparatively speaking the United States was at least trying to confront its racial problems. Those countries were not even trying to confront their problems. But I was more and more convinced that we were failing because our ideology and theory were faulty. Somehow, the Europeans seemed to have a more congruent relationship between their ideology and social reality. Meanwhile, the battle over birth control and Church authority waxed strong and preoccupied many of us. And Vietnam brought an increasing number of scholars from a variety of disciplines to the recognition of the myth of value neutrality.[6] So we signed petitions, cursed the white backlash and watched Nixon win the presidency.

In 1969 Daniel P. Moynihan was the Commencement Speaker at Notre Dame, and I was invited to be his host during his stay on campus. Since he was Nixon's urban advisor, some of us thought it an appropriate opportunity to invite him to a special gathering of social scientists to discuss an embryonic project we had in mind regarding blacks and small business. Moynihan was forthright—he told us to forget about studying the blacks, and definitely not to waste any energy on blacks and small business. The Nixon Administration had already given up the idea to try to make small business successes out of the black population. Instead, Moynihan urged us to return to the cities to study the white ethnics. He assured us that the action was fast switching to the white ethnics, and we needed to know the meaning of the revitalization of white ethnicity. We were taken aback somewhat, gave some cursory discussion to his ideas, but weren't ready to buy them.

That summer I took a group of students to a small town in Southwest Texas, along the Rio Bravo. We were invited there by the town's leaders at the urging of the local priest who had known something about my earlier research in the El Paso area. The town was 85 per cent Mexican-American (not yet psychologically chicano), but controlled economically, socially and otherwise by the anglos. We were to do a community study which presumably would help the town to better understand its problems and improve its chances for survival, since it, like many other parts of the Southwest, was in an economic slump caused by the decline of the cotton market. It was clearly our objective to strive for this goal. But the facts of economic exploitation, and discrimination in the school system, and in so many facets of community life gradually radicalized us. And what ensued was a report written from the viewpoint of the Mexican-Americans (which I have referred to in my own thinking as the making of a chicano).

By 1970 Representative Roman Pucinski was sponsoring the Ethnic Heritage Study Program in Congress; we at Notre Dame had formulated a rough proposal for an ethnic studies program at the University to incorporate black studies with those of the white ethnics who had made up so much of Notre Dame history. Rep. Pucinski heard about our effort, asked for support of his bill, and we gradually were drawn into the realization of the strength of the white ethnic movement.

Return of the Ethnic: 1971 to Present.   In 1971 I was invited to become head of the Department of Sociology at the University of Connecticut. At the same time I was becoming more and more concerned about the ethnic factor in American life, and how it intertwined with class to present dangerous problems to the society. The move also provided the opportunity to work with several other sociologists and others at the University who were themselves increasingly involved in ethnic studies.[7] And most personally, it meant the opportunity to include the study of my own ethnic group in my research. I was no longer sure about the right solutions to our racial-ethnic problems, but fairly certain that there was something wrong with the whole idea of assimilation, and also that there was some relationship between that and the American value preference for individual achievement. And here a popular Television show began to intrude itself into my thinking.

Archie Bunker and the Ethnic Factor.   For good or ill "All in the Family" must be acknowledged as one of the most popular television shows of the past decade with about one-fourth of the American population watching it regularly. I have attended a Conference on it sponsored by CBS and the American Jewish Committee, read research reports and discussed it with colleagues. Somehow I feel it fits with our concerns about ethnicity.

Archie Bunker is working class, poorly educated—and closed minded; he lives by ethnic stereotypes, clichés and elements of the American dream. He has it tough, no comfortable home in the suburb, in fact no fancy automobile. He rides the subway to work and he's hardly an example of the American dream.

But—Archie is believable—both to middle America and to suburban America. He seems like an average working class guy to working class America; he worries about his small home; he has a color TV set, and he is also beset by money bills, threats to his neighborhood and the like. If Archie lives by stereotypes, so do millions of other Americans live by these same stereotypes. Can we say with assurance that the stereotypes offered by suburban and liberal America are superior in value to these? If they are, why hasn't this fact become apparent to Archie and his followers?

Archie drinks beer, he wears a worker's coat and no tie, he bowls, his manners are working class—he dreams—and he doesn't give up. He's hardly alienated; and most important, he tolerates what he can't dominate.

He is full of prejudices, but for the most part he does not discriminate. Intentionally or not, this point seems to pervade most of the important episodes in Archie's life. The idea may not come through clearly, but the message is there, the system discriminates, discrimination is institutionalized.

Sociologists have long held that dining together is one of the most important signs of social equality and social acceptance. It is a fact that one of the most persistent activities of the family is that they dine together regularly. Archie tolerates a long-hair, jean-clad Polish son-in-law who is a sociology major. He has also learned to tolerate his Black and Italian neighbors. In much the same way that millions of other Americans have learned to tolerate "strangers" in their midst.

Let us consider "All in the Family" in the following context: (a) the four letter word was a "mortal sin" when I was young. It has been secularized in recent years, and even the clergy are heard occasionally using it. We would be hard put to make a serious claim that the society is somehow worse off for the change.

(b) There has been a revolution in sexual behavior and attitudes during the past fifty years. The mortal sins of the '30's have become optional forms of behavior today. With what effect upon society? Is this change the cause of our problems?

I would hypothesize that Archie Bunker is secularizing prejudice and thereby tending to reduce its threat to society. He has brought prejudice out into the open; it is a fact of life in this society and not easily to be eradicated. More important, in a latent and somewhat obscure manner, the show reveals that discrimination and not prejudice is the real problem. And the source of discrimination may well lie in the real estate organizations which foster block-busting tactics, the insurance companies which decide that neighborhoods are less secure with Blacks living in them, the company which protects its profits by telling Archie to fire one of his workers.

May not Archie's prejudices, which are the prejudices of all those who live in insecurity, defuse interpersonal hostilities at least as much as they support them? And may not the show cause some of the audience at least to begin to look elsewhere than to Archie's prejudices for the causes of discrimination in American society? At the same time, the show may be providing positive self-images to ethnics who have long felt neglected and devalued by American society.

Assimilation Reconsidered. It seems increasingly clear that assimilation both as theory and as ideology, along with the ethic of individual achievement and equality of opportunity, and the consensus model of American society are in need of revision, if not abandonment in favor of a more humanistic orientation.

Certainly many ethnics have been assimilated into American society; and many can say that the American success ethic worked for them. But that fact only obscures the social reality in which so many millions of ethnics still live. The assimilation-success ethic prevents us from understanding the meaning of the poverty, poor housing, poor educational opportunities, inadequate health care, and degrading job situations, and general insecurity in which so many people live. More than that, it prevents ethnics, Black, Brown and White, from appreciating the fact that there is no way out for so many millions of them.

What this ethic of assimilation-success does is to make us believe in the system as it is; those who don't make it for whatever reason, are taught to blame themselves rather than the system for their failure. This may in fact be one of the most severe shortcomings of that ethic. That the people do not see their true situation was amply illustrated by the way former President Nixon handled the white ethnics in his October 1972 campaign speech at the Statue of Liberty. The whites, including thousands of Italian-Americans, cheered him when he told them that they came to America to work and not to get a hand-out. They were oblivious to the fact that Italian-Americans constitute one of the largest welfare groups in the New York City area. This ideology leads us first to blame the Blacks, Chicanos, and

Puerto Ricans, and then ourselves, for our poverty. If Blacks only see whites, and not white ethnics, they see a false reality also. The end result is that the ethnics go around denigrating themselves as well as other ethnics for not fulfilling a dream which is only possible for a small number anyway.

But if assimilation, the melting pot, the success ethic have serious short-comings, what are the alternatives? It is clearly easier to point out the shortcomings than to be able to assert what ought to be the alternatives, either by way of social theory or of ideology. All around us there is the evidence that the ethnic factor brought to the surface means violence and conflict: in Northern Ireland, in Uganda, in the Soviet Union as in the United States. Despite these cases, I would like to offer the hypothesis that ethnic pluralism can be a viable alternative to the theory of assimilation, and that as ideology it can be developed to foster positive self-images while not necessarily denigrating outsiders. Let me suggest some possibilities.

At the social psychological level:

a—I can relax now and look with satisfaction upon my family's struggle, and upon their continuing identification as ethnics, if that is what they want. I don't have to worry now if my mannerisms are not 100 per cent American, nor if my family has learned all the "right ways" to do things. Mannerisms become alternatives, not preferred values. The dress and hair style revolution of the young has helped us also to see that we need not look down upon our different ways.

b—I have a history now, a place, an identity. My history did not begin with my assimilation into society. Nor is it dependent solely upon my ability to see myself as somehow descended from the Pilgrim fathers. And children in school may soon learn to see that WASPS aren't the only ones who helped build this society. In fact, we can begin to appreciate the society's history as preceding the WASPS; perhaps we can help de-mythologize history, remove some of the fairy tale tone from it. Moreover, we can now learn that history is made up of rather humble stuff, as well as much internal conflict. I see no necessary reason why we cannot learn to live with the conflicts and tensions that compromise the ethnic history of this society as we have learned to live with the Civil War. I would argue that we will be better off to recognize the reality of our prejudices, to bring them out into the open as Archie Bunker does. We may be better able to cope with them there than we have been when they were forced to be kept hidden just below the surface.

c—Ethnicity provides a greater sense of social identity, that is, we see ourselves as part of some collective unit, not as isolated individuals. The assimilation-success ethic focuses attention on the individual, on individual effort and achievement. Ethnicity can be a vehicle by which people come to perceive their essential interdependence, that their individual freedom lies within the larger social context. Thus, ethnicity can be one way to express and value the reality of the social; we would be more readily able to say, not just what I want for myself, but also what is good for the group.

At the structural level:

d—Ethnic groups can confront their class, status and power situation more effectively in group action rather than as individuals. In fact, as individuals they are not able to confront these situations. The focus of assimilation-success is on individual achievement. My relatives rightly say to me: "You've made it; what more do you want? If the Blacks and Puerto Ricans want to make it, let them work for it like you did." In the assimilationist framework, it is not possible to respond adequately to that challenge. Because that challenge asserts that the problem lies in individuals and not in groups or systems.

Through organized coalitions of ethnic groups such as in the recent efforts of CIAO with Blacks and Puerto Ricans in New York City, we can confront the problems of structured inequality in the society, to help people to understand that poverty and failure are built into this kind of a society, even in the promotion of the American dream. Coalitions that attempt to meet common goals may do more to help all groups than trying to promote more achievement for a few.

e—Coalitions can help block destruction of the ghettoes, either by outright plans for urban renewal, or by the slower but just as deadly process of neglect. Through coalitions, ghettoes can be made livable.

What about closed ghettoes? Ghettoes by choice? How do we confront the problem of residential segregation? Have we adequately weighted the values involved? Perhaps through coalitions we can tackle the problems of schools and livable residential areas. Blacks aren't the only ones in need of better schools. Those of us who live in semi rural areas in which our children travel several miles each way daily know the weakness of the neighborhood concept. The evidence on hand shows only that edicts from national levels have so far only exacerbated urban problems. We need research into the possibilities involved in coalition building.

The Lingering Doubts About Ethnicity. Ethnocentrism, the belief that "our ways are better than yours," is and always has been one of the great problems of ethnicity. The fact is, of course, that the white Protestant dominant group in the United States, has been the most ethnocentric of all groups, with their assimilation-success model designed for world as well as national admiration. That ethnocentrism has fostered a remarkable amount of individual freedom and material development, but at increasingly greater cost to the larger society, and indeed, to the world community. It favors the auto over mass transit.

It can even be hypothesized that assimilationist ethnocentrism has bred negative problems for us at the international level. Not only have the American people been unable to grasp fully the meaning of the changes going on in other parts of the world, but too often the rhetoric of American business and politics has seemed to be serving rather narrow interests. But this is hardly the fault of the more recent ethnics. Would not a greater tolerance for pluralism at home make possible a better understanding of pluralism abroad, and of ourselves as part of a large, disorderly international pluralist aggregation of nations?

f—And I worry about the stifling embrace of the ethnic kin group. The extended family provides warmth, a place, an identity, security, but often at the cost of personal freedom. Will a revived ethnicity impair the important movement of liberation of men and women which seems to be one of the better things happening in western society. The movie "Lovers and Other Strangers" posed the problem nicely. Many of us who find at least social psychological comfort in our ethnicity while appreciating also such changes as the liberation of the sexes may be able to show how some new model is possible, one which reveals that certain universalistic, democratic and egalitarian patterns and values are not necessarily contradictory to but can be consonant with a nonchauvinistic ethnic pluralism.

I would close with the following summary comment: ethnicity has been very important in my own life experience. I did not, as I had earlier thought, overcome it in the pursuit of assimilation and success. I believe it can be an important factor in the self-images which millions of people carry with them. By an appreciation of our ethnic heritage we can help insure that these people will develop a sense of self-worth without having to downgrade others. Ethnic groups are often the only organized groups within urban centers. What kinds of coalitions would they build if they enjoyed the knowledge which is common to business, political and other groupings? They might well develop some new alternatives for confronting the persistent inequalities of American life. The effort seems worthy of support.

NOTES

1. William V. D'Antonio and Julian Samora, "Occupational Stratification in Four Southwestern Hospitals," *Social Forces*, Vol. 41, October, 1962, No. 1, pp. 17-25.

2. For an account of the political struggle of the Mexican-Americans in El Paso, see William V. D'Antonio and William H. Form, *Influentials in Two Border Cities*, So. Bend, University of Notre Dame Press, 1965.

3. See Robert Dahl, *Who Governs?* New Haven: Yale University Press, 1961; and William V. D'Antonio and Howard J. Ehrlich (eds.), *Power and Democracy in America*, So. Bend: University of Notre Dame Press, 1961.

4. Richard Sennett and Jonathan Cobb offer a provocative analysis in class terms of the real world of the white ethnics in *The Hidden Injuries of Class*, New York: Alfred A. Knopf, 1973.

5. Nathan Glazer and Daniel P. Moynihan, *Beyond the Melting Pot*, Cambridge: The M.I.T. Press, 1963.

6. William V. D'Antonio, "Academic Man: Scholar or Activist," *Sociological Focus*, Summer, 1969.

7. See for example Harold J. Abramson, *Ethnic Diversity in Catholic America*, New York: John Wiley and Sons, 1973; and William Newman, *American Pluralism*, New York: Harper and Row, 1973.

FRANCIS A. J. IANNI

Organized Crime and the Italo-American Family

Ever since the turn of the century, the question of the role of the Italo-American community in organized crime in America has presented a major social problem for both the society and the community. On the one hand, there is the traditional view that "Mafia" or "La Cosa Nostra" are synonymous with organized crime in America and, following this logic, that organized crime is one of the more negative contributions of Italo-Americans to our society. On the other hand, the Italo-American community has answered in outrage that not logic but bias and prejudice, beginning as early as 1891 with the lynching of 11 reputed mafiosi in New Orleans and continuously reinforced by the media since that time have painted a false picture of the degree and nature of the involvement of Italo-Americans in organized crime. William James once said that wherever such a contradiction occurs, it is the result of the failure of the parties to the dispute to make relevant distinctions. This would seem to be the case here. The issue, I believe, is not whether Italo-Americans have been involved in organized crime in America—they have been just as other ethnic groups before and after them have been. Neither is the issue whether they have dominated organized crime in America—they did from the early thirties to the recent present just as the Irish and then the Jews did before them and as Blacks and Hispanics will move into control in the future. The salient issue is, rather, the relationship between organized crime as an American way of life, since it is found nowhere but in American cities, and ethnicity since minority group involvement has always been a perplexing but obvious factor in its development here. Understanding that relationship does more than erase the misplaced notion of organized crime as an Italian or even Italo-American way of life. It both places the issues in their proper societal perspective and suggests how cultural and social change can lead to reducing rather than perpetuating organized crime in America.

Recent research has begun to establish in social science, if not in the official and public view, a growing realization that organized crime is more than just a criminal way of life, it is an urban way of life in America.[1] As such, it is a viable and persistent institution within American society with its own symbols, its own beliefs, its own logic and its own means of transmitting these systematically from one generation to the next. As an integral part of economic life in the United States it can also be viewed as falling on a continuum which has the legitimate business world at one end and what we have come to call organized crime at the other. Viewed in this way, organized crime is a functional part of the American social system and, while successive waves of immigrants and migrants have found it an available means of economic and social mobility, it persists and transcends the involvement of any particular group and even changing definitions of legality and illegality in social behavior.

Having established this view of organized crime as part of American society, however, does not answer the general question of ethnic involvement patterns and, my specific interest here, the nature of the Italo-American experience. In earlier papers I have tried to demonstrate that there is no formal organization or confederation of Italo-Americans in organized crime called Mafia, Cosa Nostra or anything else.[2] There are numbers of Italo-Americans who are involved in organized crime, they do form highly organized local "families" and these groups do cooperate with each other in licit and illicit activities. But they are not held together by a national membership organization with a ruling council or even by some shared conspiracy in crime. They are joined by the looser form of obligations and protections that anthropologists have found in any clan organization. It is the universality of this clan organization and the strength of its shared behavior system which makes Italo-American criminal syndicates seem so similar and suggests a national or even international organization. Once again, the utility of this view goes beyond merely exchanging "amorality" or "criminality" for "familialism" as the descriptor for the organizational variables structuring the Italo-American experience in organized crime. Rather it suggests that understanding the changing structure and values of the Italo-American family is an important element in describing the transition of the Italo-American community through the experience of organized crime in America.

In this essay I hope to show what we already know about the changing structure of the Italo-American family, the values which shape it and the social structures which support it in its Italian heritage and in the acculturative experience. Specifically, I want to show how the changing role of women in Italo-American organized crime families reflects both the loosening of the persistence of Italian cultural values and the influence of American culture in reshaping those values. In doing so, I also hope to demonstrate that, as I learned from Leonard Covello at the outset of my research career, facts are as much a part of culture as artifacts and can not be understood as abstractions from the culture which informs them.

Ever since Josef Von Sternberg's 1927 silent film epic *Underworld* first introduced the gangster to the movie public, there has been a double imagery in the screen symbolism of the women in his life. One image is that of the "moll," the tough-talking, fast-living gangster girl. Sometimes she is his partner in crime, like Bonnie Parker in *Bonnie and Clyde,* often she is an accomplice like Holiday Tokowanda who helps Jimmy Cagney escape from prison (and later kills him) in *Kiss Tomorrow Goodbye.* Most frequently, however, she is simply his girlfriend, like "Francie," whose descent from purity into prostitution led to Humphrey Bogart's first sneer on the silver screen in *Dead End.* But she is never, never his wife. That image is a quite different one. It is the serene and loving face of the "Madonna," untouched by the ruthless and dirty world in which her husband moves. She knows he is not quite like other men, that he does not work a 9-to-5 job in some downtown office, that his business associates are evil and unsavory men, and that the police are out to get him, but she is innocent of any involvement in his criminal life and he never discusses it with her or with the children. And, along with the screen wives of *matadors* and *grand-prix* racing drivers, she spends an inordinate amount of time in church praying to the Madonna for his deliverance from the unknown sins she suspects he earns along with the fast money.

When the spectacular success of Mario Puzo's *The Godfather* made the "Mafia Family" a permanent part of popular culture, it also helped enshrine the Madonna image of the women who are a part of these families. Earlier films dealing with mafiosi had said little or nothing about their family life, concentrating instead on their criminal careers. In fact, Blondy Belle, Rico "Little Caesar" Bandello's moll in the original W. R. Burnett novel, does not even appear in the 1931 film version. But Puzo was attempting to add a human dimension to his "Mafia" family and Don Vito Corleone's clan had any number of madonnas but not one moll.

First there is Mama Corleone, the Don's wife who as a 16-year-old Sicilian immigrant marries the impoverished Vito, bears him four children, and lives with him throughout his long career in crime, seemingly with little direct knowledge about his rise to power and profit in the rackets. Every morning she is driven off to Mass by one of the Don's killer-henchmen in a vain attempt to insure that after death he will go "up there," instead of "down there." Then there is Connie Corleone, the Don's only daughter, whose husband is killed on orders from one of her brothers when he betrays the family. At first Connie berates her brother, but then, with the stoicism of the Mafia wife, she accepts the fact that "it had to be done." Sonny Corleone, the Godfather's oldest son, is married to a nice Italian girl who, despite the fact that her husband "does the job" on other women with some frequency, remains faithful to him and the code of silence even after his untimely death. Finally, there is Kay Adams, the American girl who marries Michael, the Don's youngest son and the heir-apparent to his power. At first, like any normal, educated, middle-class American girl, she wants to know what his father does to earn his obvious wealth and, more pointedly, what Michael will do when he enters the family business. But Michael explains that although she will be his wife, she can never be his partner in life because he can never share with her anything about his business affairs, can never tell her what happened at the office everyday the way other men do. Eventually, even Kay Adams Corleone comes to accept the Mafia law of *omertà*—the code of silence— and "she doesn't mind anymore" that Michael's work-a-day life is "forbidden territory their marriage can never include." In the final scenes, she goes off to church every morning with Mama Corleone to say "the necessary prayers for the soul of Michael Corleone."

Despite the fact that he was writing about mob life in the mid-forties, Puzo provided a timeless reference point for public attitudes about life in a Mafia family, and even though feminine manners and morals have changed significantly over these past 30 years, the imagery of the madonna-wife persists today. How accurate is this imagery? Has the Women's Liberation Movement had no effect on the lives of women in Italo-American families? Are the wives of the "Godfather's" sons and grandsons just as content to keep their place, remain in the background, and raise new generations of mafiosi?

In 1967, Elizabeth Reuss-Ianni, Francesco Cerase and I began an in-depth field study of an Italo-American organized crime family in New York which we described under the pseudonym, "the Lupollos" in our book *A Family Business*. For a period of over two years, we were present at and observed the behavior of members of the family in social settings which ranged from large-scale family events such as weddings or christenings, to more intimate meetings and interviews over dinner. We were able to trace the family history back over a period of four generations to their origins in Sicily and, through subsequent interviews with some of the younger members, to up-date that history to the present. What we learned about the Lupollos in that study and in subsequent interviews along with information on other Italo-American organized crime families, suggests that, at least among the wives of the younger generation members, lifestyles are changing to reflect the current values of their age and social groups.

The patriarch and founder of the Lupollo family empire, Giuseppe Lupollo, came to the United States from Sicily in 1902 as part of the largest wave of immigration in American history. He brought with him his wife, Annunziata, two young sons, Giuseppe Junior (Joe) and Calogero (Charley), and $400, a sizable sum of money in those days of impoverished immigrants. He and Annunziata also brought with them a heritage of family values, traditions and expectations which have their roots in Southern Italian culture but which have served for over 70 years to mold the Lupollos into a cohesive family business today worth over $30 million dollars.

Italy is a nation of families, not of individuals. In the South especially, from which the Lupollos originate, the family *is* the social structure and neither the Church nor the state has ever successfully challenged its supremacy. The family demands the southern Italian's first loyalty and this extended network of kinship provided a pattern of social and moral obligations which had more permanence than religion and more legitimacy than law. In Sicily, the law was viewed with suspicion and disdain because it was so often imposed by an alien government. Breaking the laws of the state was no great matter, just don't break the laws of the family. The spirit of *Mafia* derives from the fact that every man seeks protection for himself and his family. He was taught in childhood that he cannot expect this protection from the state, but only from the network of related families to which every Sicilian—man, woman or child—finds himself bound. Leonard Covello has described this pattern in detailing Southern Italian family life:

> Established on a definite but also narrow policy, the family was by no means a medium for the social training of its individual members: Rather, it precluded or at least hindered the appearance of individuals whose social outlook would transcend family interests and bring into life a more closely integrated community.[3]

The pattern of roles within the southern Italian family grows out of this familialism and mirrors the divine family in Catholicism. The stern, authoritarian father is the patriarch who commands complete and immediate obedience. The true *paterfamilias*, he projects the family's power and status in the community. The mother, like the Madonna, subservient to the father; her humility, fidelity, and willingness to bear all burdens, enshrine the honor of the family and win her the respect of her children. Daughters, like mothers, are humble, and their chastity is a matter of great moment; in Italy, wars have been fought over a daughter's honor. The son is Christ-like in his obedience to his father and his respect for his mother. Whenever he is in danger, pain or anguish, he calls out to either his *mama* or to *La Madonna* for aid or sympathy.

Giuseppe settled in the "Little Italy" section of New York's lower East side and used his $400 savings to set up two small businesses. One was a legitimate business enterprise in which he imported foods from Sicily to sell to his Italo-American neighbors. The other was an illegal store-front bank and card parlor through which he provided both a place to gamble and the one sure source for loans to the hard pressed immigrants. This storefront was the beginning of what later became a multi-million dollar gambling and loan sharking empire. Giuseppe was a shrewd businessman but he also used his Sicilian heritage of familialism to considerable advantage. "If he told us once he told us a thousand times," his son Charlie remembers, "you couldn't trust the judges and the politicians to do anything for you because they were crooks who hid behind the law. The only protection was to take care of yourself and to make sure that you had people around you that you could count on when the time came. Pop always said he trusted his family first, relatives second, Sicilians third, and after that, forget it!" Again, Covello has described this pattern as it existed in the South of Italy in his childhood:

This was the pattern of southern Italian living. First came the immediate family. Then the Covello clan with its innumerable relatives. Then our loyalty extended in ever-diminishing waves from our street to our neighborhood, until it encompassed the whole town; so that anyone who came from outside the town itself was called a *forestiere*, or foreigner.[4]

When Annunziata married Giuseppe in Sicily, she had become part of his family of parents, brothers and sisters, cousins, aunts and uncles, just as he had become part of her extended family. When she came to the United States, however, she left her family ties behind and became a Lupollo. Life for her was a bounded network of other Italian immigrant women hemmed in by the linguistic and cultural walls of the Italian ghetto. Restricted by tradition from having any contact with men other than her husband, she was almost completely confined to social contacts with other neighborhood women. Not only were these neighbors all Italian, many of them came from the same village as Annunziata and had known her and her family in childhood. Within the "Little Italys" of America, Italians have tended to congregate with others from the same province and even from the same village. In Annunziata's neighborhood, for example, Elizabeth Street was Sicilian from one end to the other, while the Neapolitans inhabited most of Mulberry Street. On Elizabeth Street, neighbors from the Sicilian city of Sciacca huddled together in the same tenements, just as people from Palermo lived together in other blocks. More than any other immigrant group, the Italians succeeded in bringing their village culture with them, and that village culture set the standards for Annunziata's behavior and beliefs just as surely and just as completely as it had in

Sicily. So, for Annunziata, the traditional role of the southern Italian peasant wife—seeing only relatives and neighbors who were themselves often relatives—made her life a thing apart from her husband's growing legal and illegal enterprises. It would be more romantic than real to suggest that she was not, however, aware of Giuseppe's business activities, illegal as well as legal, for, unlike the embezzler whose illegal acts are a sideline, organized crime was the major part of Giuseppe's everyday life. *"Chi tace, afferma,"* "Silence gives consent," says an old Sicilian proverb.

By 1915, Giuseppe Lupollo was an established and feared "man of respect" in Little Italy. He had achieved considerable financial success, and over the subsequent decades, the family businesses continued to expand. On the legitimate side, such businesses as real estate, garbage and refuse hauling and disposal, were added. The small importing business had expanded into a chain of groceries and bakeries which later became a nationally known food products company. On the illegal side, family ventures grew even more rapidly and included bootlegging during prohibition as well as the continuance of the loan sharking and gambling operations which spread outside of Little Italy to other sections of New York City and Long Island. In addition, the family itself expanded. By 1920, both of Giuseppe's sons were married and providing grandchildren to the family. Joe married the daughter of an important organized crime figure in New York and the marriage tied the two families together in business as well as social relationships. Charley, younger and better educated than Joe, chose his own wife, Giuseppa Alcamo, who, like Charley, had graduated from high school shortly before their marriage. Through these marriages and other kinship ties, three other lineages—the Alcamos, the Salemis and the Tuccis entered the family and the family businesses as well. As Giuseppe's business enterprise prospered, he delegated responsibility to others but always with the cardinal rule: Keep the business within the family.

As the Lupollos prospered, they began to move out of the Italian ghetto, first to Brooklyn and later to upper-class areas of Long Island and New Jersey. But despite their growing wealth, the family continued to live conservatively. Their house in Brooklyn appeared no more luxurious than any others in their neighborhood. Giuseppe acted and dressed the role of a successful Italo-American businessman. He did not permit himself, or his children, to take on the lavish life style they could well have afforded. Annunziata seems to have changed least of all. Her daughter-in-law, Giuseppa, says of her, "She never seemed to change anything. The furniture in the house was better and there was somebody to drive her to see her children and grandchildren. But her clothes, her hair, nothing changed. Except she put more money in the poor boxes at church."

Annunziata had never really made any close friends in Manhattan, and so moving to Brooklyn did not represent any problems for her. Her children and grandchildren formed the center of her life, and what social contacts she did maintain were with other kinsmen. Joe and Charley continued to provide her with grandchildren. Joe had four sons—Anthony (Tony), Marko (Marky), Giuseppe III (Joey), and Salvatore, and a daughter Marianian. Charley had two sons—Pasquale (Patsy) and Calogero Junior, and three daughters named Clare, Helen and Annunziata. It was these grandchildren who first began to break away from the old traditions of the family. Joe and Charley had been raised in Little Italy and had little or no contact with non-Italian youngsters. They started working for Giuseppe at an early age and their wives lived little differently from Annunziata. In fact, much of their life centered around Annunziata who took it as her responsibility to see that they behaved properly and did not cause their husbands any embarrassment with their business associates or in the community. Giuseppa, Charley's wife, describes her early days living with Charley's family as a period in which she felt she had no family other than Charley until she was finally accepted as a Lupollo. Although Giuseppa was Sicilian, she came from a different district than the Lupollos and so Annunziata did not know much about her family. That, together with the fact that Charley had not sought out his parents' advice in choosing a bride, created tensions in the family, particularly with Annunziata. The young couple moved in with his parents and Giuseppa still remembers that sometimes Charley's mother would pointedly set the dinner table for just three people—herself, her husband and Charley. Gradually, if grudgingly, Annunziata accepted her new daughter-in-law, particularly after grandchildren began to arrive.

In 1940, when he was almost 70 years old, Giuseppe turned over control of the family businesses to Joe, who continues to run them today. Despite his retirement, Giuseppe and Annunziata continued to live in Brooklyn and to remain enveloped by their children and grandchildren. There were occasional visits to the summer homes of their children and even one or two trips to Florida, but neither could escape the web of kinship which they had built nor, really, did they want to. Old Giuseppe died in 1950 and Annunziata went to live with Charley and his family.

It was in the post-World War II period, the third generation of the family, that the major changes in life style for the women of the family began to shape the role of the wives. Many of the children of Giuseppe and Annunziata left the family business and set up their own lives. Joe Lupollo's youngest son Sal graduated from medical school and practices medicine in New Jersey. His wife is active in charities, particularly those benefiting blind children. Charley's daughter Clara is a registered nurse and married a physician. She, along with her husband and children live on Long Island and few, if any, of their neighbors associate them with the Lupollo crime family. His son Charles went to law school in the south and then moved to Arizona, where he is in the real estate business. The four third generation members of the Lupollo lineage who remained in the family business—Joe's sons Tony, Marky, and Joey, and Charley's son Patsy, all live on Long Island. Their wives and families are integrated into the communities where they live quietly. Their wives are much like their neighbors; they shop and socialize in the community, go into New York City to shop for clothing and to attend the theater and are active in local church affairs. If they do differ from their neighbors, it is in the reticence with which they talk about their husband's jobs and the caution they must use in using their considerable wealth for fear that federal tax officials may become suspicious.

What led to these changes in life style, the changing role of women and the defections of wives from the old traditions, was their own sense of liberation as they moved outward and upward from the tightly-knit Italian communities in which they were reared. New friends, new experiences, greater contact with American social values and morals certainly had their effect. But to some extent, it also resulted from the changing place of their husbands in the world of organized crime. Not only were their husbands moving gradually out of organized crime into more legitimate areas of business enterprise, but the strength of mob control over members was diminishing. Part of the unwritten code of Italo-American organized crime syndicates is the strong injunction against telling one's wife about business activities since to do so would not only be unmanly, it would be potentially dangerous as well.

It is in the fourth generation of the family—the children of Marky, Tony, and Joey Lupollo, of the Alcamos, the Tuccis and Salemis—that the greatest change has taken place. It is also in the fourth generation that the women of the family are most obviously and openly in rebellion against the traditions which kept their mothers at home and restricted all social activity for women at least, to within the family group. For one thing, the Lupollos are steadily moving toward legitimation. It is reasonable to predict that by the next generation none of the Lupollo's will be actively involved in organized crime. Of the 27 fourth generation men in the family, only four are involved with the illegal enterprises. Unquestionably, some of the movement is motivated by the need to legitimate money which is received in illegal activities. But much of the movement away from crime results from the normal process of social and occupational mobility which has characterized all ethnic groups in the United States. The Lupollos are following this pattern. Tony Lupollo, for example, has five children. His two daughters have both married outside the family, one of them to a judge's son. Paul, the only son working in the Lupollo family business, has been with the family realty company in Brooklyn ever since he graduated from an Eastern university. The other two sons are still at college. One is a student and the other is an English professor. Marky Lupollo has two daughters. One is a teacher married to a dentist, and the other is working on a Masters in psychology.

Few of the fourth generation of Lupollos have followed their fathers into the family business, and most of the women have married professional or business men frequently, but not always Italian. As in all families, each of the fourth generation wives among the Lupollos is an individual married to a different personality among the four sons who are still in the family business. Freddy Lupollo, for example, is considered the family "ladies man" and spends a good deal of time making the rounds of the night spots in New York City. His wife Monica gets little sympathy from the other wives because, they agree, she brought it on herself. Monica is Irish and met Freddy when both were in college. They were married in 1967 against the wishes of Freddy's family. The family objection became even stronger when, soon after their marriage, they began going out frequently with her friends from college who lived in the New York area. By 1968, their "defection" from the family had become so pronounced that there was open criticism about Monica, her ancestry, and Freddy's lack of masculinity in following her around. Whenever the older women of the family got together socially, they talked of little else besides Monica and her airs. Comments ranged from "she thinks we're not good enough for her" to speculation that Monica was not so much interested in her friends as she was in their husbands. It was Freddy's mother who bore the brunt of the collective displeasure and finally, in exasperation she went to see Monica and spoke harshly to her about what she was doing to her son. Monica stopped seeing her friends for a while, but evidently in the last few years, has been seeing a number of her former girl friends during the day, while Freddy is away. It is this rebellion to family wishes, say the old women knowingly, that leads Freddy to seek his pleasures in the city.

Tommy Lupollo is the family "jock," an avid and expert golfer who plays tennis with his non-Italian neighbors on Long Island two or three times every week. Angie, his wife, is also into sports and plays golf and tennis sometimes with her husband and sometimes with neighbors. Both Tommy and Angie attend football and soccer games religiously. Angie feels strongly that current injunctions against the involvement of girls in the more traditionally male dominated sports such as Little League baseball is insulting and detrimental to children's images of femininity, the family's closest approach to women's liberation. But, when asked if she would take an active role in pushing to remove these barriers, she said she would not: "The last thing they need is to have some character like Howard Cosell announce that the mob has now infiltrated girls' athletics."

Paulie and his wife Mary have no children and, much to the consternation of his parents and other older Lupollos, do not plan to. Mary is very involved in civic affairs, and would like to become active in local and perhaps even national politics someday. Paulie, who works with his father in the family business is prone to saying that she would "clean up the mess," if she did, but does not really take her seriously. When this occurs, Mary becomes furious, and Paulie usually backs off. None in the family really believes she will ever run for office, but Mary seems determined.

These young women and others in the family have grown even farther from the old traditions and would find it hard to recognize the familialism which their mothers and grandmothers practiced as anything more than a ceremonial requirement that they all get together on holidays and feast days and at weddings and funerals.

Even in Sicily, the strength of the rustic code which placed *onore e famiglia*—honor and family—above all else, is beginning to fade. In 1968, when we were doing field work in Sicily, a celebrated case of abduction and rape was causing a stir throughout the island, and even on the Italian mainland. A young shepherd in a mountain village in the heart of the *Mafia* district surrounding Palermo, was *stonnato*—stunned by the thunderbolt of love—on seeing a beautiful young girl in a neighboring village. But she and her family refused his request to call on her. Finally, he decided to settle the matter in the time-honor fashion of the Sicilian hills. He and a number of his male relatives kidnapped the girl and carried her off to the mountains, where the shepherd raped her. Then they returned her to her family to await the inevitable result. The tradition for as long as anyone could remember required that the girl should marry her despoiler, since her honor and the honor of her family was at stake, for now, no one else in the village could ever marry her. But she did not love him, and so she refused. This was unusual enough, but her father not only stood by her in her determination, he denounced the youth to the police and testified against him in court. The girl's determination and her father's courage won the hearts of the townspeople, and not only did they not ostracize and shame the family publicly, they even sent a petition to the Italian government in Rome asking that the girl's father be named a Knight of the Italian Republic. The girl subsequently married a soldier from northern Italy who was stationed in her village.

Yet, while among the Lupollos and other Italian-American organized crime families, the symbol of the madonna-wife, isolated and insulated from her husband's business life is disappearing under the force of acculturation to American social values, some of the old heritage still remains. One of the favorite stories among the Lupollos tells of old Giuseppe's wife visiting with some of her grandchildren in Phil Alcamo's lavish New York apartment. Phil's apartment is tastefully decorated and except for the many autographed photographs of political and entertainment personalities, it is not very different from that of any wealthy business or professional man in the city. Throughout the visit Annunziata kept looking at the lavish collection of paintings on the wall. As they were leaving, one of her granddaughters turned to Annunziata and asked her why she had been so quiet during the evening. *"Manga nu Santa,"* she replied in Sicilian dialect, sadly shaking her head . . . "Not even one Saint's picture."

The kinship model which ties Italo-American criminal "families" together is now disappearing. After three generations of acculturation, the Italo-American family is losing its insistence on father-obedience and mother-respect and the authority structure in the crime "families" is changing, too. What remains to be seen is if these cultural and social facts are as compelling to the American view of the whole of Italo-American community and if they will inform public policy on organized crime as well.

NOTES

1. See, for example, Joseph Albini, *The American Mafia* (New York: Appleton-Century Crofts, 1971); Francis A. J. Ianni, *A Family Business* (New York: Basic Books, 1972); and Dwight Smith, *The Mafia Mystique* (New York: Basic Books, 1975).
2. Francis A. J. Ianni, "Mafia and the Web of Kinship," *The Public Interest*, Winter, 1971.
3. Leonard Covello, "Social Background of the Italo-American school child," unpublished Ph.D. dissertation, New York University, 1944, p. 245.
4. Leonard Covello, *The Heart is the Teacher* (New York: McGraw-Hill, 1958), p. 7.

JERRE MANGIONE

*On Being a Sicilian American**

Being a Sicilian in the United States has never been a picnic. From the time the Sicilians first began migrating to this country in large numbers, they found a hostile land. The only words of welcome were those of the poet Emma Lazarus, inscribed on the base of the Statue of Liberty, and they were written in a language foreign to them. One would have thought they would have had a sympathetic welcome from the German and Irish immigrants, who had preceded them and who knew from experience how difficult it was to make a new home in a new country. But these older immigrant groups had no love for the Sicilians or for any Italians, for that matter. As far as they were concerned, the new immigrants were intruders who represented a threat to their jobs and were deserving of nothing but scorn. The contempt they helped to generate with such terms as "Dago" and "Wop" spread throughout the country.

Because of their swarthy complexions Italians were not considered members of the white race in some parts of the South. One Southern employer was quoted as saying: "It makes no difference to me whom I employ—Negro, Italian, or white man." The Southerners often resented the Italians because they treated Negroes as their equals. In a small Louisiana town five Sicilian immigrants, who had become friends with some of the local blacks, so enraged some of the townspeople that they picked a quarrel with one of them over a goat, then lynched all five of them. In some parts of the South, Italian children were forbidden by law to attend white schools. And in South Carolina a state law prevented Italians from migrating to that state.

In all parts of the country the period between 1880 and the start of World War I, when Italian immigration was at its height, were dark years for the Sicilian and other Italian immigrants. In addition to the hostility of the older immigrant groups, there was that of the native Americans and

* Copyright by Jerre Mangione (All rights reserved).

of the press in general. The Italians had reason enough to fear all of them. During the 1890's at least 22 of their countrymen had been lynched. In the cities they lived in crowded ghettos for mutual protection. Their situation in New York City was especially reprehensible. Although there were no lynchings there, there existed a criminal indifference to the pressing needs of the half-million Italian immigrants crammed into Manhattan's East Side, described by Arrigo Petacco as "a kind of an antheap in which suffering, crime, ignorance and filth were the dominant elements."

Virtually without any police protection, the Italian immigrants in Manhattan found themselves in the same wretched position they had been at home—at the mercy of exploiters and criminals. William McAddo, then New York Police Commissioner, despairing of bringing them law and order, wrote: "The lower East Side, where the Italians live, represents an insoluble problem for the police." This hopeless attitude was reinforced by the fact that of the 30,000 police in New York at the start of the century only eleven spoke Italian—the language of a quarter of the city's population. "It was precisely this absence of 'dialogue'—in the literal sense —between immigrants and policemen," observes Petacco in his excellent book *Joe Petrosino*, "that was to help the growth of the Mafia."

In their hostility campaign against the Italian immigrants the newspapers in all parts of the country promoted the canard that they were largely a criminal lot who carried stilettos and belonged to some secret criminal organization, such as the Mafia and the Black Hand. (That situation has not altered much; even a respected newspaper like the *New York Times* continues to exploit the sensational aspects of words like "Mafia" and "Cosa Nostra.") In the early years of the century when the American press's vilification program was at its height, a number of fair-minded Americans (especially teachers and social workers) felt compelled to protest that the great majority of Italians were honest and law-abiding persons. They cited studies which indicated that crimes by Italian immigrants were of a lower percentage than crimes committed by native-born Americans. But the press, pandering to the bigotry of their readers, ignored all such protests.

From the start, the word "Mafia," which was especially prominent in the headlines, created a great deal of confusion in the public mind about the nature of that criminal organization. The public was kept ignorant of its origins and of its connection with American crime. The term had such drawing power that to newspaper editors, who placed circulation above all other considerations, it seemed like good business to let the public go on thinking that the Mafia was a gigantic network that enveloped nearly everyone with an Italian name. Neither the American press nor the Italian American newspapers made any attempt to explain that the Mafia was

comprised of only a tiny percentage of the entire Italian American population, and that many of the *mafiosi* were not from Sicily but were products
of our own American slums. Nor did the newspapers explain that most
of the victims of the *mafiosi* in this country were the Italian immigrants
themselves.

Early in the century, the image of the Sicilians in Rochester, New York,
where I was born and reared by Sicilian immigrant parents, was so bad
that the immigrants felt it necessary to take some affirmative action that
would demonstrate they were a civilized people of high moral standards,
despite their poverty and their general lack of formal education. They
decided to present the Passion Play, a dramatization of the suffering, death,
and resurrection of Jesus Christ. Several hundred Sicilians, among them
some of my relatives, banded together for the project. The large cast
included milkmen, masons, shoemakers, bakers, tailors, factory hands and
ditchdiggers. Those who were not in the play contributed their services
as costume makers or helped raise money for the production.

After weeks of rehearsals, the company selected a date for the presentation: October 12, Columbus Day, perhaps in the hope that the Americans
in Rochester would discover the good qualities of their much-maligned
Sicilian neighbors. But, alas, for some unexplained reason, most of the
Americans who had been invited to the presentation failed to show up;
those who did were far outnumbered by the Italians in the audience.
Fortunately, the performance of the players generated such excitement as
to create a demand for an encore. The next time, the auditorium was
packed with both Americans and Italians, and the applause, according to
my parents who were present, was tremendous. The next day the same
newspapers that had been featuring Sicilian crime on the front pages
devoted the same space to rave reviews of the production. And the same
editors who had been describing the Sicilians as uncouth and dangerous
produced glowing editorials thanking the immigrants for their contribution
to the community's culture.

But it takes more than a single stage production to change public
opinion. Within a year, the newspapers were back to their old routine of
smearing Sicilians.

As a child who hoped to achieve some prestige among his peers my
Sicilian relatives (who numbered almost one hundred) were a distinct
disappointment in the sphere of crime. The only murder in our family was
that of a gentle, dreamy-eyed uncle who was killed by mistake at a wedding party when he tried to stop a fight between two drunks, one of whom
was armed. Another uncle also got into trouble but he too was the victim
rather than the criminal. My uncle Stefano, who ran a small jewelry business from his living room, was robbed by two *paesani* who tied him to a

chair, then cleaned out his safe. What shocked my uncle as much as the robbery was the fact that a well-meaning neighbor had called the police without consulting him.

Eventually, my relatives were to respect the motives of the American police, but in those early years they could not distinguish between them and the corrupt police system they and their ancestors had known in Sicily. So it was that when the police arrived, my uncle gave a vague account of the robbery, and was unwilling to guess at the identity of the thieves. As a result, the newspaper accounts broadly hinted that my uncle had plotted the robbery in order to collect the insurance. No one bothered to check out the fact that there was no insurance; the robbery had wiped him out completely.

In an attempt to recover the stolen goods, my uncle visited a *paesano* who was reputed to be a big wheel in the local underworld, and provided him all the information he had not given the police. The *paesano* was horrified that a man as "respected" as my uncle would be robbed by two of his compatriots. He promised "on my honor" to do everything possible to recover the stolen jewels. A few days later he apologetically reported that the thieves, on seeing the news stories of the robbery, had taken fright and left for Sicily; there was nothing he could do.

None of my relatives thought it strange that my uncle should go to a *mafioso* for help in his circumstances; nor did they have any doubt that if the police and the newspapers had not interfered, my uncle would have been able to recover his jewels. Within the strict code of Sicilian morality, a "respected" person like my uncle, who had a good reputation for dealing with people fairly, did not deserve to be robbed. The fact that the robbery had taken place suggested that a mistake had been made, one that could be rectified by the boss of the robbers.

My relatives did not condone people who were *mafiosi*; they simply expected that if you couldn't trust the police to deal with you with the proper respect, you trusted those who were in a position to enforce your rights as a respected person. This line of thinking can be traced to the origins of the Mafia, which began to flourish in Sicily when the newly founded Italian Republic ignored the problems of law-enforcement on the island. At first the Mafia groups meted out justice for people who could not get it from the regular authorities but after a while they degenerated into criminal self-serving gangs who, by means of terror and violence, imposed their own code of law on the people—a code that forbade, on penalty of death, any cooperation with the police.

As a young child constantly surrounded by Sicilian relatives, the public image of the Sicilians did not concern me much. A far greater worry was the question of who I was. It was a confusion I shared with my brothers and my sisters. Were we Americans or were we Sicilians? Neither our parents nor our teachers could provide us with an answer that satisfied any of us. Being the oldest child in the family, I was the first to be confused, especially as my first language was Sicilian. For reasons of love, our parents, who were afraid of losing communication with their own children, forbade us to speak English at home.

My feeling of being an outsider in or out of our home may have begun with that edict. Or it may have started when I was finally permitted to play with the other children on the street—the children of Poles, Jews, Germans and other Italians. They sneered and jeered at me, as was their custom when any new boy tried to join them. Their loudest sneers were directed against my baptismal name of Gerlando, which they reduced to Jerry as soon as they had decided to accept me in their group. Out of such action came the awareness that I, like many other children of immigrants, was doomed to live a double life, the one I led at home with my Sicilian parents and relatives, and the other that took place on the street and at school.

As I have shown in *Mount Allegro*, most of my relatives lived within a few blocks of one another. That was about as far apart as they could get without feeling they were living as hermits in a desolate and lonely land. Rochester, like so many Eastern American cities, had an extensive "Little Italy" but our neighborhood was not part of it. The Poles and Jews in it outnumbered the Italians and the Jews outnumbered everybody else. At one time I had so many Jewish playmates that one of them began spreading the rumor that I had been left on my parents' doorstep by a Jewish mother.

There was no sense of ethnocentricity in the neighborhood. They were all immigrant families concerned chiefly with the problem of economic survival. Two of the groups, the Jews and the Sicilians, were also concerned with the problems of prejudice. My father constantly worried about the damage being done to the honor of the Sicilians by the newspapers that maligned them and by the employers who would not hire them. So sensitive was he about the reputation of the Sicilians that when he learned that Boy Scouts carry knives, a weapon that was commonly associated with Sicilian crime he forbade his sons to join the Scouts.

For my father and for many other Sicilian immigrant parents the American world was fraught with alien mores that offended them and corrupted their children. They were appalled, for example, that American boys and girls were permitted to date without having a chaperone along. In Sicily this would have been unthinkable. My relatives were also shocked to learn that American sons and daughters could become engaged and marry without obtaining permission from their parents. Such customs were antithetical to their own and, in their view, invariably destroyed the sanctity of the family and the authority of the father. In Sicily the father could expect (and receive) absolute obedience from every member of his family. Here he was relatively powerless; on reaching legal age, his children could do as they pleased.

Understandably, it took most Sicilian immigrants a long time to surrender to the American way of life—some of them never did. When it happened, the immigrants blamed Destiny for sending them to a materialistic land where respect and family honor, in their judgment, were disdained with impunity. Perhaps the most painful concession they had to make was permitting their daughters the same kind of freedom that all other American-born girls enjoyed. One Sicilian father, at least, was never able to make that concession. When he discovered that his 17-year-old daughter was secretly dating an *Americano*, he trailed the young couple one night and, while they were kissing goodnight, pounced on the young man and bit off a piece of his ear.

If we children had our own way, our parents would have dropped all of their Sicilian ideas and customs and behaved like "Americans." Like most children, we were mindless conformists. More than anything else, we wanted to be regarded as Americans, though we could not be certain what they were like. Among our relatives anyone who spoke English and was not an Italian was promptly categorized as an "American." Movie stars probably came closest to our conception of what Americans must be like. But in the face of having to speak Sicilian and eat Sicilian, it seemed futile to try to imitate them. Some of our teachers were obviously American but it was impossible to imitate them—they knew too much, had too much power, and entertained curious ideas about children of Italian origin, believing, for example, that if you had an Italian name, you were bound to be brilliant in such subjects as Latin, music and art.

Our parents were as guilty as the teachers in this respect, particularly in misjudging our talent for music. As the oldest child, I was the first victim of my mother's campaign to make musicians of all her children. Diligently she hoarded nickels so that she could pay the piano teacher who called once a week, but instead of practicing scales, I would be hiding somewhere reading a book (my mother held that too much reading could drive a person insane; so nearly all my reading at home was done in secret). As a student of the piano I was a complete flop. But my mother's faith in my musical abilities seemed to be indestructible for a time. To support her optimism she had developed the remarkable theory that once I found the right musical instrument to match my talents, I would become a concert artist in no time.

Well, after the piano came the violin. And when it became all too evident, even to my mother, that the violin was not my instrument, I was given guitar lessons. My brother, who had just finished demonstrating that the piano was not his instrument, took my place at the violin. Eventually my mother gave up on both of us, not because she had lost faith in her theory but because she wanted to give my two sisters a chance to develop their musical genius, and there were not enough nickels to pay for all of our instruction. We were all miserable failures as musicians, and it is still a profound mystery to everyone in the family where my brother's two sons, Chuck and Gap Mangione, who have achieved considerable success as composers and performers, got their musical talent. Certainly not from their father, or grandfathers. The only possible conclusion is that in some miraculous fashion they must have acquired it from my mother's wishes and dreams.

In a poor immigrant family like ours any form of education beyond that required by law was considered a great luxury. If the means could be found for sending one of the children to college, the child usually chosen was the eldest son. In their struggle to plant roots in this country, many an immigrant family dreamed of producing a doctor or a lawyer. It was said of Italian families that if a son could tolerate the sight of blood, he would be trained as a doctor; otherwise, he went to law school. Becoming a doctor was considered the supreme achievement but few could afford the years of professional training that entailed. So they compromised, and their sons became lawyers, dentists, pharmacists or teachers instead. Most families, however, could not send their children past high school, and were obliged to console themselves with the hope that the grandchildren might achieve some profession.

Since the sight of blood did not appeal to me and I lacked the aggressive personality commonly associated with lawyers, it was decided I should become a pharmacist. In preparation for such a career, on my birthday my family presented me with an elaborate chemistry set. But one day, while experimenting in my cellar laboratory, a test tube exploded in my hands, almost setting myself and the house on fire. That ended my career as a pharmacist. My ambition to become a writer may have begun at the age of ten when my uncle Luigi, who was easily attracted to non-Italian widows, commissioned me to ghostwrite his love letters. The first letter must have been a disaster. In my ignorance of women, I emphasized my uncle's passion for the widow's luxurious home rather than his passion for her. There was no reply to that letter but my uncle, not realizing what I had written, attributed her silence to her Anglo-Saxon frigid nature, and went on paying me to write letters to other widows—none of whom he ever married.

Generally, there was little communication between my relatives and the non-Italian world. Nowhere was this more evident than at St. Bridget, a near-by Catholic Church where most of my relatives worshipped. The parish priest was a short-tempered Irishman, who deeply resented the fact that most of his congregation now consisted of Italians, many of whom did not understand a word he said. His fierce demands from the pulpit for contributions were often mistaken by the Italians as diatribes against the devil. My brother and I deplored his obvious dislike of the Sicilians in his congregation, particularly his habit of bullying them for not contributing enough money for the support of the church. One Sunday morning, while the priest was passing the collection plate, we witnessed a scene that caused my eleven-year-old brother to explode. When the priest reached the pew in front of us, a poor Sicilian widow we knew dropped a nickel into the collection basket only to have it thrown back in her face. Before I could stop him, my brother was on his feet shouting at the priest: "You can't do that. She's poor. She can't afford any more." The priest was too stunned to say anything. My brother was trembling, frightened by his impulsive action. I took him by the hand (I am sixteen months older) and we made a hasty exit.

Instinctively, most Sicilians kept away from the "Americans," if it was at all possible. They shopped in Italian stores, and frequented Italian dentists, doctors, lawyers, shoemakers and barbers. Nearly all of their business and social life was conducted in their native tongue. In Rochester, as in other cities, this separation was to continue long after the immigrants had been here. Psychologically, this was an unfortunate but understandable situation. In a new country filled with foreigners whose language and customs were incomprehensible, they depended on one another's company more than ever.

The Sicilians were always having parties, mostly family affairs, not only for birthdays, saints days and anniversaries, but also when a child was baptized, when he received first Communion, when he was Christened, and when he was graduated from school. Being together engendered in them a feeling of emotional security. The arrival of a new immigrant from Sicily, or the opening of a new barrel of wine was still another excuse for another reunion. Weddings, which were the most elaborate of all the celebrations, were usually held in large halls (sometimes rented from unions) so that all the relatives and their children, as well as all their friends, could be accommodated. And the dancing would last long after the newlyweds had departed, far into the night, even among the smallest children.

Sicilians were quite strict with their children—they could not speak at the table, for example, unless they were first spoken to by an adult. Yet the children were never excluded from the company of the grownups. They were permitted to go to bed as late as the parents did, regardless of age, and they usually accompanied their parents no matter where they went, be it a funeral or a picnic. Babysitters were then unheard of among Sicilians. Being a Sicilian child was like living under a loving dictatorship.

Even though it meant living a double life—being Sicilian at home and American elsewhere—as children we enjoyed the company of our elders. It was only when they were being "Sicilian" in public that we felt embarrassed by them. I had a particular dread for picnics in public parks when Sicilian food was being consumed with pagan abandon, the sound of their talk and laughter drowning out all other sounds, while near-by some American family sat sedately and quietly nibbling on neatly trimmed sandwiches. Mistaking the high spirits and easy naturalness of my relatives for vulgarity, I worried about what the Americans might think of them, not realizing then that their reaction might be one of envy.

Living in two worlds, our general impression of Americans was bound to be confused by our relatives' ambivalent opinions of them. On the one hand, they were highly critical of their lack of moral standards and the liberties they permitted their children. On the other hand, they sometimes admired their energy and enterprise and even took to imitating some of their habits, such as drinking orange juice in the morning and wearing pajamas at night. And although they criticized Americans for their willingness to exploit immigrants, they envied them for their ability to achieve materialistic success.

The wide gulf between the Sicilian world and the American one went beyond differences of custom and language. At the center of the gulf was a basic difference in philosophy. Ingrained into the ancient Sicilian soul by centuries of poverty and oppression were strong elements of fatalism which the Sicilians called *Destinu*. The Sicilian immigrant believed, just as all his forebears had, that *Destinu*, the willingness to resign oneself to misfortune, was the key to survival. To refuse to believe that a force beyond human control predetermined the fate of all people was to court disaster, according to the traditional Sicilian. The fact that he and his family had, in effect, defied *Destinu* by crossing an ocean in the hope of changing their lives did not occur to them; they continued to believe in *Destinu* long after their arrival here.

The philosophy that the children of immigrants acquired in American schools was diametrically opposed to that of their parents. There was nothing fatalistic about it. Repeatedly the teachers talked of freedom, free enterprise and free will, and constantly stressed the individual's capacity to change and improve his situation. Some of them went so far as to say that if you were smart enough and played your cards right, you might even become President of the United States. Inevitably, the children became aware of this basic disagreement between Sicilians and Americans, and it accentuated their dissatisfaction for being obliged to lead a double life—a dissatisfaction which, in most children of immigrant parents, generated serious identity problems as they became adults.

Psychologically, at least, the immigrant parents were better off than their children. *They* had no identity problem. With their old world wisdom, they could accept the fact that they were living among foreigners with foreign customs, and, in accordance with Sicilian tradition, learned to make the best of it. Contrary to the expectations of the melting pot theorists, they retained their individuality; they did not "melt down." However, they did become Americanized in at least one significant respect. It took them a long time but gradually they began to move away from their faith in *Destinu*. The longer they lived here, the more they sensed that it was they themselves, not destiny, who had the power to change their lives. It was probably the best thing that happened to them as strangers in a new land.

For all their wisdom, they failed to understand the dilemma of their American-born children who were being pulled in two opposite directions, on the one hand by their parents with their insistence on old world traditions, on the other by their teachers, whose new world ideas were often at variance with those of the parents. In this inadvertent tug of war the offspring of the Italian parents was often left with confused impressions of identity which were never resolved. In most instances the influence of the parents prevailed, and the offspring remained trapped in their environment for the rest of his life, afraid of venturing out into the American mainstream. He developed, in effect, a ghetto psychology which, incorporating the darkest fears and suspicions of his immigrant forebears, made him resistant to social change.

Some of us escaped that fate by our decision to explore the world beyond that of our immigrant parents. I initiated my own explorations by going to a university in another city, not out of any lack of love for my relatives but simply because I suspected that as long as I remained among them, I would never have a clear sense of my own identity. Only after I had been separated from them for a number of years did I begin to see them objectively and to appreciate their great wisdom and their superb talent for living, qualities which I rarely encountered in my new American world. While I could never go home again, except for visits, my association with my relatives gave me a *root* feeling, a sense of the past that I needed in order to cope with the present.

PELLEGRINO NAZZARO

Fascist and Anti-Fascist Reaction in the United States to the Matteotti Murder

In June, 1924, the Socialist Deputy Giacomo Matteotti was murdered by Fascist "squadrists." He was done away with after a courageous condemnation of the atmosphere of terror and the grave irregularities committed by the Fascists in the general elections of April, 1924. Through acts of terrorism and intimidation, Fascists had been able to secure an unexpected, strong majority in the Italian Parliament. Matteotti's slaying raised, however, one single cry of indignation and horror in Italy and abroad. Aware of this situation of general distrust for the regime, Mussolini rushed in, writing personal dispatches to diplomatic agents and chargé d'affaires abroad. Mussolini instructed them to spread word that Matteotti's murder had "aggravated the domestic situation of Italy, since Fascism was faced now with more intrigues." Though the actual executors of the crime had been secured to the Italian judiciary authorities, who would certainly render full justice to the victims, Mussolini suggested that the diplomatic authorities abroad insist in pointing out the general atmosphere of uneasiness with which Fascism was confronted. Furthermore, he invited them to insist in stressing that the murder had, at least for the time being, suspended the process of national reconciliation he had initiated.[1]

On June 18, Gelasio Caetani, Italian Ambassador to the United States, cabled Mussolini assuring him that the American press in general had reported the Matteotti "incident," without any "sharp or unfavorable direct reaction against Mussolini and the Italian government." Particularly, *The New York Times* had commented on the "incident of Matteotti," using words of respect and sympathy on behalf of Fascism, Mussolini, and the Italian government.[2] On June 21, continuing in his informative program, Caetani briefed Mussolini on the latest developments of the Matteotti affair. He reported that, with the exception of the Italian-American anti-Fascist and a few American newspapers, such as *The World* of New York City, the majority of the American press continued in maintaining "an

objective position, with comments of sympathy for the Italian government."
Moreover, Caetani assured Mussolini that, in an interview with the Associated Press, he had carefully observed Mussolini's instructions. Especially, he had emphasized the deep sorrow and grief expressed by the head of the Italian government and the nation at large. Finally, he had carefully presented the three issues Mussolini had recommended: (a) that the murder had been committed by vicious elements who had infiltrated the Fascist Party with the evil intention to subvert it; (b) that justice would be meted out with severity to the material executors of the cynical crime; (c) that the recent domestic events would fortify Fascism in its program of moral and national regeneration.[3]

Even while Caetani gave Mussolini these sympathetic assurances, anti-Fascist manifestations against Il Duce and his repressive regime were not late in coming. On June 26, following an extensive press condemnation, an anti-Fascist manifestation was held at Carnegie Hall in New York by Italian and American anti-Fascist organizations. The chief topic was the kidnapping and slaying of the Socialist Deputy Matteotti. In a three hour oratory, Mussolini, the Fascists of Italy and America, President Coolidge, and the Ku Klux Klan were denounced. At the cry of "Down with Mussolini and Fascism," the 2,500 people attending the meeting denounced Fascism, its leaders, its doctrine, its methods, and its terrorism. At a certain point, New York City Municipal Court Justice Jacob Panken shouted that the cry "Down with Mussolini and Fascism" was not enough. The cry should be "Down with Capitalism." The crowd immediately agreed. When one of the main speakers, Charles Erwin, former editor of the suspended Socialist newspaper, *The New York Call*, addressed the audience demanding the immediate resignation of the Italian Ambassador Caetani, clashes with punching, kicking, shoving and yelling occurred among the crowd. Evidently Fascist elements had infiltrated the crowd with the task of disrupting the meeting. Several policemen and the entire Bomb Squad intervened. After order had been restored, Erwin continued reading a letter addressed to President Coolidge, demanding the immediate resignation of Ambassador Caetani, who had "avowed himself a member of the Fascists." Furthermore, Erwin demanded that the American Congress pass immediately a resolution denouncing Italy, because "a nation governed by such a body does not deserve recognition as a sister nation to the civilized states of the world." The spirit of Mussolini that had poisoned all of Italy had gained strength through American recognition, concluded Erwin. Another speaker, Arturo Giovannitti, proposed a permanent "state of war between the workers of the United States and the government of Fascism in Italy." Elizabeth Gurley Flynn, third speaker, asserted that the murder of Matteotti had been approved by Mussolini because the Socialist Deputy was going to uncover scandals in Mussolini's government which "would have made the Teapot Dome scandals look sick."[4]

Even though it may be regarded as a pure coincidence, on June 28, *The Saturday Evening Post* started publishing a series of articles written by Richard Washburn Child, former American Ambassador to Italy. The articles examined the nature, the doctrine, the structure, and the goals of Fascism in Italy. The first article, "The Making of Mussolini," was a lengthy, biased, and apologetic essay on Mussolini as person, political leader, and statesman. The second article, "Open the Gates," appeared on July 12. In it, Child stressed that Fascism was a movement of youth. Like springtime, Fascism had blossomed throughout Italy from 1920 to 1922, the year of the March on Rome. The October Revolution in Italy was described as "a rain-soaked Revolution," carried out in the spirit of the Crusades and in Mussolini's idea of moderation. The series concluded, on July 26, with the article, "What Does Mussolini Mean." According to Child, Fascism meant full power and full responsibility. Moreover, Mussolini's immediate achievements had been work for unemployed, duties set above rights, a spirit of service, pragmatic vision for the most impellent problems of Italy without illusions. All these issues made Mussolini a "glutton for work."[5] "What a propitious moment," Caetani wrote Mussolini on June 27, "for such a series." *The Saturday Evening Post*, with an overall circulation of two million copies, had to be considered "an important and influential paper throughout the United States." The publication of Child's series and, above all, the very fact that Caetani notified Mussolini about the forthcoming series advances some conjectures on the role and function of the series. Given the timing, it must be inferred that the series, written by a sympathizer of Fascism, served to offset anti-Fascist propaganda against Mussolini in the United States, which had become extremely aggressive in the aftermath of Matteotti's murder. Even though the periodical's publishers cannot be charged with connivance with Fascism, nevertheless it seems that, reflecting its conservative line, the magazine expressed more approval than disapproval of Fascism. The very fact that the series appeared when Matteotti's slaying had spurred indignation and horror in Italy and abroad and was written by a diplomat well known for his sympathy toward Fascism leads one to believe that the series had been planned. Caetani rejoiced for such a series. In his dispatch to Mussolini, he commented:

By a happy event, ex-Ambassador Child has started publication of a series on Fascism in the weekly magazine, *The Saturday Evening Post*. . . . From what has been written in the first article, I foresee a sympathetic analysis of the Fascist Revolution.[6]

Furthermore, Mussolini's strategy aimed at presenting Matteotti's murder as slowing down his program of national reconciliation in Italy seemed to have captured the imagination of many American correspondents. In analyzing the press coverage of that period, it emerges unequivocally that Mussolini had succeeded in producing a remarkable mystification of Matteotti's case for the American government and the people as well. On June 29, *The New York Times* published Arthur Livingston's article, "Power of Mussolini Is Shaken by Murder." The author of the article condemned the material assassination of Matteotti. However, he found enough evidence to perpetuate the newspaper's quasi-defensive attitude toward Fascism. "In the past five years," wrote Livingston, "Mussolini has accomplished wonders as a political organizer. He has worked miracles as general manager and repairer of a collapsing State. But he is still confronted by one failure that threatens at any moment to upset him. He has failed to pacify Italy. He has failed to discipline the elements to which he owes his power." Assertions of this nature supported the thesis that Matteotti's murder had to be held as the immediate consequence of the still unstable political situation reigning in Italy. Hence, Mussolini's direct responsibility in the murder of the Social Deputy had to be excluded. "The kidnapping of Matteotti, member of the Parliament," continued Livingston, "brings the Italian public face to face with the fact that it is governed not by a legal State but by a crowd of selfish politicians." Thus, Fascism was faced with a tremendous task at that time: to bring into the mainstream of legality and order strong concentrations of disorderly forces, which still operated in Italy.[7]

A pro-Fascist attitude was taken also by the weekly magazine *Outlook*. According to editorials published in this magazine, the charges moved against Mussolini were merely a Communist invention, because "neither murder nor conspiracy has been proved." In connection with the disappearance of the Socialist Deputy, the magazine asserted that "violently partisan accusations" had been put forth against Mussolini by his foes. Furthermore, the magazine seemed to give special credit to the version offered by the Italian Ambassador in Washington. In fact, it quoted extensively Caetani's comments on the affair. In doing so, the magazine followed the identical interpretive pattern of *The New York Times*, *The New York World*, and *The Saturday Evening Post* of Philadelphia. As far as the material crime was concerned, *Outlook* gave this interpretation. The murder had to be ascribed only to those criminal elements "who exist in every party no matter how respectable and in every country." Even though Fascism was, indeed, passing through a serious moment of political adjustment, nevertheless such an unfortunate and regrettable event should not justify any accusations of Mussolini's integrity. The Communists and the Socialists had staged, instead, a denigratory campaign against Mussolini, asserting that Matteotti's kidnapping and murder were Mussolini inspired. According to the magazine, these charges had been made "in an inflamed state of mind by radicals of the extreme type" and should have not been taken seriously unless and until they were proved. The magazine gave also credit to Mussolini's immediate and intelligent action in the political sector. In rejecting as ominous, vicious, and unfounded the accusations moved by the extremists, Mussolini continued to defend the process of national reconstruction undertaken in Italy. Therefore, with ability and skill, Il Duce had been able to neutralize another maneuver of the Opposition that tried to use the incident of Matteotti to overthrow the regime. The story of Mussolini's extraordinary talent in reforming Italy had to be understood as the result of a counter-revolution. Italy was still suffering from a dangerous and corrosive propaganda of Bolshevism and Anarchism, which had rendered all the previous governments inefficient and supine. Though Mussolini's counter-revolution was producing sporadically serious manifestations of violence and lawlessness, nevertheless, he deserved credit for rescuing Italy from a perilous situation. A government established through a revolutionary act was bound to guarantee sooner or later "merciless justice against the dastardly political and personal murderers" and a national state of affairs where "constitutional guarantees and thoroughgoing representative self-government" would be as a result definitely established.[8] Pursuing this philo-Fascist line, the magazine published, on August 6, an article "After the Matteotti Murder." In it, the correspondent from Rome, special envoy of the magazine, stressed Mussolini's new program to get rid of those Fascist elements who had elected violence for violence's sake. The article advanced, and for the first time, the hypothesis that the murder of the Socialist Deputy might have been instigated by those dissident groups that formed the extremist and revolutionary fringe of the Fascist Party. In fact, in denouncing the crime, Mussolini had clearly admitted that the murder of Matteotti had been "worse than a crime—a blunder." The crime, however, would give Mussolini a firm grip to bring Fascism to normalization. Decidedly, the process of normalization would not be smooth due to the reaction and opposition of those Fascist "squadrists" who were too frightened to become normal citizens. Nonetheless, Mussolini would finally triumph over his internal and external enemies. "Yet those who think that Fascism is finished commit a grave error," continued the article. "Rome itself remembers only Matteotti; but the rest of Italy remembers the Socialist regime and threat that Fascism destroyed." Under Socialist control of almost two thousand municipal governments, Italy had witnessed a period of "ceaseless strikes, of the blackmail of society, of brutal murders." After all, Fascist violence paled

in a drawing up of the mournful balance of Socialist and Communist out-
rages. In spite of Fascist violence, life in Italy had been safer and quieter
under Fascism, concluded the article.[9]

From June to August, the American press at large concentrated on
Matteotti's murder, hypothesizing on the consequences it might bear for
Fascism in Italy. *The New York Herald Tribune*, the *Brooklyn Eagle*, the
Baltimore *Sun*, the Chicago *Evening Post*, the Philadelphia *Public Ledger*,
all agreed that the murder might have shaken Mussolini's political position
(The crime itself has proved unmistakably that the Fascist regime in Italy
was as much an opponent of democracy and parliamentary institutions as
of liberty).

In July, *The Nation*, a periodical which had led all the way in anti-
Fascist opposition among the English language magazines, published an
article "Why Matteotti Had To Die," by James Fuchs. It was the first
unbiased and objective presentation of the Matteotti affair to the American
people. After having presented the political situation generated in Italy
since the Fascist coup d'état of October, 1922, the article analyzed the
motives that had instigated the slaying of the Socialist Deputy. According
to the article, Matteotti was murdered for three reasons:

1. Because he wanted to reveal the true story of the corruption and
abuses committed by the Fascists in the general elections of April, 1924;

2. Because he was about to incriminate the chief participants in the
after-election act of terrorism;

3. Because he would have forced judicial action against the main
corruptionists in the elections. This legal action would have provided the
invalidation of enough mandates to deprive Mussolini's government of its
majority.

The whole article proved unmistakably that Matteotti's murder should
not be considered, as Mussolini had affirmed, as an isolated and sporadic
act of criminal offense executed by the "squadrists" of the left wing fringe.
On the contrary, the crime was the immediate responsibility of Mussolini
himself and his entire Fascist regime. The article concluded that Matteotti
had to die because he was about to prove to the civilized world that "Italy
had lost its rank as a nation with a representative government." Thus, the
article brought to the attention and analysis of the American nation the
most tangible acknowledgement of the despotic aims of Fascism in Italy
and in the whole world.[10]

The criticism staged by *The Nation* and other anti-Fascist newspapers in
the United States was not sufficient to change the pattern maintained by the
overwhelming majority of the American press, which continued to be
pro-Fascist and pro-Mussolini oriented. In particular, *The Literary Digest*

published in August and September, 1924, a series of articles in each of which the reaction to Matteotti's murder was assessed differently. However, each article ended with a note of praise for Mussolini's efforts in defending Italy from the attacks of subversive and Communist elements:

> The present parliamentary majority retains not only the right but also the duty to assume the most important responsibilities before the possible political consequences of recent grave events, especially because the oppositions are so various and discordant that Italy cannot depend upon them for any solution.[11]

Against this pro-Fascist front, represented by both the American conservative and liberal press, the anti-Fascist press of Italian language staged the most courageous and massive propaganda campaign. Throughout the United States, the anti-Fascist Italian press was relentless in condemning and accusing Mussolini and his regime for the assassination of Matteotti. In New York City, *Il Martello, Il Proletario, La Notizia, L'Era Nuova, La Giustizia, L'Adunata dei Refrattari, L'Umanità Nuova*, and from November, 1925, *Il Nuovo Mondo*, all published editorials accusing Mussolini of the slaying of Giacomo Matteotti. Their campaign, relentless, courageous, and well planned, continued until the fall of Mussolini in 1943. In particular, *Il Martello* with its impressive anti-Fascist campaign became the vanguard of the Fascist opposition in the United States. It even proclaimed, on December 5, 1925, a nation-wide campaign of boycott. In an appeal to all Italian-American Anti-Fascists, the newspaper invited them to follow the following guidelines of boycott:

> Workers, comrades: the best method to defeat our common enemy is to cut off monetary assistance and profit.
> If your doctor is Fascist: boycott him.
> If your lawyer is Fascist: boycott him.
> If your tailor is Fascist: boycott him.
> If your shoemaker is Fascist: boycott him.
> If your retailer is Fascist: boycott him.
> If your grocer is Fascist: boycott him.
> If your newspaperman is Fascist: boycott him.
> If your druggist is Fascist: boycott him.
> If your barber is Fascist: boycott him.
> If your landlord is Fascist: boycott him.

If you know that Banks, Movie Theatres, Drug Stores, Insurance and Travel Agencies are owned by Fascists, boycott them. Do not buy products which bear the label "Made in Italy." You must boycott, wherever you are and always. In this way, we can weaken the Italian monster. It is like a horse, if it has no oats, it changes course.[12]

Articles of condemnation of Fascism and its methods of terrorism were published in *La Parola, Il Lavoratore*, and *The Daily Worker* of Chicago.

The leading role was held by *Il Lavoratore*. In an editorial on July 1, 1924, the newspaper accused Fascism of having transformed Italy from a civilized and democratic country into "a swamp of death, assassination, and terror." On July 28, another article appeared, declaring Fascism and the Italian government "to be drowned in a sea of innocent blood." Moreover, the black shirts, considered in Italy the heroes of the Fascist revolution, were portrayed as the "black souls" of Fascist degeneration.[13] In Detroit, the anti-Fascist opposition was led by *La Voce del Popolo* and *La Luce*. In Pueblo, Colorado, two newspapers, *Marsica Nuova* and *Il Pupo*, carried on relentless attacks against Fascism and Mussolini. On May 9, 1925, *Il Pupo* published an article, "A Strong State," written by Vincenzo Vacirca, ex-Socialist Deputy, who had been expelled from Italy for his affiliation with the Socialist Party. Vacirca criticized not only the slaying of Matteotti, but also the most recent aggression suffered by another Socialist Deputy, Giovanni Amendola, who had been beaten almost fatally by the "squadrists." The incident of Amendola, according to Vacirca, proved unmistakably that the theory of the "strong State," introduced by Mussolini to defend all citizens from treacherous elements, was a legend. Fascism had espoused the doctrine of violence for violence's sake.[14] In Boston was published *La Nazione*; in Pittsburgh, the *Unione Figli D'Italia*. On August 24, 1924, an editorial in the *Unione Figli D'Italia* affirmed that the body of Matteotti one day would rise to indict the assassins and vindicate himself before the tribunal of the world. However, the proletariat of the world will assign the great sentence to Mussolini and his regime.[15] In San Francisco, California, *L'Italia* and *Il Corriere del Popolo* were published. In an article "What is the Fatherland," *Il Corriere del Popolo* affirmed that the ideal concept of the nation can develop only in a democratic country. A dictatorial system cannot admit or believe in the concept of Fatherland. The dictator is himself the country. Therefore, people should idolize him. Consequently, the idea of nation is mere abstraction.[16]

These newspapers carried a relentless anti-Fascist campaign, which intensified in the aftermath of Matteotti's murder. However, it is important to point out that their activities were not limited to the United States. Rather, they extended to Europe and to Italy in particular. According to archival sources, discovered in Rome's Central State Archives, from June, 1924 to July, 1925, over 20,000 copies of the mentioned newspapers were seized by the Italian Post Office throughout the nation. Mussolini and DeBono sent confidential dispatches to the Provincial Postmasters inviting them to seize all "subversive newspapers, literature, and propaganda materials aimed at introducing radical and subversive ideas in Italy." Special attention had to be given to all newspapers arriving from the

United States.[17] Indeed, Mussolini and the Foreign Ministry had been informed directly from America about the smuggling in of anti-Fascist materials. On June 10, 1924, an Italian "squadrist" living in Pueblo, Colorado, sent Mussolini a lengthy memorandum containing a list of addresses of persons in Italy who received "subversive propaganda."[18]

This shows that Matteotti's murder not only raised a cry of indignation and protest, but also was the turning point of a world-wide anti-Fascist campaign conducted in communal spirit by the American, French, English, Canadian, Mexican, and Latin American anti-Fascists. It was a most constructive and articulate anti-Fascist struggle, which eventually ended with the downfall of Fascism and Mussolini.

As far as the fortune of anti-Fascism in America, things seemed to have developed in various directions. As we have seen, the Matteotti affair had raised protest and indignation even in the United States. However, the press had dissociated Mussolini from responsibility for the material execution of the crime. This superficial solution of the case had been sufficient to create problems for the Italian-American radicals, Socialists, and Communists. Furthermore, such an interpretation had drawn a demarcation line between Mussolini's sympathizers and his foes. In addition, it had divided profoundly the Italian colony in America. To most Americans, the Italian-Americans had to be divided into two different breeds of countrymen. On the one hand were those who heartily supported Mussolini and his regime of law and order. To these groups went the moral and spiritual support of the American majority. On the other hand were those who, having espoused the cause of Socialism, appeared in the eyes of the Americans to be subversive, radical, revolutionary, and enemies of law and order. To these groups went popular contempt and governmental harassment.

The June 26 manifestation at Carnegie Hall was not the only one staged by the anti-Fascists in America. In the aftermath of Matteotti's murder they intensified their activity. Meetings, rallies, and public manifestations took place in many cities throughout the United States. Police and the entire Bomb Squads were on the alert. Since these manifestations were carried on with the shouting of anti-Italian and anti-American slogans, police intervened and made arrests. On other occasions, the manifestations were prevented on the charge that they were being held by Italian radicals. This situation of police repression inflamed some of the American public.

On June 30, a letter of protest was addressed to *The New York Times* by Emanuel Aronsberg, a New York City resident. The author of the letter stigmatized the "turbulent and violent gathering" at Carnegie Hall. The presence of Charles Erwin, former editor of the extinct Socialist daily, *The New York Call*, offered further arguments of protest. Erwin's request for the immediate resignation of Ambassador Caetani and the ominous attacks against the Fascist government of Italy had to be considered unwarranted. In fact, Erwin had never, in the past and as editor of the Socialist *Call*, criticized or expressed concern or indignation for the continued imprisonment and execution of his Socialist friends, the Mensheviks, at the hand of the Bolsheviks in Russia. According to Aronsberg, what was good for his Russian friends seemed to be objectionable for Mussolini:

> Such is the crabbed logic of the Socialists. They have two standards of morality and justice, and still they howl and rave when they get once in a while a taste of their own medicine from Mussolini. . . . In these circumstances, the protest of Mr. Erwin and his Socialist friends against Mussolini sounds like rank hypocrisy, and no man or woman who believes in a single standard of legality, equality, and justice, will read it without a smile of contempt and scorn.[19]

On July 4, in Philadelphia, the police arrested seven persons during an anti-Fascist meeting held to protest the assassination of Matteotti. Among the arrested were C. William Thompson, editor of the Socialist newspaper *The New Jersey Leader*, and Emedio Pistilli, Chairman of the meeting and President of Local 21, United Shoe Workers of America. They were charged with inciting to riot.[20] On June 29, a massive manifestation took place in Boston to commemorate the sacrifice of the Socialist martyr. According to *Il Lavoratore*, which covered the event, over 70,000 persons gathered in the city of Boston from Quincy, Haverhill, Lawrence, Brockton, Cambridge, East Cambridge, Roxbury, E. Weymouth, and Providence. Speeches were delivered by Arturo Giovannitti, Gildo Mazzarella, Giuseppe Merenda, and Fred H. Moore. Anti-Fascist manifestations were reported in Pittsburgh, Erie, Dunmore, and Plains in Pennsylvania; in Baltimore, Maryland; in Syracuse and Rochester, New York; in Cleveland, Ohio. In Detroit, Michigan, over 500 workers attended, in mid-July, a meeting sponsored by the anti-Fascist groups of Michigan. Speeches were delivered by Luigi Ceccoli, Romolo Bobba, and Nicolà Di Gaetano. In Chicago, Illinois, the manifestation was a remarkable success. Chicago was the editorial city of *Il Lavoratore*. Its wide circulation had spurred anti-Fascist feelings among the Italian-American community. The meeting was headed by Antonio Presi, editor of *Il Lavoratore*. Speeches were delivered by Enea Sormenti and Alvaro Badillo. Manifestations of minor intensity took place in hundreds of towns where the Italian community was present.[21]

However, these manifestations of protest against Fascism did not seem to have interested or attracted the attention of the vast majority of the American people. On the contrary, they were considered as a strictly Italian affair. Moreover, in those areas like New York, Chicago, Boston and Philadelphia where they attracted American attention, they were interpreted as dangerous explosions of Anarcho-Communist-Socialist propaganda. As such, they needed to be followed carefully by American authority. Taking advantage of this paradoxical development, Ambassador Caetani went to Rome to confer with Mussolini on the situation of Fascism in America and the reaction of the Americans to the Matteotti case.

The Italian Premier expressed his personal satisfaction for the conduct and behavior demonstrated in the Matteotti affair. Warm reception was given the news that the American press and public opinion at large, with very rare exceptions, still maintained perfect equanimity in judging Mussolini, Fascism, and its methods from the standpoint of domestic Italian events.[22] On November 21, Mussolini had another chance to persuade himself that the Americans nurtured great sympathy for Fascism. Carlo Vinti, editor of a New York pro-Fascist paper, visited Mussolini, expressing the devotion of the Italian-American colony and of the American Fascists as well. Mussolini charged him to convey his warm greetings to the members of the Fascist Party of America.[23] The overall situation of American reaction to Matteotti's case gives indication that Mussolini had not lost a bit of the popularity he had enjoyed among the Americans. During the Matteotti affair things seemed to swirl in the opposite direction, but afterward a general atmosphere of normality prevailed. So, Mussolini had won the Matteotti case with a prudent strategy. To complete the scenario, on January 11, 1925, Mrs. John Adams Drake, President of the American Free Milk and Relief for Italy-Society, met Mussolini in a special audience in Rome. She expressed such a deep sympathy and enthusiasm for Il Duce that Mussolini authorized her appointment as the first American Woman Fascist.[24]

As far as the philo-Fascist Italian-American press is concerned, *Il Progresso Italo-Americano* held a leading role. In a series of editorials between 1924 and 1925, the newspaper maintained a philo-Fascist heralding role. In December, 1923, the newspaper had already asked for a clear answer from those political parties representing the constitutional Opposition in Italy. Among other things, it asked them what intention they nurtured toward Fascism and if they approved of Mussolini's program of national pacification. By the end of December, with an article "Political and Social Doctrine of Mussolini's Fascism," the newspaper examined Fascist ideology from the March on Rome to the period of stabilization of the Fascist government. In this period Fascism had regenerated Italian prestige, economy, and industry. Furthermore, the role of Fascism in the life of the nation was considered vital and unreplaceable. On July 5, 1924, in the aftermath of Matteotti's murder, the editorial proclaimed that, in spite of the criminal act, Fascism would never abandon Italy to the Opposition. By no means, continued the article, could the Matteotti incident justify the request advanced by the Opposition that Mussolini relinquish his power and step down. Such a decision would generate an atmosphere of chaos and would imply yielding the power to Bolshevism. On July 6, another article, "Italo-American Relations," reported an interview with Professor Vincenzo Giuffrida of the University of Rome on the future prospect of Italo-American economic cooperation. This possibility was considered feasible, since Italy had offered sufficient guarantees of economic prosperity and political stability. Nancy McCormack provided, on July 13, an article, "When Mussolini Poses," a sentimental portrayal of Il Duce, whom she describes as impressive, strong, and fascinating. On July 16, the newspaper examined in depth the nature of the political crisis produced by the Matteotti incident. The crisis was ascribed to those extremist groups that had infiltrated the Fascist Party. The article recalled that Fascism was born as a heterogeneous movement and that Mussolini had been able to blend together and harmonize different groups with divergent aims. In so doing, Il Duce had proved to have the skill and the talent of the statesman. In two articles, on July 26, "From Achilles to Lychaon," and on August 5, "The Council of Fascism vs. Revisionism and Militarism," the newspaper appealed to party factions to set aside their ideological differences and proceed toward the realization of the goals of the Fascist revolution. National regeneration and pacification should be the primary objectives of Fascism.[25]

In addition to this widely circulated newspaper, an extended network of local philo-Fascist newspapers, disseminated throughout America, provided a propaganda marathon for Fascism. *Il Corriere del Bronx*, edited by Bernardino D'Onofrio, defined Mussolini as the "apostle of liberty and justice." In New Haven, Connecticut, Antonio Pisani edited *Le Forche Caudine*. He maintained that Fascism had wiped out Feudalism in Italy. In Chicago, *La Tribuna* praised Mussolini not only for his program of national regeneration but also because he had made Italian workers abroad more respected human beings, with dignity and national pride. Another Chicagoan newspaper, *l'Italia*, praised Fascism and Mussolini because he had restored the destinies of Imperial Rome. *La Gazzetta di Massachusetts*, published in Boston, advised America to suppress the *Volstead Law* and adopt, for those who did not agree on the issue of Prohibition, Fascist remedies: castor oil and *manganello*. *La Stella d'Italia* of Greensburg, Pa., affirmed that Fascism was the ideology of the future for Italy and the world. *La Tribuna* of Portland, Oregon, defended Mussolini and his philosophy of national regeneration and pacification. *Il Vaglio* of Wilkes-Barre, Pa., praised Mussolini's strong methods used to restore law and order in Italy. *Il Corriere di Syracuse*, of Syracuse, New York, edited by Luigi Fulco, was a pro-Fascist newspaper that endorsed from its first issue (1922), Fascism and its methods of government. *La Stampa Unita* of Rochester, New York, was edited by C. G. Lanni.

On July 18, 1924, in the aftermath of Matteotti's murder, Davis Salomon, in a speech delivered in the Amalgamated Hall of Rochester to commemorate the Italian martyr, stressed that "the act of killing Matteotti had kindled fires of rage in a million hearts. Nothing will satisfy us, or quench these fires, until every ounce of this martyr's blood has been paid for in restitution." To Matteo Teresi of *La Stampa Unita*, these expressions were fruit of a radical mentality and served to inflame the Americans against the Italians. Continuing in its relentless pro-Fascist campaign, *La Stampa Unita*, on May 15, 1925, reprinted an article, which had appeared earlier in another Rochester newspaper, *The Rochester Journal-Post Express*. The article, "What Butterflies Do We Seek?" analyzed Mussolini's achievements in Italy since 1922:

> Mussolini today, ruler of Italy, is one of the most powerful men produced by modern history, or ancient history, either. In his Fascist black shirts, he rallies his legions . . . Mussolini is a man of strong words and of strong action. Of late, the murder of Matteotti, attributed to the Fascists, appeared to shake Mussolini's hold on the people. But Mussolini did not dodge that issue. He has never dodged any . . . Mussolini is powerful. Force is a great thing. But his real power is mental courage.[26]

The philo-Fascist propaganda of these newspapers was of moderate tone, and therefore, effective, incisive, and well-planned for the American mentality. On the contrary, the anti-Fascist propaganda was torn between its desire to give heed to Fascist principles, which had destroyed democracy and freedom in Italy, and anti-Fascist ideological interests expressed in the anti-capitalist style of Marxism-Leninism doctrine. In fact, Tresca's *Il Martello*, Giovannitti's *Il Veltro*, and Presi's *Il Lavoratore* interpreted their anti-Fascist opposition and struggle in terms of Marxist-Leninist strategy and doctrine. Not only did they advocate an alliance of all anti-Fascist forces of North America, Canada, and Mexico, in order to form an anti-Fascist Popular Front, but also they advocated Bolshevism as the only alternative to Fascism. In an article published in *Il Lavoratore*, on October 25, 1924, entitled "Neither Fascism nor Liberalism, but Bolshevism," the opposition maintained that the capitalist bourgeoisie in the world had reached the highest stage of reaction against the working classes. Capitalism was using and hiring Fascist henchmen to perpetuate its program of exploitation and repression. Fascism, under the mien of the henchmen of capitalism, represented the most perverse and abject form of capitalism. Therefore, the alternative was not only Democracy versus Fascism, but also Bolshevism versus Capitalism.[27]

This sort of propaganda, mixed in a chain of public manifestations that police often interpreted as *mobs* staged by Italian radical and Communist groups, provided to inflame popular reaction against Italian-American anti-Fascism. On October 1, 1925, the Italian Delegation to the Washington Parliamentary Conference was attacked in New York. The incident culminated in the wounding of two Fascist delegates by Italian Communists, residents in New York City. The occasion served further the purpose of Fascism in Italy and abroad. The Fascist press waxed indignant reaction.[28]

On October 28, four hundred anti-Fascists "rioted" in front of the Hotel Pennsylvania, making "several attempts to break through a police cordon." Inside, the Fascists were celebrating the third anniversary of the March on Rome. The celebration was to honor Captain Paul C. Grening, of the *President Harding*, who had rescued in mid-Atlantic the crew of the Italian freighter *Ignazio Florio*. Guests of honor were Alessandro Sardi, former Italian Minister of Public Works; Consul General of New York, Emilio Exerio; and General Mastro Mattei. The celebration was chaired by Dr. A. Previtale, Vice-President of the Fasci of North America. The anti-Fascist "mob" was led by Carlo Tresca and Pietro Allegra. The situation required police reinforcement. The rioters, with cries of "Down with the Fascists," intended to penetrate the hotel. The anti-Fascists' behavior led to a general protest in New York. Next day, *The New York Times*, in an editorial, "They Should Go Home For Fighting," announced that the "newcomers," in stretching American charitable hospitality, had manifested "bad manners by attempting to fight out quarrels of their home land." The article continued in its wide condemnation of anti-Fascist behavior:

As it happens to be anti-Fascists who have chosen repeatedly to break through, upon them must fall condemnation. The police hardly could have used too much severity in repressing the riotings. . . . If any Italian in the United States thinks that things are going badly in Italy, his duty is to go back there and rearrange them. He cannot help his country by mobbing Fascists on steamship docks and in hotels here.[29]

In a letter to *The New York Times*, on November 8, Frederick F. Lily portrayed the feeling of the majority in New York City on the continued riots staged by the anti-Fascists. Even though a single act of protest did not reflect necessarily the viewpoint of millions of people living in the city, nevertheless, it can be used as a parameter to assess the kind of frustration these manifestations of outbursts had produced. According to the author of the letter, most people "were getting a little bit tired of these mobbish manifestations." Since anti-Fascism appeared to play a very limited part in the outbursts, Lily saw in them "Communism camouflaged." Therefore, he invited the authorities to be seriously concerned about those pseudo-anti-Fascists elements who, on the contrary, were radical disseminators of Communist propaganda.[30]

In conclusion, Matteotti's murder did not undermine the position of Fascism in America. Instead, it made it stronger and elevated by the paradoxical support and sympathy of the vast majority of the American people. For most Americans, Mussolini had acted with courage and wisdom in not yielding to the illegitimate demands of the Socialists and Communists in Italy. He had secured the material executors of the criminal act to justice. Therefore, he had discharged his duty with honor, competence, and impartiality. In the meantime, he had defended himself and his regime from the attacks of the Opposition, which had tried to use Matteotti's case to overthrow Mussolini and plunge Italy into another period of political disorder and economic instability. In the eyes of the Americans, Fascism appeared more than ever the innocent victim of a prepotent Socialist-Communist-Radical conspiracy in Italy and in the whole world.

NOTES

1. *Documenti Diplomatica Italiani, Settima Serie*, 1922-1935, vol. 3, 160.
2. *Documenti Diplomatici*, Cit., 163.
3. *Documenti Diplomatici*, Cit., 182.
4. *The New York Times*, June 27, 1924, 21:7.
5. *The Saturday Evening Post*, June 26, pp. 1, 2, 156 and 158; July 12, pp. 5, 55, 56, 57 and 58; July 26, pp. 23, 87, 88 and 90, 1924.
6. *Documenti Diplomatici*, Cit., 201.
7. *The New York Times*, June 28, 1924, VIII, 4:6, and June 26, 1924, 22:2.
8. *The Outlook*, July 2, 1924, 340-41 and 348-51.
9. *The Outlook*, August 6, 1924, 538-39.
10. *The Nation*, July 30, 1924, 114-15.
11. *The Literary Digest*, August 9, 1924, 16-17, and September 13, 1924, 21.
12. *Il Martello*, December 5, 1925, 1.
13. *Il Lavoratore*, July 1, 1924.
14. *Il Pupo*, May 9, 1925, 3.
15. *Unione Figli D'Italia*, August 24, 1925.
16. *Il Corriere del Popolo*, July 24, 1925.
17. Ministero dell'Interno, Dir. Gen., P.S. Div., AA.GG. e Riser., 1924, Cartella 86, Cat. F.4. *Stampe Sovversive Provenienti dall'Estero*.
18. Giacomo Di Tella to Mussolini, *A Letter From Pueblo, Colorado*, June 10, 1923. I.F.M.D. n. 3262, 014661-64.
19. *The New York Times*, June 30, 1924, 14:7.
20. *The New York Times*, July 4, 1924, 6:7.
21. On the anti-Fascist meetings and demonstrations, *Il Lavoratore* made extended coverage. See these July, 1924, issues: 1, 17, 19, 23, 24, 25, 28.

22. *The New York Times*, July 27, 1924, 31:4.
23. *The New York Times*, November 21, 1924, 21:4.
24. *The New York Times*, January 12, 1925, 15:2.
25. For the mentioned articles, see *Il Progresso Italo-Americano*, December 28 and 30, 1923; July 5, 6, 13, 16, 18 and August 5, 10, 1924.
26. *La Stampa Unita*, May 15, 1925, 1.
27. *Il Lavoratore*, October 25, 1924, 2.
28. *The New York Times*, October 1, 1925, 5:2.
29. *The New York Times*, October 30, 1925, 20:5.
30. *The New York Times*, November 8, 1925, 14:5.

HUMBERT S. NELLI

Chicago's Italian-Language Press and World War I

Italy remained in the minds of her emigrants whether or not they intended to return. News of the mother country provided a link during at least the early years of settlement overseas. The Italian-language press provided the sought-for information, including coverage of Italian domestic and foreign happenings. Articles contained news about the king, parliament, natural disasters, the Pope and the Church, migration of Italians to Latin America and Africa, diplomatic maneuvers and entanglements of the Kingdom of Italy, military and naval armaments, Italian colonial ventures in Africa, and local events like marriages, deaths, and festivals.[1] The assassination of King Humbert in 1900 was the major news event of that or any other year prior to World War I. The main continuous news item about Italy during the late 1890's concerned the exploits of the Calabrian bandit, Giuseppe Musolino. Captured in 1902, Musolino faced trial in May and June of that year, prompting minute coverage and verbatim transcripts of the proceedings. *L'Italia's* feature report on September 27 was titled "Visit with Musolino." While it deplored Italy's lack of concern with the welfare of immigrants in America, the colonial press generally supported the Kingdom in its dealings with the Church, in military and diplomatic ventures, and when natural disasters struck.

Bourgeois and proletarian papers alike agreed in condemning the Church's temporal claims. Papers like *L'Italia, Il Progresso Italo-Americano, La Tribuna Italiana Transatlantica* opposed the Church, in this regard, primarily out of loyalty to the Kingdom. Oscar Durante, editor of *L'Italia*, bluntly stated in 1890 that he—and, he believed, a majority of Italian immigrants in Chicago—fully supported the State in disputes between Italy and the Church, for "the Pope . . . is the relentless enemy of our unity and liberty."[2] The Protestant *La Fiaccola* and the leftwing *La Parola dei Socialisti* and *Il Proletario* also upheld the Kingdom, in part to embarrass the Church and in part to further their own particular objectives. Thus *Il Proletario* and *La Parola* participated in the commemoration of September 20 and applauded Italian unification, both as a vigorous anti-Catholic action and as a method of winning the support and confidence of Chicago's Italian community.[3]

While socialists and anarchists relished armed activity against (or at the expense of) the Church, they strongly opposed patriotic manifestations among Italians in America[4]—a position difficult to clarify or to maintain. The bourgeois press gloried in fancied diplomatic and military successes of Italy in the Abyssinian venture in the 1890's and the Libyan War of 1911-1912, while socialist journals emphasized the disastrous consequences of such activities and lamented the waste of money better used by the Italian government to educate its people.[6]

Interest in Italy and activities within the home village generally declined after years of residence in Chicago. Local news from various towns and districts in Italy, extensive during the early years of immigration, declined in quantity almost to the point of nonexistence after 1900. Taking its place was increased coverage of Italian national news, indicating a widening of immigrant horizons. At the same time, identification with America gradually replaced that with Italy. In addition, during and after World War I it was not necessary, as it had been in previous years, to turn to an Italian-language paper for news of Italy; with the Kingdom's increased prominence after 1915, American papers expanded their coverage.

The periodicals exhibited an intense interest in World War I, news of which drove everything else off their pages. *La Fiaccola* was the sole exception, continuing to concentrate upon internal—that is, religious—affairs. In newspaper coverage of war news, major and usually sole concern centered on the Italian front. Activities in the Western and Eastern fronts, the Balkans, the Middle East and the American home front took definite back seats to the Austro-Italian phase of the war. Events elsewhere were included only when they affected the fortunes of Italy.

As early as May, 1916, the bourgeois press favored America's entry into the war on the side of the Allies. Papers condemned German propaganda and spy activities in the United States, considering them immoral and evil, but printed nothing concerning Allied efforts to bring the Republic into the war.[7] America's declaration of war against Germany won warm press support[8] but, particularly after Caporetto, editorials argued that Americans should help Italy as well as other Allies.[9] The declaration of hostilities against Austria was characterized as a blow for humanity against "the feudal and most Catholic but by no means Christian Austria."[10] Even after the involvement of the United States in the war, Italy continued to receive most attention and space in the papers.[11]

The various papers differed in amount of war news and in editorial support of the Kingdom. *Il Progresso Italo-Americano*, a New York newspaper which was widely read in Chicago, presented the most complete war coverage, devoting all of page one and most of its news sections to hostilities. Advertising still occupied at least four of the eight pages of each day's issue. War news included a daily account of activities on all sections of the Italian front—land, sea and air; public statements of Italian generals; rumors and opinions of Italian newspapers; accounts of enemy atrocities; statements, official or unofficial, of the Italian government; claims of battle successes, capture of enemy soldiers, reports of enemy dead and wounded; and hints of enemy peace overtures.[12]

L'Italia could not equal its New York rival either in extent or depth of coverage, but it did offer the most complete news of any of Chicago's Italian-language papers. It emphasized, of course, the Italian front. News accounts from and of the fighting sectors were supplemented by articles of Italian writers and Italian-American war correspondents. These reports included statements of Italian war aims, progress and conduct of the war, speeches and activities of national leaders and comments about the battle spirit of the Kingdom's army.[13]

La Tribuna Italiana Transatlantica did not attempt to compete. It specialized instead in opinion and interpretation—both shunned by *Il Progresso Italo-Americano* and *L'Italia*—and in special features, particularly opera and Italian theater. For example, in October, 1917, it reported no specific news of the Caporetto debacle. The actual defeat remained unmentioned until 1918, although on November 3, 1917, *La Tribuna Italiana Transatlantica* devoted page one to the problem of revitalizing the Italian war effort. Retreat of the Italian troops to the Piave and fighting there during November and December, 1917, received about equal coverage with the opera season in Chicago.[14]

La Fiaccola generally relegated war news to page 4, its final one. Articles about the fighting appeared occasionally on other pages, although these were exceptions to the general custom. Major interest and news coverage continued to focus on the religious battle between Protestant and Catholic groups in the United States and the evils of the Church in Italy. Everything else, including World War I, received incidental coverage. Thus page one of the issues in December, 1916, features a series by Charles Fama, M.D., on the topic "What is the Religion of Italians of Today? Are they not all Roman Catholics?" An article in September, 1917, concluded that the real enemy of humanity was "His Holiness" and not the Central Powers.[15]

Socialist and anarchist journals opposed the war from the beginning to end, viewing it as an opportunity for capitalistic enrichment at proletariat expense. In the opinion of *La Parola dei Socialisti*, capitalist "jackals" fed on proletariat corpses.[16] These periodicals saw only one value to the war: in its aftermath, contended *Il Proletario*, would come the long-awaited downfall of the capitalistic system.[17] Socialists and anarchists alike believed the Bolshevik Revolution to be the first step in the fulfillment of their hopes, and gave it their strong support.[18]

Except for the leftwing press and *La Tribuna Italiana Transatlantica*, the journals emphasized news rather than editorial opinion. This policy varied from paper to paper but generally preferences and attitudes showed themselves through treatment of news items, special articles and use of descriptive terms like "our front," "our army," "our latest victories." On the other hand, *La Tribuna Italiana Transatlantica*, like the leftwing papers, emphasized editorials over straight news reports. It also resembled socialist and anarchist tabloids in its use of a conspiracy theory, by means of which it explained Italian military failures. While *L'Italia* blamed events at Caporetto on lack of munitions, for example, Alessandro Mastro-Valerio, editor of *La Tribuna*, assigned responsibility to specific individuals and groups: "Giolitti, the Jesuits, the neutralists, the pacifists, the German-ophiles, and the Austria-siding socialists of Italy, these are the saboteurs of the war of liberation."[19] Before Caporetto, *La Tribuna Italiana Trans-atlantica* accused the Church—and particularly the Jesuits—of preferring Germany and opposing Italy; after October, 1917, editorials expounded the idea that the Vatican, in league with the Central Powers and internal enemies of the Kingdom, had agreed to work together for Italy's defeat.[20] The paper accused socialists in the United States as well as "Lenin, Trotsky and the other Bolshevik traitors" of being secretly allied with the Kaiser to bring Italy to her knees.[21] Feelings tended to run high in all the papers.

Apparently the average immigrant shared little in these wartime emotions. Italy, for example, considered it the duty of emigrants to return and fight. Many reservists did, indeed, do so: Gino Speranza, Special Correspondent of *Outlook* in Italy, estimated that by April, 1916, between 60,000 and 70,000 Italian-Americans had answered the call to arms.[22] The mass of the immigrants, however, did not. As a contemporary economist and historian Robert Foerster, noted, they remained in the United States and worked "for unprecedentedly high wages."[23] The papers claimed (probably at the insistence of the consul) that all able-bodied immigrants ought to return to Italy to fight; but most of the periodicals deemed it inadvisable to emphasize this obviously unpopular argument.[24]

Homeland Italians reacted with anger and contempt to emigrant disinterest. In May, 1917, the Reverend Augusto Giardini, a recent arrival from Italy, expressed this attitude when he complained that "Mother Italy" needed her sons on the Isonzo and not on the Hudson. The editor of *La Fiaccola* found it expedient to explain in a postscript to his article the immigrants' attitude toward the war. The newcomers, the papers pointed out, now had homes and families in America. To them "any num-

ber of sentimental considerations do not offset the strength of these facts."
Returning to Italy "to defend the graves of their fathers and ignore the
needs of their children" seemed neither wise nor desirable.[25] Besides, guilty
consciences could be salved by financial contributions to the Italian war
effort and to postwar calls for money.

That many Italian-Americans were as unwilling to contribute money
as they had been to offer their lives is clear from press complaints about
immigrant reluctance to buy Italian government bonds.[26] To a certain
extent this disinterest in the war fortunes of Italy applied as well to the
involvement of the United States.[27] On the other hand, the press and most
immigrants loyally supported the American war effort. These activities
included opposition to "Prussian militarism," purchase of American war
bonds and service in the American army. This favorable attitude applied
to the bourgeois Italian journals only. Socialist periodicals opposed American, as well as Italian, military ventures.[28] Mastro-Valerio's reaction to
the American declaration of war in April, 1917, was "Long Live America!
Long Live Wilson!! Long Live Democracy!!! Down with Prussianism!!!!"

While German-American newspapers were suspected and even accused
of wartime disloyalty, studies conducted during and after World War I
found the bourgeois Italian-language papers to be "uniformly loyal" to the
United States.[30] The Italian press opposed Germany as well as the German-
language papers in the United States. It applauded governmental action to
control these allegedly anti-American organisms of expression.[31] While
proud of American fighting achievements and Italian-American contributions to the war effort in the United States, the major interest of the colonial papers remained focused on Italian military activities. The journals'
prime hope was that

> . . . the Italy that will emerge from this war will not be the humble servant
> of the past but, enlarged and suffused with a new breath of life, will inspire
> awe in the concert of nations, and will attract a great new respect to her
> sons scattered throughout the world.[32]

With the end of the war, the powerful emotions and hopes formulated
during the fighting burst forth in the pages of the journals. As Oscar
Handlin observes, "It was a time for reaping the fruits of victory. Only
there were no fruits. Peace did not come. In the aftermath, all the tensions
and sacrifices of war brought no more than a pervasive sense of betrayal."[33]
All immigrant groups, and the American public in general, shared this
disillusionment. Immediately following the war's end in November, 1918,
disputes broke out between Italians and Yugoslavs. Hysteria, accusations
and hostility raged in colonial newspapers. Except for *L'Avanti!* and *Il
Proletario*, they supported all Italian demands and violently denounced

Yugoslav ingratitude. The concensus was that Italy deserved all its hoped-for rewards in accordance with history, racial superiority, economic needs, geography and provisions of war-time treaties with Allied nations and the Slavs.[34] The journals castigated the "hypocritical propaganda conducted by the Yugoslavs in America," as well as the anti-Italian leanings of the American press.[35] Mastro-Valerio in particular blasted the "bias, slander, false news concocted in the offices of certain [American] newspapers." Members of the Italian Chamber of Commerce pleaded "as American citizens, for the love that we bear this country of our adoption and for its honor, . . . that the United States will never consent to be a participant in this injustice, unparalleled in history, or in this crime against humanity."[36]

La Tribuna Italiana Transatlantica firmly believed that primary credit for the Allied victory belonged to Italy. "Italy won the war when she declared her neutrality . . . . [She] won the war at Piave." Furthermore, "Germany gave up only after the Italian victory of Vittorio, the greatest victory of universal history." Equally successful at sea, Italy's navy "destroyed almost all the Austrian fleet." Italy's allies, however, were jealous of her contributions and accomplishments and were therefore attempting to revive Austria through Yugoslavia; "but Italy at the cost of her last drop of blood must defeat this monstrous and nefarious plot."[37]

Similar views of Italy's contributions to the Allied victory appeared in other journals. *L'Italia* maintained that the battle of "Vittorio Veneto saved the world from ruthless Teutonic domination." *Il Progresso Italo-Americano* quoted unnamed German newspapers to the effect that "but for Italy's defection from the Dreibund we would have won the war!" and "but for Italy's victory at Piave, that opened our rear to invasion, we would never have surrendered to Foch!"[38] The periodicals agreed that the valiant Kingdom was now being denied the rightful fruits of victory. The Treaty of London and Wilson's Fourteen Points were to be repudiated to benefit Yugoslavia at Italy's expense: her former allies had deserted her in favor of the enemy.[39] The Italian Chamber of Commerce summed up the attitude of Italian-American papers and societies in general:

> The responsibility for the war is shared alike by the Yugoslavs, formerly subject to Austria, and by Germany and it is difficult to understand why, while the latter country is to be severely punished, its accomplices, the Croats and Slovaks of Austria, are to be glorified and have been made the object of so much tender care and solicitude by the American delegation to the Peace Conference, notwithstanding the fact that in this war they were fighting the United States, as well as Italy and other Allied nations.[40]

The consul played an important role in encouraging this support of Italian demands by the colonial press and societies. For example, he often led postwar protest meetings against Yugoslav demands, and was in a position to ensure that the Italian press fully publicized them.[41] The journals and societies warmly applauded and stoutly defended Gabriele D'Annunzio's occupation of Fiume on September 12, 1919. *Il Progresso Italo-Americano* led the way in establishing a press-society subscription to be sent the hero to show Italian-American support of "D'Annunzio's feat."[42]

In line with their support of the Kingdom, the periodicals attacked Wilson and the League of Nations.[43] In 1920 Wilson's policies and actions constituted, to the Italian-language press, the principal issue in the presidential campaign; the journals relished Harding's victory over Cox.[44]

The Italian newspapers were divided in their response to Wilson's October, 1918 appeal. *Il Progresso Italo-Americano* rallied to the President's support. *L'Italia* showed indifference to Wilson's statement and remained uninterested during the entire campaign. *La Tribuna Italiana Transatlantica*, which had ignored the campaign previously, reacted violently to the appeal and called on Italians to vote Republican. *La Fiaccola* made no mention of the campaign in any issue.[45]

In 1920, *L'Avanti!* and the socialists, viewing both Harding and Cox as "the candidates of Wall Street" and enemies of labor, chose to support Eugene Debs. *Il Proletario* as usual, took notice neither of the campaign nor of the election.[46]

L'Avanti! also disapproved of the entire peace settlement procedure, as well as Wilson, the League of Nations, Italian "pretensions" to Fiume and other territory, and the arrogant "reign of Czar D'Annunzio" in Fiume. In the immediate postwar period *L'Avanti!* supported Bolshevism and looked forward to worldwide revolution.[47] Even during this period of class solidarity and seeming victory for socialism, Italian nationalism made its appearance in the pages of this paper: on May 3, 1919, *L'Avanti!* contained a long article supporting Italian claims—"Down with Wilson, Long Live Italy." However, at the same time it strongly opposed the conservative government in power in Italy, and in 1919 eagerly anticipated the revolution. By 1920 it had abandoned this position and hoped that control of the country would pass to socialists through parliamentary means.[48] The socialist press quickly recognized the dangers presented to leftwing plans by Fascism and as early as 1919 condemned the ideas and tactics of Mussolini and his followers.[49] By January, 1922, the paper (now *La Parola del Popolo*) and the Socialist Party had shifted to a bitterly disillusioned anti-Communist and anti-revolutionary position, although they never modified their anti-Fascist stand.[50]

The bourgeois press, in contrast, was in mortal fear of socialism and of Bolshevik intentions in Italy. It saw Mussolini as a savior from these dangers.[51] Durante echoed the views of other editors when he declared that Fascism was necessary in Italy in order to satisfy "the needs, destiny and salvation of the nation." The methods employed by these Fascist servants of "the national will," argued Mastro-Valerio and Durante were necessary in order to protect democracy; besides, they were forced on the Fascists by socialists and communists.[52]

It is obvious from the foregoing that the press and societies strongly supported Italy during and after the war. They gloried in (and often exaggerated) her wartime successes, and suffered with her alleged postwar humiliations at the hands of former allies. At the same time, the press and most of the immigrants considered themselves to be loyal Americans. Claiming that there was no conflict in this duality of interests, the papers stressed that the one loyalty reinforced the other.[53] The reason for the stubborn clinging to Italy even after years of residence in America and in full knowledge of the true attitude of the Kingdom's government toward them can be found, in part, in American attitudes toward the immigrants. Even before 1914 Americans were generally unfavorable toward Italians, as the newcomers well realized.[54] To the natives they had long been "dagos," objects of ridicule and contempt. As early as 1888 *Il Messaggiere Italo-Americano* lamented:

> Here is the ugly word, here is the ugly appellative that Americans and non-Americans, gentlemen and knaves, bootblacks and journalists enjoy hanging on every human being who might have had the misfortune of being born under the sky of Italy! . . . Dago is the first word which falls from the lips of one who intends to mock or insult an Italian.[55]

While the meaning of "dago" had to be explained to people in Italy, immigrants in America were painfully aware of its connotation and deeper meaning.[56] The press and the immigrants in general, however, desired acceptance, if not respect. That they supported and glorified Italy in large part to gain this acceptance from the American community is clear from the responses of the press to American criticism of immigrant life and labor, and in the demands for recognition of Italian contributions to civilization.[57] Thus Italian-Americans magnified Italy's achievements as a defence against American contempt for current social and economic problems facing the newcomers.[58] It is probable that neither press nor immigrants recognized their motives in identifying with Italy in order to be accepted as Americans.

In these facts lies the real importance of Mussolini to the immigrant community. The newcomers no longer had to point to ancient glories and dead heroes, for Italy in Mussolini had a living leader who was admired and respected by many Americans and Englishmen, if not always by his native countrymen. Edward Corsi points out that the praise lavished on Mussolini and his system by "the press and leaders of public opinion in this country," combined with Fascist propagandist activities among the immigrants, "tended to strengthen the immigrants' impression that Italy under Il Duce had come into her own." Caroline Ware quotes "a strongly anti-Fascist Italian-American girl," who, in spite of her opposition to Mussolini and his program, declared, " 'You've got to admit one thing: he has enabled four million Italians in America to hold up their heads, and that is something. If you had been branded as undesirable by a quota law, you would understand how much that means.' " Handlin claims that "among some Italians of the New World, admiration for Mussolini implied not so much approval of Fascism as gratitude for the achievement of having earned the respect and fear of the great powers of the earth." Giuseppe Prezzolini, who, during the Fascist period was director of Columbia University's Casa Italiana (then a center of Fascist activities and propaganda) maintains that immigrant exaltation of Italy under Mussolini was revenge against the Anglo-Saxon master race which had humiliated Italians during the previous fifty years. "For the first time," Prezzolini continues, "Italy gave the appearance of a country of which they could be proud."[59]

Probably closest to the truth is Corsi's observation that "the overwhelming majority of Italians in America have never been Fascist, nor, for that matter, Anti-Fascist. They have approved of Fascism not as a political ideology or as a form of government, but as something good for Italy." Alberto Traldi, of *Il Progresso Italo-Americano*, agrees with this idea, contending that the immigrants' conservatism encouraged their support of Mussolini: they traditionally accepted or supported the existing government of Italy simply because it was in power, and not through any strong ideological beliefs.[60]

To many immigrants and second generation Italian-Americans, however, journalistic support given Mussolini when he came to power seemed to prove that the press had chosen loyalty to Italy over its ties to the new world. These critics often ignored the cultural factors involved in the attitude of the papers, as well as the facts that during the 1920s many responsible American and English observers also supported Mussolini while the only solid opposition to him came from socialists and communists.[61]

The emphasis upon "Americanization" during and after the war also played a part in the decline of the press. Rash outbursts over the peace settlements and warm support of Mussolini antagonized and alienated the second generation as well as many of the immigrants. Reading "foreign" papers appeared, also, to be incompatible with "American" ways. Of grave concern to Americanizers was the question of press loyalty and of the hyphenates served by the papers, especially the German-Americans. Theodore Roosevelt's demand that "there should be but one language in this country—the English," was based on the belief of many that "there is not a loyal German-language paper in America."[62] Although studies on the problem of immigrant devotion to the United States found the foreign-language press to be loyal, except for anarchist, socialist and a portion of the German press, the crusade against German and radical journals brought the entire foreign-language press under suspicion. Fred C. Butler, for example, found that many intelligent Americans loudly demanded "the abolition of everything published in any language they cannot understand."[63]

Wartime super-patriotism combined with the rise of Bolshevism and postwar fear of radicalism to contribute to the passage of restrictive legislation. In the final analysis, curtailment of immigration was the key factor in the decline of the Italian-American press. The laws reduced the steady flow of new readers who were essential to the continued functioning and prosperity of the journals. Few newcomers arrived to replace the bulk of the pre-1914 immigrant generation as it died out or outgrew its need of the foreign press. Italian-language periodicals declined appreciably in numbers and subscribers, but the major ones—*L'Italia, La Tribuna Italiana Transatlantica* and *Il Progresso Italo-Americano*—retained readers or absorbed them from papers which could not solve the increased problems. Even these papers, however, lost readership.[64]

Between 1921 and 1931 at least ten papers went out of business, including *L'Idea* which had claimed a readership of 34,000 in 1919. In 1935 *La Tribuna* ceased operations. *L'Italia*, which had declined in readership from 38,426 in 1921 to 27,310 in 1930, jumped to 33,006 in 1935 as it absorbed readers from its defunct rivals. By 1943, however, its circulation had decreased to 28,000, and in 1957, to 5,968.[65]

At their worst, Italian-language newspapers kept the immigrants tied to the past and to a world that had never really existed for them, often exaggerating, as they did so, the isolation and uniqueness of the immigrant group. At their best, they helped the immigrants to see themselves as Americans, with concrete obligations toward their new homeland. At the same time, the journals encouraged newcomers to retain their ties with the country of their birth and to take pride in a heritage as Italian-Americans.

NOTES

1. *Il Messaggiere Italo-Americano*, July 5, 13 and 24, 1888; *L'Italia*, Dec. 2 and 16, 1893; Jan. 1 and 6, June 30, Dec. 15, 1894; Apr. 20, May 25, June 1, 1895; July 13 and 27, Dec. 21, 1901; Jan. 13, Apr. 12, 1902; June 17 and 24, Aug. 5, Sept. 9, 23 and 30, Oct. 7, 14, 21 and 28, 1905; July 27, Aug. 3, 10 and 17, Sept. 28, 1907; Jan. 2, 9, 16 and 23, 1909; Nov. 2, 9 and 23, 1909; Nov. 2, 9 and 23, 1913.

2. *L'Italia*, Oct. 20, 1890; also Sept. 15, 1888; Nov. 5, 1890; *Il Progresso Italo-Americano*, Nov. 3, 1890; Apr. 30, 1895; *La Tribuna Italiana Transatlantica*, Oct. 27, 1906. For a discussion of the technical aspects of Chicago's Italian-language press see Humbert S. Nelli, *Italians in Chicago, 1880-1930: A Study in Ethnic Mobility* (New York: Oxford University Press, 1970), pp. 158-170.

3. "The Pope is not Italian," claimed *La Fiaccola*, Jan. 30, 1913. It strongly supported legislation then before the Italian parliament directed against the Catholic Church (Feb. 13 and 27, 1913); *Il Proletario*, Sept. 15, 1911; *La Parola dei Socialisti*, Sept. 27, 1913.

4. *La Parola dei Socialisti*, July 10, 1909.

5. See, for example, *L'Italia*, July 21 and 29, Aug. 18, 1894; Oct. 26, Dec. 21, 1895; Jan. 18 and 25, Mar. 14 and 28, May 30, June 13, 1896; Aug. 5, Sept. 16, 1911-Oct. 20, 1912; Jan. 5, Aug. 3, 1913; Jan. 18, 1914; *La Tribuna Italiana Transatlantica*, Sept. 30, 1911-Oct. 19, 1912; *Il Progresso Italo-Americano*, Sept. 30, 1911-Oct. 17, 1912; *La Fiaccola*, Sept. 19-Oct. 17, 1912; *Bollettino della Camera di Commercio Italiana*, November, 1911. Concerning the "glorious" achievements of Italy, Giuseppe Prezzolini, *The Legacy of Italy* (New York: S. F. Vanni, 1948), pp. 302-303, comments that the military actions of the Kingdom were uniformly disastrous from the days of the Risorgimento to World War II.

6. *La Parola dei Socialisti*, Jan. 25, 1913; July 4, 1914.

7. *L'Italia*, May 7, 14 and 28, Aug. 6, Dec. 24, 1916.

8. *La Tribuna Italiana Transatlantica*, Apr. 7, 1917; and *L'Italia*, Apr. 8, 1917. On press support of the Liberty Loan Campaign see, among others, *L'Italia*, Oct. 14, 1917; *Il Progresso Italo-Americano*, Jan. 18, 1918; *La Tribuna Italiana Transatlantica*, Apr. 27, 1918.

9. *La Tribuna Italiana Transatlantica*, Sept. 8, Nov. 17, Dec. 1, 1917.

10. *Ibid.*, Dec. 15, 1917; *Il Progresso Italo-Americano*, Dec. 8, 1917.

11. For example, *L'Italia* made no mention of the United States in the war until March 10, 1918, when it printed an item containing the fact that one million American troops were in France.

12. For example, "In the North Our Troops Assume the Offensive and Reconquer Positions on the Col Caprile," Dec. 18, 1917; "Emperor William will make his New Peace Proposal Today," Dec. 24, 1917; "A Great Air Battle in the Sky over Treviso," Dec. 28, 1917; "119 Austro-Germans Made Prisoners," Jan. 18, 1918; "Our Political and Military Problems Discussed in the Chamber," Feb. 15, 1918; "Austrian Barbarities," Apr. 28, 1918.

13. Among others in *L'Italia*: "The Spirit of Italian Combatants and the Strength of the Armies," Alighiero Castelli, May 6, 1917; "The Importance of Italian Success in the Last Battle of the Isonzo," Tomaso Monicelli, Sept. 30, 1917; "Our Trentino," Pietro Pedrotti, Nov. 25, 1917; and "From the Isonzo to the Piave," Rino Alessi, Jan. 13, 1918.

14. *La Tribuna Italiana Transatlantica*, Dec. 8, 1917; Mar. 2, 1918.

15. Among others, "In the War Zone," Alighiero Castelli, Jan. 11, 1917; "Methodists at the Front in Italy," Walling Clark, and "Neutrality," Giovanni Thom, Apr. 19, 1917; "Italy Makes Albania Free and Independent," June 14, 1917; Dec. 7-28, 1916; Sept. 6, 1917.

16. *La Parola dei Socialisti*, Aug. 22, 1914, and interview with Mr. Egisto Clemente, April 29, 1964.

17. *Il Proletario*, Aug. 1, 8, 15, 22 and 29, Sept. 12, 1914.

18. *La Fiaccola* (Soc.), Mar. 9 and 16, June 22, 1916; *Il Proletario*, Jan. 7 and 26, Feb. 23, Mar. 30, 1918. The directors of *La Parola dei Socialisti* found it desirable to change the paper's name four times between 1916 and 1921 in order to evade wartime postal restrictions on radical as well as German-American newspapers and magazines. The name used from 1916 to early in 1918 was *La Parola Proletaria*, when it was changed to *La Fiaccola*. Later the same year it became *L'Avanti!* (Avanti! after Mar. 1, 1919) and in 1921 it was called *La Parola del Popolo*.

19. *L'Italia*, Nov. 4, 1917; *La Tribuna Italiana Transatlantica*, Nov. 3, 1917. It is interesting to compare the views of recent scholars concerning Caporetto. Englishman D. Mack Smith, an authority on Italian history, attributes the defeat to a "crumbling of morale" of the fighting men: *Italy, A Modern History* (Ann Arbor: University of Michigan Press, 1959), p. 311. American scholar René Albrecht-Carrié maintains that the rout was due to the fact that "the command and the rear gave them [the common soldiers] inadequate leadership and support respectively": *Italy, From Napoleon to Mussolini* (New York: Columbia University Press, 1950), p. 102. Military historian Cyril Falls agrees essentially with the judgment of Albrecht-Carrié. Caporetto, he argues, "was due more to bad leadership than to bad soldiers, though pacifist and treasonous influence played their part": *The Great War, 1914-1918* (New York: Capricorn Books, 1959), p. 309.

20. *La Tribuna Italiana Transatlantica*, Apr. 28, Sept. 8, 1917; Nov. 10, Dec. 1 and 15, 1917; Feb. 9, Mar. 2 and 16, May 4, June 29, July 13, Sept. 21 and 28, 1918.

21. *Ibid.*, Mar. 30, 1918. Also Mar. 16, Apr. 6, May 18, June 8, 1918. The attitude of *L'Italia* and *Il Progresso Italo-Americano* was, by contrast, rather moderate. After July, 1918, *L'Italia* seemed almost to have lost interest in hostilities. Until the end of the war it printed less about the fighting than it had previously.

22. Gino C. Speranza, "The 'Americani' in Italy at War," *Outlook*, CXII (April 12, 1916), 861.

23. Robert F. Foerster, *The Italian Emigration of Our Times* (Cambridge: Harvard University Press), p. 399.

24. For example, *La Tribuna Italiana Transatlantica*, Feb. 2 and 9, 1918; *L'Italia*, Feb. 10, 1918.

25. *La Fiaccola*, May 3, 1917.

26. For example, *L'Italia*, Dec. 1, 1918; *La Fiaccola*, Mar. 18, 1920.

27. This attitude is seen in La Guardia's account of constituent reaction to his support of the conscription bill: "Quite a few of my constituents did not like my vote in favor of the draft bill. There were Socialists and others in my district opposing the war." Fiorello H. La Guardia, *The Making of an Insurgent, an Autobiography: 1882-1919* (New York: Capricorn Books, 1961), p. 145.

28. Among others see: *La Tribuna Italiana Transatlantica*, Jan. 22, Feb. 3 and 10, Mar. 3, 17, 24, and 31, Apr. 7, 14 and 21, May 19, June 1, Sept.

8, Dec. 15, 1917; Apr. 13, 20 and 27, May 24, June 15, Nov. 9, 1918; *L'Italia*, Apr. 8 and 29, May 13, July 8, 1917; Feb. 10, Mar. 10, Apr. 28, July 7, Sept. 15, 1918; *La Fiaccola* (Soc.), June 22, 1918.

29. *La Tribuna Italiana Transatlantica*, Apr. 7, 1917.
30. For example, Glenn Frank, "Our Foreign Language Press," *Century Magazine*, LXLIX (March, 1920), 638.
31. "The Senate Against the German Press," *La Tribuna Italiana Transatlantica*, Sept. 22, 1917.
32. *L'Italia*, June 10, 1917.
33. Oscar Handlin, *The American People in the Twentieth Century* (Boston: Beacon Press, 1963), p. 136.
34. For example, *L'Italia*, Nov. 17, Dec. 1 and 22, 1918; Jan. 19 and 26, 1919; *La Tribuna Italiana Transatlantica*, Nov. 30, Dec. 7, 14 and 21, 1918; Jan. 4 and 11, 1919; *La Fiaccola*, Nov. 21 and 28, Dec. 26, 1918; Jan. 9 and 23, 1919; *Il Progresso Italo-Americano*, Nov. 24, 25, 27 and 28, Dec. 1, 3, 5-31, 1918; Jan. 2-30, 1919.
35. *L'Italia*, Feb. 9, 1919; also *La Tribuna Italiana Transatlantica*, Jan. 4, 1919; *Il Progresso Italo-Americano*, Mar. 2, 1919.
36. *La Tribuna Italiana Transatlantica*, Jan. 18, 1919; *Bollettino della Camera di Commercio Italiana*, August, 1919.
37. *La Tribuna Italiana Transatlantica*, Jan. 25, 1919.
38. *L'Italia*, Nov. 2, 1919; *Il Progresso Italo-Americano*, Mar. 3, 1919.
39. *L'Italia*, Jan. 26, Feb. 9 and 23, Mar. 2 and 9, May 18, July 6, 13, 20 and 27, Nov. 16, 1919; *La Fiaccola*, Jan. 23, Mar. 13, 1919; Jan. 22, Feb. 26, July 22, 1920; *La Tribuna Italiana Transatlantica*, Feb. 15, Mar. 1 and 8, May 3 and 10, June 7, July 5, 1919; *Il Progresso Italo-Americano*, Feb. 16, 19-28, Mar. 1-31, 1919; and almost every issue through the remainder of the year. While no scholar now would credit Italy with winning the war for the Allies, there is disagreement as to who was responsible for the victory in Italy. Falls, *op. cit.*, p. 387, contends that "the presence of British and French troops was enormously important." Equally important, he argues, were Austrian weaknesses. On the other hand, Luigi Salvatorelli, *A Concise History of Italy, From Prehistoric Times to Our Own Day* (New York: Oxford University Press, 1940), pp. 618-619, dismisses the "few French and English divisions" in Italy as mere exchanges for Italian divisions sent to France (a point ignored by Falls), and credits the victory to national spirit. Giuseppe Prezzolini, *The Legacy of Italy*, p. 303, believes that Italians did well considering the difficulties faced, but that even with a numerically superior force the Kingdom achieved victory "only when the Austrian Empire was completely disorganized internally." For the attitude of the Allies and the U.S. toward Italy and its interests, see René Albrecht-Carrié, *Italy at the Paris Peace Conference* (New York: Columbia University Press, 1938), pp. 52-56.
40. *Bollettino della Camera di Commercio Italiana*, August, 1919.
41. *L'Italia*, Dec. 22, 1918; also *La Parola dei Socialisti*, Jan. 16 and 30, 1915; *Bollettino della Camera di Commercio Italiana*, February, July, 1919; *L'Italia*, Feb. 2, 1919; Sept. 26, 1920.
42. *L'Italia*, Oct. 19, Nov. 2, July 20, 1919; *Il Progresso Italo-Americano*, Sept. 21 and 24, 1919; *Bollettino della Camera di Commercio Italiana*, October, 1919; *La Tribuna Italiana Transatlantica*, Oct. 18, Nov. 1, 1919.

The *Unione Siciliana* was one of the leading organizations in supporting the seizure of Fiume. *La Tribuna*, Oct. 4, 1919 and *L'Italia*, Oct. 19, 1919. *Il Progresso* initiated the subscription on September 26, 1919.

43. *La Tribuna Italiana Transatlantica*, Feb. 22, Sept. 20, 1919; Oct. 30, 1920; *L'Italia*, Nov. 2, 1919; *Bollettino della Camera di Commercio Italiana*, August, 1919.

44. *La Tribuna Italiana Transatlantica*, Aug. 14 and 21, Sept. 4 and 18, Oct. 2, 9 and 23, Nov. 6, 1920; *L'Italia*, Sept. 26, Oct. 10, 24 and 31, Nov. 7, 1920; *La Fiaccola*, Nov. 4 and 11, 1920.

45. *Il Progresso Italo-Americano*, Oct. 26, Nov. 1, 2 and 5, 1918; *L'Italia*, Oct. 6, 13, 20 and 27, Nov. 3, 1918; *La Tribuna Italiana Transatlantica*, Nov. 2, 1918.

46. *Avanti!*, Aug. 7 and 21, Oct. 2, 16, 23 and 30, Nov. 6, 1920.

47. *Ibid.*, Dec. 1 and 31, 1918; Feb. 15 and 22, Mar. 15 and 29, June 7, Aug. 2, 1919; June 19 and 26, Sept. 11, 1920; Mar. 5, Apr. 16, 1921.

48. *Ibid.*, July 19, Aug. 30, 1919; July 3 and 17, 1920; May 28, 1921.

49. *Ibid.*, Jan. 15, July 19, 1919; *La Parola del Popolo*, Dec. 24, 1921; Jan. 28, 1922.

50. *La Parola del Popolo*, Jan. 28, 1922.

51. *L'Italia*, Nov. 23, Dec. 7, 1919; July 25, 1920; Apr. 24, May 1, 1921; *La Tribuna Italiana Transatlantica*; June 21 and 28, July 19, 1919; Jan. 29, Feb. 26, Apr. 2, May 28, June 18, 1921; *La Fiaccola*, May 13, June 3, July 8, Sept. 16, Oct. 28, Nov. 18, 1920.

52. *L'Italia*, Jan. 2, June 26, 1921; *La Tribuna Italiana Transatlantica*, June 25, 1921.

53. *L'Italia*, Sept. 22, 1888; Aug. 17, 1889; Apr. 5, 1890; July 5, 1902; Aug. 24, 1913; May 13, 1917; July 28, 1918; Mar. 30, 1919; July 27, 1920; *La Tribuna Italiana Transatlantica*, Mar. 16, 1918; *La Fiaccola*, May 3, 1917.

54. Giuseppe Giacosa, *Impressioni d'America* (Milan: L. F. Cogliati, 1908), p. 169; *L'Italia*, Jan. 4, June 28, 1902; *Il Messaggiere Italo-Americano*, July 17, 1888.

55. *Il Messaggiere Italo-Americano*, July 13, 1888.

56. Luigi Villari, *Gli Stati Uniti d'America e l'emigrazione italiana* (Milan: Fratelli Treves, 1912), p. 290, explained in footnote 1 that it was "an expression of disrespect which is applied to the Italians in the U.S."

57. This is described in Humbert S. Nelli, "The Role of the 'Colonial' Press in The Italian-American Community of Chicago 1886-1921," unpublished Ph.D. dissertation, University of Chicago, June 1965, Chapter III.

58. For example; see *L'Italia*, Jan. 5, 1895; Nov. 9, 1919; *Il Messaggiere Italo-Americano*, July 5, 1888.

59. Gaetano Salvemini and George La Piana, *What to Do with Italy* (New York: Duell, Sloan and Pierce, 1943), chap. iii; Edward Corsi, "Italian Immigrants and their Children," *Annals*, CCXXIII (September, 1942), 105; Caroline F. Ware, "Cultural Groups in the United States," *The Cultural Approach to History*, ed. C. F. Ware (New York: Columbia University Press, 1940), p. 63; Oscar Handlin, *The Uprooted* (Boston: Little, Brown & Co., 1951), p. 296; Giuseppe Prezzolini, *I Trapiantati* (Milan: Longanesi & Co., 1963), p. 63.

60. Corsi, *loc. cit.*, p. 105; Interview with Mr. Alberto Traldi, June 9, 1964.

61. For example, see two articles in *La Parola del Popolo. Cinquantesimo Anniversario*, IX, No. 30 (December, 1958-January, 1959): "Il movimento fascista fra gli italiani d'America," 69-72, and Charles Fama, "Fascist Propaganda in the United States," 91-93. In contrast to World War I, Italian-American socialists participated fully in U.S. efforts against the Axis during World War II. See *La Parola . . . Anniversario*, "Il contributo degli Italo-Americani per la liberazione dell'Italia," 74-85.

62. *New York Times*, Mar. 29, 1918; *Capital* (Des Moines, Iowa), reprinted in the *New York Tribune*, Aug. 13, 1917.

63. Among others: Glenn Frank, "Our Foreign Language Press," *Century Magazine*, LXLIX (March, 1920), 636-638; M. O. Whitton, "The Spirit of the German Press," *Smith Alumnae Quarterly*, No. 9 (February, 1918), pp. 93-97; C. W. Park, "The Strategic Retreat of the German Language Press," *North American Review*, No. 207 (May, 1918), pp. 706-719; F. P. Olds, "Disloyalty of the German-American Press," *Atlantic Monthly*, No. 120 (July, 1917), pp. 136-140; Robert E. Park, "Foreign Language Press and Social Progress," National Conference of Social Work, *Proceedings* (1920), XLVII, 493-500; Lucy M. Salmon, *The Newspaper and Authority* (New York: Oxford University Press, 1923), pp. 214-222; Fred C. Butler, "Problem of the Foreign Language Newspapers," *American City*, XXII (February, 1920), 117-118; "Influence of the German and Other Foreign Press," *Literary Digest*, LXIV (February 28, 1920), 31-32; "Foreign Language Papers Pleading for Life," *Literary Digest*, LXV (April 3, 1920), 24-25.

64. Nelli, "The Role of the 'Colonial' Press in the Italian-American Community of Chicago, 1886-1921."

65. Chicago Public Library Omnibus Project, *Bibliography of Foreign Language Newspapers and Periodicals Published in Chicago* (Chicago: Works Project Administration, 1942), pp. 71-74; N. W. Ayer and Son, *American Newspaper Annual* for the years 1921-1957. *L'Italia* went out of business temporarily during the 1960s but is again being published in Chicago.

MICHAEL PARENTI

The Blessings of Private Enterprise

A Personal Reminiscence

When my grandfather died in 1956, my father took over the family bakery. The bread he made was the same bread that had been made in Gravina, Italy for generations. After two days standing it was fresh as ever, the crust having grown hard and crisp while the inside remained soft, solid, moist and tasty. People used to say that our bread was a meal in itself.

The secret of the bread had been brought by my grandfather all the way from the Mediterranean to Manhattan, down into the tenement basement where he had installed wooden vats and tables. The bakers were two dark wiry men, *paisani da Gravina*, who rythmically and endlessly pounded their powdery white hands into the dough, molding the bread with finesse and strength. My grandfather, and then my father after him, used time and care in preparing their bread, letting it sit and rise twice in one night, using no chemicals and only the best quality flour. The bread was baked slowly and perfectly in an old brick oven built into the basement wall by my grandfather in 1907, an oven that had secrets of its own.

Often, during my college days, I would assist my father in loading up the bread truck at 5:00 A.M. on Saturday mornings. We delivered in the Bronx to Italian families whose appreciation for good bread was one of the satisfactions of our labor. Papa's business remained small but steady. Customers, acquired slowly by word of mouth, remained with us forever. Papa would chat with them everyday on the route, taking nine hours to do seven hours work. He could tell me more than I wanted to know about their family histories.

In time, some groceries, restaurants and supermarkets started placing orders with us, causing us to expand our production. Papa seemed pleased by the growth in his business but I felt a vague uneasiness about making commercial deliveries to such unconsecrated places as the Jerome Avenue Supermarket. I began to wonder where it would all lead.

Some months after Papa had begun to build his new clientele, as if to confirm my worst qualms, the Jerome Avenue Supermarket manager informed him that one of the big companies (I can't recall if it was Wonder Bread or Tip Top) was going into the "specialty line" and was offering to take over the Italian bread account. As an inducement to the super-market, the company was promising a "free introductory offer" of 500 loaves. With that peculiar kind of generosity often found in merchants, the supermarket manager offered to reject the bid and keep Papa's account if only we would match the big company's offer at least in part, say three hundred loaves. "Their bread is paper compared to mine," Papa protested. But his artisan's pride proved no match for the entrepreneur's manipula-tions, and he agreed to deliver 300 free loaves, twenty-five a day for almost three weeks to the supermarket in order to keep their account, all the while cursing them under his breath. This situation, known to the layman as "extortion," is referred to in the business world as a "deal."

During deals of this sort, however, my father developed certain tricks of his own. By artfully flashing his hands across the tops of the delivery boxes he would shortcount loaves right under the noses of the store man-agers: "Five and five across, that's twenty-five, Pete," he would point out, when in fact it was only twenty-three. We would load 550 loaves for the morning run and he would sell 575. Not since the Sermon on the Mount had bread reproduced itself so well.

"Papa," I said to him after one of his more daring performances, "You're becoming a thief."

"Kid," he said, "It's no sin to steal from them that steal from you." [*Individual competition in the pursuit of private gain brings out the best of our creative energies and thereby maximizes our productive contribu-tions and advances the well-being of the entire society.* Economics 101]

I left for a few years to go to graduate school, only to return home in 1959 without a penny in my pocket. I asked my father to support me for a semester so that I might finish writing my dissertation. In return, I offered to work a few days a week on the bread truck. Papa agreed to this but he wondered how he would explain to his customers and to his bakers that his son was twenty-five years old and still had no full-time job.

"Kid, how long can you keep going to school and what for?" he asked. "All those books," he would remind me, "are bad for your eyes and bad for your mind."

"Well," I said, "I'm getting a Ph.D." To this he made no response. So I put in a few days a week hard labor on the truck. Nor did Papa com-plain; in fact, he needed the help and liked having me around (as he told Mama who told me).

When the bakers asked Papa how come, at the age of twenty-five, I was working only part-time, he said grimly and without explanation: "He's getting a Ph.D." Hearing this, they looked away politely, thinking that I was coming down with some kind of blood disease. That was why I didn't work full time, they figured. So everyone was satisfied and I was treated with understanding.

On the day my dissertation was accepted and I knew I was to receive my Ph.D., I proudly informed Papa. He nodded and said, "That's good." Then he asked me if I wanted to become a full time partner in the bread business working with him on the truck every day.

I almost said yes.

One day the health inspectors came by and insisted we could not leave the bread naked in the store aisles in open display boxes, exposed to passers-by who might wish to touch or fondle the loaves with their germ-carrying fingers. No telling what kind of infected pervert might chance into a supermarket. So my father and I were required to wrap each loaf in a plastic bag, thus increasing our production costs, adding hours to our labor, and causing us to handle the bread twice as much with our germ-carrying fingers. But now it looked and *tasted* like modern bread because the bags kept the moisture in, and the loaves would get gummy in their own humidity inside their antiseptic plastic skins instead of forming a crisp, tasty crust in the open air.

Then some of the bigger companies began in earnest to challenge our restaurant and store trade, underselling us with an inferior quality Italian bread. At about this time the price of flour went up and the landlord from whom our family had rented the bakery premises for a half century, or rather his son, raised our rent substantially.

"When it rains it pours," Papa said. So he tried to reduce costs by giving the dough more air and water, and spending less time on the preparation. The bakers shook their heads and went on making the imitation product for the plastic bags.

"Papa," I complained, "The bread tastes like rubber and paper."

"What's the difference? They still eat it, don't they?" he said with a tight face.

But no matter what he did, things got more difficult. Some of our old family customers complained and began to drop their accounts. And a couple of the stores decided it was more profitable to carry the commercial brands. Not long after, my father disbanded the bakery and went to work driving a cab for one of the big taxi fleets in New York City.

This essay, with some change, appeared in ITALIAN AMERICANA (Autumn, 1974).

JOANNE PELLEGRINO

An Effective School of Patriotism

Political emigration played a unique and vital role in the Risorgimento. Refugees from political oppression in the several Italian states, either through condemnation or self-banishment, sought asylum in the more liberal nations of Europe and in the Americas. Exile very often meant more than finding merely their own personal safety. These expatriots continued to labor for the ideals for which they had fought in Italy, and seldom abandoned their efforts to make Italy one, independent and free.

The importance of the political emigration of the Risorgimento extends beyond the refugees as an active revolutionary force. They were also a cultural and moral force in the countries in which they found a haven, often exerting a powerful influence on public opinion in favor of the cause of Italian unification. These factors demonstrate the significance of the Italian political emigration of the Risorgimento expressed by Alessandro Galante Garrono:

If Italy was anything alive and viable in Europe and in the world . . . it is owed in great measure to the political emigration . . .[1]

This political emigration had its root in the French Revolution beginning with Filippo Buonarroti and others of a French outlook, but it also included Italians opposed to the Revolution who fled to England. A great surge in emigration did not take place until 1820-21, following the unsuccessful *moti*[2] in Naples and Piedmont. Switzerland, Tunis, Corsica and Algeria joined France and England as places of asylum, while Spain held a special fascination because of its Constitution of 1812 and its revolutionary government. 1830-31 witnessed another great wave of emigration sparked by the insurrections in Modena and the Papal States, causing Garrono to assert:

1831 was truly the critical, decisive year in the story of our political emigration.[3]

To the familiar places of exile at this time was added another—America.

The ranks of expatriots swelled almost to the proportions of a mass movement with a rigorous self-examination taking place, many times directed toward eventual action in Italy. Mazzini in London dominates this period, which was climaxed in 1848-49 with the return of many of the exiles to fight in the First War of Independence or under the standard of the Roman Republic.

Defeat of both these efforts brought yet another surge in political emigration, while the Second War of Independence of 1859 and the expedition of Garibaldi's *Mille* saw many exiles return again to fight for unity and independence. This time they were successful. With the formation of the Kingdom of Italy in 1860, uniting all the peninsula except Rome and the Veneto, the hopes of most Italian patriots were realized and the essential historical function of Italy's political emigration of the 19th century had been accomplished.

Italian political refugees of the Risorgimento sought asylum in many lands and continents, from England to Algeria and the nations of the Americas. The emigration to each particular country is significant for a variety of political and sociological reasons, but it is interesting to note this comment Mazzini made in 1842,

. . . the Italian immigration in France and in England is a disgrace compared to that of America.[4]

Mazzini was referring to the spirit of the refugees in these nations and their zeal in fighting for the Italian cause. He had based his assessment on the idea that a patriot's fervor somehow diminishes as he found himself closer to Italy. Mazzini concluded that in England and France the exiles more often took matters for granted, while those in distant lands, as America, were more enthusiastic. While it is evident that Mazzini was most likely referring to both North and South America, it would be noteworthy to investigate his implication as it concerns at least part of the Americas—the United States.

The political emigration of Italians to the United States as an historical phenomenon is significant for a number of reasons. The presence of the Italian exiles had a strong influence on American opinion concerning the struggle for Italian unity, and exposure to America and her way of life in some measure influenced the ideas of these refugees.

Many of the exiles were prominent in the political life of Italy before their stay in America; others were to become so on their return. Several exiles became United States citizens and remained here, with three serving as consuls of their adopted country.

The years 1831 to 1860 provide valid boundaries for study because of the great increase in emigration after 1831, and its virtual cessation after 1860. The years also encompass those during which the most noteworthy refugees came to America. The political emigration of Italians to the United States from 1831 to 1960 is a phenomenon which possesses significance for the histories of both nations.

PROFILE OF THE REFUGEES

The political emigration of Italians to the United States was only a very small portion of the total European immigration of 1831-1860 to America, which is estimated at approximately 4,910,590.[5] Of these, according to the statistics of the Regio Commissariato Generale della Emigrazione, 13,254 were Italians.[6] But the exact number of those coming to the United States for political reasons is difficult to ascertain. Economic conditions were undoubtedly the chief motivation for migration here, but it never will be known in how many instances disquieting political situations gave an added impetus to the decision to leave Italy.

It is most probable that several hundred Italians did come to America between 1831-1860 for more purely political reasons. They came to escape a land constrained by the Treaty of Vienna of 1815, where Lombardy and the Veneto were under the direct rule of Austria and the Duchies of Modena, Parma and Lucca in her sphere of influence; where Tuscan was governed by a Hapsburg grand duke, albeit with moderation, and the Papal States were under stringent Church control; where a Bourbon despot reigned in the Kingdom of Naples and at least a modicum of freedom was found in the Kingdom of Sardinia. For these men the United States was a land of personal freedom, a nation whose struggle for independence they had read in Carlo Botta's history of the American Revolution.

Of these political refugees there was a nucleus of about fifty men whose names emerge from that unacknowledged mass and who merit historical investigation—either for their contributions to the fight for Italian unification or their life in their adopted country. Names like Garibaldi, Avezzana or Confalonieri are more familiar than some others of this group like Tinelli, Argenti or Albinola. Nevertheless their experiences in America all demonstrate how their exile was in the words of H. Nelson Gay, "an effective school of patriotism."[7]

The most important years for political emigration to America were 1831 to 1860, although a number of refugees did come to the United States because of the unsuccessful *moti* of 1820-21 in Sicily and Piedmont. The 1830's are dominated by exiles from Austrian-controlled Italy—the "Martyrs of Spielberg" as the American press hailed them, men from

Lombardy-Veneto who were convicted of high treason and membership in secret sects in a series of secret trials from 1819 to 1835.

Although refugees from Italy's troubled political situation continued to find a haven in America, as Antonio Gallenga in 1836 and G. F. Secchi de Casali in 1844, it was not until the fall of the Roman Republic in 1849 that another larger group emigrated here. Pre-eminent among them was Giuseppe Garibaldi who had led the defence of the Republic, and the exiles included General Giuseppe Avezzana, Quirico Filopanti, Col. Bovi-Campeggi, and Gugliolmo Gajani. Until the decline of emigration after 1860, political refugees continued to come to the United States from Italy, with the 1850's characterized by the arrival of groups of lesser-known exiles whose prison sentences had been reduced to deportation to the United States.

A generalized profile of these refugees is difficult, even if it is limited to the nuclear group of fifty. There was no "typical" refugee. The safest generalization is self-evident—all these men were at least political activists, if not outright revolutionaries in Italy. Many of the older men were Carbonari, and the younger adhered to Mazzini's *Giovine Italia*. Politically the majority were republicans with some monarchists like Secchi de Casali or Maroncelli among them. There were almost all proscribed men by their respective governments, some having been sentenced to death *in absentia*.

Many, like the Spielberg patriots, had suffered imprisonment for varying periods of time. Some voluntarily chose the United States as a land of exile, while others were deported here by the governments of Austria, Naples or the Papal States, often on the condition that refusal for deportation would mean continued imprisonment. Several exiles came directly here from unsuccessful revolutions or threats of arrest in Italy, while a few had at first sought asylum in England, France, Tangiers, Spain or Mexico.

Geographically the refugees came from all the Italian states, with perhaps Lombardy having the largest and most renowned group in the Spielberg prisoners. Sardinia was represented by Garibaldi and Avezzana, and Naples by De Attelis and Chitti. Bachi, D'Alessandro and Minnelli were Sicilians, and Gajani was from the Papal States.

Socially and economically the Risorgimento was dominated by liberal nobles and the middle class, by those who were like Pellico, "an equal distance from the rich and poor."[8] Records of Italian state prisoners in Spielberg support this judgment. For 39 Italians for whom an occupation is given, 33⅓% were landowners and 10% merchants. 20% were professional men—lawyers, writers, pharmacists—while 7.5% were civil servants, and an equal number students. 10% were clerks or had no profession, and only one prisoner was listed as poor or having no possessions.[9]

The socio-economic background of the refugees to America reflects this upper middle-class bias with the nobility represented by Counts Confalonieri and DeAttelis. Garibaldi and Avezzana were military men, but for the greater part in Italy these exiles had been teachers, lawyers, literary men, judges or court officials, merchants and manufacturers, and very often landowners.

For the most part these refugees came to America without families. Very many, especially the Spielberg prisoners, were unmarried. Confalonieri's wife had died while he was in prison, and Luigi Tinelli's wife chose not to follow her husband, although this would have been permitted by Austria. Garibaldi was another widower, his beloved Anita having died in their desperate retreat from Rome in 1849. Maroncelli brought his wife to America and they were later joined by her brother.

Although several exiles married in America, this absence of family may have contributed to the fact that so many returned to Italy either for visits or to remain permanently. Undoubtedly the primary motivation for this return was political—to fight for unification and to remain after that fight had been successful—but the lack of permanent ties in America may have played a role in these decisions.

In addition, the majority of the exiles were not young revolutionaries in their twenties. Most of them were in their 30's and 40's due to years of imprisonment or intrigue at home, another factor which may have made adjustment to American life more difficult.

PIERO MARONCELLI

Piero Maroncelli, a native of Forli, was one of the first of this group of exiles to arrive on American soil. His coming to America in 1833 as chorus master for an opera company was not unheralded. An American newspaper commented:

> Maroncelli, the friend and companion of Pellico, is now with us. May he be received as his talents, his virtue and his long sufferings for the cause of liberty require and merit.[10]

Silvio Pellico and his book of recollections of confinement in the Austrian prison of Spielberg, *Le Mie Prigioni*, were well-known to literary Americans, having been favorably reviewed by *Norton's Select Journal* and the *American Quarterly Review*.

Maroncelli, his cellmate in Spielberg, had been Pellico's friend in Milan before their prison experience, and they belonged to the same circle of young liberals, eager for reform and freedom, which expressed its views in the short-lived journal *Il Conciliatore* (1818-1819) of which Pellico was the editor.

Both he and Maroncelli were Carbonari[11] and in 1820 both were arrested by a Special Commission to eradicate such liberal thought from Austrian Italy. They were sentenced to death commuted to long term imprisonment in the dungeons of Spielberg.

This Spielberg imprisonment forms the heart of *Le Mie Prigioni* which reaches its climax with the amputation of Maroncelli's leg by the prison barber-surgeon because of a tumor undoubtedly aggravated by the terribly unhealthful prison conditions. Their pardon by Francis the First came in 1830 after eight years of confinement.

Maroncelli, who was born in 1795, was a musician by training having studied at the Naples Conservatory. After his release from Spielberg, he chose Paris for his place of exile, but in 1833 he came to America with his new wife Amalia, hoping to make a better life here.

Critically the couple was well received, as a review of Rossini's *La Gazza Ladra* in the November 18, 1833 issue of the *New York Mirror* attests.[12] Maroncelli also won the friendship of a number of Americans interested in the Italian cause, especially Andrews Norton, professor of Sacred Literature at Harvard and father of Charles Eliot Norton. It was though the help of Andrews Norton that Maroncelli undertook to publish a new edition of *Le Mie Prigioni* in English together with his own *Additions*. The book appeared in 1836 and won the admiration of the *American Monthly Magazine*.

It was for his *Additions*, essays and poetry that Edgar Allan Poe admired Maroncelli as a literary man and included him in his autobiography *Literarti*. He also described him as a friend:

Maroncelli is strong-willed, frank, generous and chivalrous . . . his love for his country is immense and he devotes himself with great fervor to spreading Italian literature in America.[13]

Although for a time he had considered moving to Boston, Maroncelli and Amalia remained in New York where he taught music and Italian. His circle of friends included Catherine Sedgwick and other Americans favorable to the Italian cause. Maroncelli was not as active in political affairs as some other exiles, although he generously helped those refugees who followed him. He did have an interest in the social and political theories of Charles Fourier and Edward Swedenborg and frequently attended Fourier meetings.

An eye condition he mentioned as early as 1836 rapidly led to blindness, compounded by mental illness. He died blind and insane 10 years later. Signora Maroncelli was forced to sell his library of over 900 volumes, but even the notice of sale attests to the friendship he won in America, not only for himself, but also for the cause of Italian unification.[14]

MARTYRS OF SPIELBERG

In October 1836, the *New York Times* carried the following news item:

The Austrian Imperial Brig *Ussero* . . . had on board Italians whose punishment for alleged political crimes the Austrian Emperor had commuted to perpetual exile in America . . .
We sincerely trust that these worthy victims of despotism may be able to find a hospitable sympathy in our country.[15]

It was with these and similar sentiments that Felice Foresti, Gaetano Castillia, Pietro Borsieri, Felice Argenti, Giovanni Albinola, Luigi Tinelli, Cesare Benzoni and Alessandro Bargnani were welcomed to America. All these men had either been prisoners in Spielberg or were about to be sent there, and were recipients of an amnesty granted by the new Emperor Ferdinand II on March 4, 1835.

Felice Foresti, a judge at Crespino, was arrested in 1819 on charges of being a Carbonaro and founding a cell at Rovigo. His death sentence was commuted to 20 years at Spielberg. In a trial of a secret sect similar to the Carbonari, the Federati of Milan, Count Confalonieri, Pietro Borsieri and Gaetano Castillia were condemned in 1821. Giovanni Albinola and Felice Argenti were tried almost 10 years later and suffered about one year's imprisonment. Although condemned to Spielberg in September 1835 for activities in the *Giovine Italia*, Luigi Tinelli, Cesare Benzoni and Alessandro Bargnani never were actually imprisoned there, taking immediate advantage of the imperial clemency.

Little is known of Bargnani or Benzoni, although the latter was a young legal student at the time of his arrest. Both Albinola and Argenti remained in the United States, Argenti dying in San Francisco in 1862 and Albinola becoming a successful merchant in New York and friend of his compatriots until his death in 1883.

Both Pietro Borsieri and Gaetano Castillia eventually returned to Italy. Borsieri, a nobleman from Milan described his arrival in New York in words which reveal his literary profession. The harbor . . .

. . . presented itself crowned with two charming islands and [was] solemn in its beauty . . . At that moment my heart opened. The sight of a welcoming land which presented itself after so many days of endless water and sky, smiling with such beauty, melted my sadness into tears.[16]

However he returned to Europe later that year and died near Lake Maggiore in 1852.

Borsieri's companion on his return was Gaetano Castillia, a Milanese jurist, who was implicated in the Federati plot of 1821. After a stay in

America where he gained the friendship of the Sedgwicks, Castillia also returned to Italy where he served as a Senator of the Kingdom of Italy until his death in 1870.

Two of these Spielberg prisoners distinguished themselves in America and became citizens and consuls of their adopted land. Yet Italy was not forgotten. Speaking of Felice Foresti, H. Nelson Gay commented:

No other Italian resident in America worked harder than he to diffuse knowledge of this cause [Italian independence] and the feeling of its justice.[17]

Foresti had been born in the province of Ferrara in 1789 and received a law degree from the University of Bologna in 1809. He practiced in Crespino in Austrian Italy until his arrest. In New York Foresti taught Italian to earn his livelihood and in 1839 he was appointed Professor of Italian at Columbia University.

Foresti's political convictions remained unfaltering throughout his years of exile in the United States. He was a republican and Howard Marraro calls him the official representative of Mazzini in America.[18] He was virtual head of the Italian community in New York and was one of the organizers of a school for poor Italian children. A naturalized citizen, Foresti was appointed U.S. consul at Genoa in 1858 by James Buchanan, but died a few months later, being buried with the full diplomatic honors of his adopted land.

Luigi Tinelli also became a U.S. consul and participated actively in American life. He was born in Lombardy in 1799 of a noble family and received a degree in law. After the uprisings of 1821, he fled to England and then Spain, but returned to Italy where he was active in the *Giovine Italia* until his arrest in 1833.

In America Tinelli devoted himself to the manufacture of silk as he had done in Italy, and he was awarded a gold medal by the Institute of American Industry. In 1841 Tinelli was appointed U.S. Consul-General in Oporto, Portugal, where ironically he signed the death certificate of Carlo Alberto who died there after his abdication.

When Tinelli returned to New York in 1850, he resumed his commercial interests and opened a law office. Together with his two sons, he distinguished himself fighting with the Union Army in the Civil War and died in New York in 1873.

FEDERICO CONFALONIERI

Federico Confalonieri was one of the "Martyrs of Spielberg" well-known to Americans and one of those to remain here the shortest time—

barely seven months. He is especially important because of his extensive political and social activities in Italy before his arrest and his acknowledged position as leader of the Milanese liberals. During his short stay in America, his correspondence is laced with perceptive comments on the country and its systems, which demonstrate how at least one exile viewed the United States.

Count Confalonieri arrived in New York on February 21, 1837, separately from the other Spielberg refugees, as he had to remain longer at the detention center of Gradisca due to ill health. It was also because of this broken health that he declined an invitation to welcome him at a formal dinner, offered by twenty three distinguished New Yorkers including Albert Gallatin, William Cullen Bryant and Theodore Sedgwick, Jr.

Federico Confalonieri was born in 1785 of a family of the Milanese high nobility loyal to Austria, but his convictions followed the new liberal philosophy which included independence for Italy. He had traveled extensively through Europe and had engaged in a series of social projects including the opening of two schools for poor children in Milan.

Confalonieri was the impetus behind the liberal journal, *Il Conciliatore*, staffed by Pellico and Borsieri among others, which "hinted at politics in witty parables and boldly proclaimed its patriotism."[19] It was soon suppressed and the Count's arrest followed in December 1821 after the failure of the Piedmontese uprising of earlier that year. His life was spared only at the personal intercession of his wife, Teresa before Francis I and the Empress.

Confalonieri was known to Americans especially through Maroncelli's 1836 *Additions* to *Le Mie Prigioni* and accounts of his trial in the *Edinburgh Review*, which were summarized in the press as his arrival in America approached. For a time the Count remained in New York among the circle of Americans sympathetic to the Italian cause and became a close friend of Catherine Sedgwick. In the spring he took a whirlwind tour of the United States together with another exile, Giovanni Albinola. Everywhere he was greeted with affection and enthusiasm, and he reflected whether Austria may not have hurt herself by sending the refugees to America.

Confalonieri's trip took him south through Philadelphia, Baltimore, Richmond and Charleston, and then through Georgia and Alabama to New Orleans. Here he had ample opportunity to witness some of the defects of American society:

> Slavery marks a boundary line between the States of the North and those of the South which seems to be sometimes one of civilization, industry and morality.[20]

Confalonieri admired the natural beauty of America, like Niagara Falls, but some of what he saw politically and socially disillusioned the European liberal and idealist in him:

The present generation is not that of Washington . . . Irreligion, immorality, the most unbridled greed have invaded the present population: and the lofty sacrifices . . . the civic and domestic virtues, have all felt their fateful influence.[21]

Confalonieri had always viewed his exile in America as temporary and sailed for England from New York on August 8, 1837, a day he described as "classic and solemn."[22] He settled eventually in Paris where he became a friend of Cavour on the latter's visits there. He died in Switzerland in 1846 while returning home to Milan.

Although the Austrian authorities tried to prevent a public demonstration at the funeral, the rites evoked a huge outpouring of both the Milanese people and nobility. His funeral was the first of a series of patriotic demonstrations in Milan culminating in the Cinque Giornate of 1848 and caused a contemporary to comment:

Living he had been a martyr; in death he had to be the prophet of patriotism.[23]

GIUSEPPE GARIBALDI

The political repression which was well-settled in Italy in the 1840's undoubtedly reduced political emigration to America. It was not until the turmoil of 1848 followed by the fall of the Roman Republic in 1849 that another significant group of refugees became exiles in America. Pre-eminent among them was Giuseppe Garibaldi.

This was not the first American exile for Garibaldi. From 1835 thru 1847 he had been in South America where he led the Italian Legion against rulers he considered despots. More importantly, he developed the tactics of guerrilla warfare which he employed so effectively in Italy. Born in Nice July 4, 1807 and a sailor by profession, Garibaldi became a member of the *Giovine Italia* and it was for his Mazzinian activities that he was condemned to death *in absentia* in 1834 and forced into exile.

With the outbreak of revolution in Italy in 1848, it was an eager Garibaldi who returned to offer his sword to Carlo Alberto. He was refused. Nevertheless he led a band of volunteers which won several brilliant but short-lived victories. The declaration of a republic drew him to Rome in February 1849 and his desperate, heroic defense of the Roman Republic won him the admiration of the world.

Through various involved twists of fate and opportunity, Garibaldi found himself an exile in New York on July 30, 1850. The Italian tricolor was raised at the Quarantine Station on Staten Island in his honor and the *New York Herald* welcomed him:

Few men have achieved so much for the cause of freedom, and no one has accomplished so many heroic acts for the independence of a fatherland as General Garibaldi has for Italy.[24]

He declined a gala reception in New York ostensibly because of poor health, but in reality pressure had been put on the organizers by Catholics, especially the Irish, who were loath to see a man who had fought the temporal power of the Pope, so honored.

Garibaldi's stay in New York was brief and otherwise uneventful. For a while he remained with compatriots in Yonkers or Manhattan, but his longest stay was with his Florentine friend and inventor, Antonio Meucci on Staten Island. Here he joined the local volunteer fire department and became a third degree Mason in the Tompkins Lodge No. 401. His memoirs describe this time of exile:

There was no luxury at the home [Meucci's], however, nothing was lacking of the primary necessities of life, both in lodging and food.[25]

Garibaldi continued to shun offers of honors and he often contributed money he received to less fortunate exiles. American and foreign visitors frequently visited him at Staten Island where the little community of exiles engaged in candlemaking to support themselves.

Garibaldi's original idea had been to sail again, this time under the American flag, a nation he loved and deeply adored. For this reason he had filed initial papers for citizenship which led in later years to his occasional claims of being an American citizen. In April 1851 an opportunity to command a ship presented itself, and although it was not an American vessel, Garibaldi left on an extended voyage to the Orient.

On his way home to Italy in September 1853, Garibaldi again visited the United States briefly, primarily Boston and New York. This shorter stay in America was more important historically than that of 1850-51.

Sometime during his American exile and voyage to the Orient, Garibaldi's political ideas underwent a change, which first manifested itself in 1853 in America. He noted with distress the discord among the expatriots, especially in New York which were usually along monarchical versus republican lines and he wanted to effect a reconciliation. On September 19, 1853 he wrote from Boston to Felice Foresti:

I have decided to work actively (as much as possible) toward the conciliation of Italians of whatever opinion, and I sincerely wish to see you guide the plan, in New York especially, where above all you are esteemed and loved. I would like you to see Valerio, to whom I am writing on this matter, and to speak with him on this undertaking. I will write to Avezzana, Forbes, Gavazzi, and if it is possible I will also return to New York.[26]

Valerio was the Sardinian Consul General in New York and the following letter Garibaldi wrote him from Boston on September 22, 1853 shows the direction of the understanding Garibaldi sought to achieve:

Concerning the idea manifested to you of reconciliation among the Italians, I have written to various of the most influential men proposing as a program: To muster around the Italian flag of Piedmont whatever many have been their conviction of a system for the past and [to do this] decisively; not having any other means than this, to reunite Italy to that Government, fighting all the foreigners that oppress her.[27]

This realization of the leadership role of Piedmont in the struggle for Italian unification, manifest during Garibaldi's American exile, was later raised by him during the expedition of the *Mille* with its motto: *Italia e Vittorio Emmanuele*. It contributed immeasurably to making Italian independence a reality.

ROMAN REPUBLIC EXPATRIOTS

The fall of the Roman Republic in July 1849 brought with it to the United States refugees besides Garibaldi, many of whom had played important roles in the short life of that Republic. General Giuseppe Avezzana had been Minister of War and Marine and Quirico Filopanti, secretary of the Triumvirate. Luciani and Gajani had served in the Roman Assembly, while many like Colonel Bovi-Campeggi had fought in its desperate defense.

Giuseppe Avezzana was not new to revolutionary activity or exile in America when he arrived in New York in September 1849. Born in Piedmont in 1797 he chose a military career and in 1821 had participated with Santorre Santarosa in the insurrection in Piedmont. He was condemned to death *in absentia* and fled to Spain and finally New York in 1834, after having lived in Mexico where he fought in the Civil War.

General Avezzana became a prominant member of the Italian community in New York in the 1830's and a naturalized citizen. Doggett's *New York Business Directory* for 1841 and 1842 lists Joseph Avezzana as a commission merchant with offices at 47 Pearl Street.[28] He was an organizer of the Italian Guard in 1843 and a president of the Società Italiana di Unione Fratellanza e Beneficenza.

Avezzana returned to Italy late in 1848 and on April 18, 1849 was nominated Minister of War and Marine for the Roman Republic. In turn he named Garibaldi one of its Generals. With the fall of the Republic through the help of the American Chargé d'Affaires Lewis Cass, Jr., and under an assumed name, he escaped from Italy to return home to accolades in the press and a personal welcome by the Mayor.

The General continued to work for the cause of Italian unity while in New York. He was one of the "prominenti" to whom Garibaldi directed his new political thoughts in 1853. In November 1859 he became president of the New York Garibaldi Fund Committee, which was raising money for arms for Garibaldi. By September 1860 he had joined Garibaldi at Caserta, and he served in the Trentino campaign of 1866 and at Mentana in 1865. Avezzana was elected a deputy to the Italian Chamber and died in Rome in 1879.

If Avezzana's life was one of action, that of Quirico Filopanti was more intellectual. He was secretary of the Triumvir of the Republic and lived in New York briefly in 1850. A mathematician and philosopher, he struggled in poverty in New York for several months before returning to Italy where he was elected a deputy of the Italian Chamber in 1876. He was a member of the Far Left and remained so until his death in 1894.

Among others of this group were Guglielmo Gajani, a Roman jurist and member of the Republic's Assembly, as was Luciani. Righini and Oregoni, who had also served in Garibaldi's Italian Legion of Montevideo, fought with him in the defense of Rome, and like him chose exile in America, at least briefly.

ALSO IN SEARCH OF FREEDOM

The diversity and scope of the Italian political emigration to America can also be seen in some of the lesser-known refugees whose lives perhaps do not always fit into previous classifications.

A number of the refugees were Sicilians, exiles from the Revolutions of 1821 or 1848. Ignazio Batolo, alias Pietro Bachi, was a native of Palermo who fled to Boston in 1824. He was appointed to teach Italian at Harvard and won the friendship of George Ticknor and William H. Prescott. After playing a minor role in the Sicilian Revolution of 1848, he returned to Boston where he died in 1853.

Another Sicilian was the poet Pietro D'Alessandro, a sensitive young follower of Ugo Foscolo, who arrived in Boston in 1833, most likely in voluntary exile. Through him, Americans came to know the feelings of at least one expatriot.

In 1842 Henry Theodore Tuckerman anonymously published some of D'Alessandro's letters in the *Southern Literary Messenger*. But by that time the young poet, who had taught Italian in Boston, had returned to Sicily where during the Revolution of 1848, he headed a department in the Ministry of Foreign Affairs. He accompanied Ruggiro Settimo, leader of the Sicilian Provisional Government, into exile in Malta and died there in 1855.

Among the Neapolitan refugees was Orazio De Attelis, the Marquis Sant'Angelo, born of a noble family in 1774. Before settling in New York in the early 1840's, the flamboyant Marquis had participated in the Moscow campaign as an aide of Murat, opposed the Bourbons in Naples in the Revolution of 1821, fought under the liberal banner in Spain and lent his sword to the battle for independence in Mexico. He had lived in New Orleans where he was a founder of a multi-language newspaper *Correo Atlantico.*

A naturalized citizen, DeAttelis was an active member of the Italian community in New York. Perhaps his most important contribution was organizing the Italian Guard there in 1843. After fighting in Genoa and Rome on his return to Europe in 1848, he died in Civitavecchia in 1850.

The editor Secchi de Casali called Luigi Chitti, "the glory of the Neapolitan political emigration."[29] A scientist and economist, he was born in 1784 in the province of Reggio Calabria, the southernmost region of the Kingdom of Naples. He followed his father into exile after the fall of the Parthenopean Republic in 1799, and after a while he returned, to leave again after the failure of the Revolution of 1821.

A president of the Bank of Ghent, Chitti had among his friends and associates Cavour, Richard Cobden and Sir Robert Peel. The date of his arrival in the United States is uncertain, but in the 1840's and 1850's he was working with Casali in New York on the *L'Eco d'Italia.* He died here in 1853 with Felice Foresti delivering the eulogy.

The Piedmontese journalist Antonio Gallenga represents a situation where exile in America is definitely credited with a change in political views. A close friend of Mazzini and a member of the *Giovine Italia,* he had also participated in a desperate scheme to assassinate Carlo Alberto. After living in exile in Tunis and Tangiers, Antonio Gallenga arrived in Boston in 1836.

Here Gallenga taught Italian and engaged in journalism. More significantly, two biographers credit his five-year stay in America with modifying his political views from those of a radical revolutionary to those of one favoring more democratic means to achieve the goal of Italian unification.[30]

Gallenga returned to Italy in 1848 and he advocated union under Piedmont, for which he was applauded by Cavour. He became a member of Parliament, but returned to America briefly to cover the Civil War for the London *Times.* He died in Turin in 1895.

In addition to these exiles, many Italians sought refuge in the United States about whom little more is known than their name, if that much.

The 1850's especially were characterized by this type of emigration, with the arrival of groups of refugees on the same ship, often sent from the Papal States or Sardinia.

With the realization of Italian unity and independence in 1860, the cause of this political emigration was removed, and the year marks the virtual end of this unique type of Italian immigration to America during the 19th century.

EXILE PRESS AND POLITICS

The Italian exiles in America were very conscious of their *italianità* and had a vigorous sense of community. They formed welfare groups and societies, and organized Italian military units. Above all they engaged in political activity via committees, rallies and demonstrations whenever the opportunity presented itself to further the cause of independence and unity.

This sense of community was particularly evident in New York where the majority of the refugees gathered. It was especially fostered by their own press. The *L'Eco d'Italia* came into being in 1849 and was the foremost Italian language newspaper in New York for this period. *L'Eco* was the creation of a dauntless refugee from Piacenza, Giovanni Francesco Secchi de Casali, who came to America in 1844 and had contributed articles to such American publications as the *Whig American Review*, the *Tribune*, the *Herald*, and the *Evening Post*, edited by William Cullen Bryant who was favorable to the Italian cause and later became a personal friend.

L'Eco progressed from a weekly to a daily, and was printed entirely in Italian, containing news of America as well as that of Italy. Theater reviews, business news and excerpts from books were included, but politics dominated the four-page paper. It served as an indispensable means of communication among the exiles and indefatigably supported the efforts of refugees to further the cause of Italian unity.

Politically *L'Eco d'Italia* was moderate and favored a monarchy; it saw the House of Savoy as the means of Italian unification. Its republican counterpart for one short year was *Il Proscritto* which was published from 1851-1852 and had been proceeded by an even shorter-lived version, *L'Esule Italiano.*

Il Proscritto was strongly Mazzinian in sentiment and carried regular reports from his paper, *Italia e Popolo*. The paper's tone was much more polemic than *L'Eco* and spoke of the "betrayal" of Milan and Novara, the Salasco armistice and the abdication of Carlo Alberto. *Il Proscritto* was equally anti-Papal, calling the Papacy, "the first cause of our decay in the intellectual, moral and political ranks.[31] After it ceased publication, no republican organ replaced it. In later years Secchi de Casali commented that it was "edited with much ability and with equal intolerance and rancor."[32]

An Italian language press also existed in a limited extent in other American cities, such as *La Gazzetta Italiana* in Philadelphia, which published during the 1850's and *L'Eco della Patria* founded in 1859 in San Francisco. The *Correo Atlantico* of New Orleans was begun in 1836 by the Marquis de Attelis, the Neapolitan exile.

The republicans were most active, however, with Foresti founding a Congrega Centrale of the *Giovine Italia* in New York in 1841. Loyal republicans like Tinelli or Gajani lectured widely for the Italian cause. During the Crimean War funds were raised to aid the families of poor Italian soldiers.

Many refugees wanted to return home to fight for their homeland in 1859-1860, but in a letter to Secchi de Casali, Cavour urged the exiles to remain in America and help financially and morally instead. Garibaldi's exposition of the *Mille* evoked a huge outpouring of emotion and over $100,000 for arms was realized. Even thousands of miles from their home, the exiles retained a strong patriotic spirit and fervor.

AMERICA AND THE REFUGEES

In all these efforts, the refugees were aided by a small, but influential group of Americans who were sympathetic to the Italian cause. These Americans were often interested in Italian culture and through it came to see the need for Italian political unification. These were men and women like Harvard Professor Andrews Norton, and later his son Charles Eliot Norton, Henry Wadsworth Longfellow, James Russel Lowell, and New Yorkers like William Cullen Bryant, Theodore Sedgwick and his sister Catherine, and politicians like Senator Lewis Cass and his son, the American consul who had aided Avezzana.

These Americans helped the immigrants materially in making the difficult adjustment to the American way of life and more importantly organized rallies and meetings to keep alive the spirit of Italian unity. There was a definite growth in sympathy for the Italian cause among Americans at large because of the work of these dedicated friends of the Italian exiles.

How did the exiles view their new, if temporary, home, these friends and the vastly different circumstances into which they had been thrust? We have already heard the views of Confalonieri of this expanding nation bursting forth economically and socially from the Jacksonian era. What did the others think? Many of the exiles were informed about America before arrival here especially through Carlo Botta's history of the Revolution.[33]

Among Italian liberals, the American republic and her institutions were esteemed and idealized. For some, like Confalonieri, the practical reality proved a rude shock, but men like Garibaldi never wavered in their esteem of the United States. Pietro D'Alessandro, for example, delighted in the freedom of thought and speech here.

It is significant to note that several of the exiles became American citizens, among them Maroncelli, Avezzana, Foresti, Tinelli and DeAttelis, while Garibaldi had filed his preliminary papers. Some exiles returned to Italy, sometimes temporarily, and of a sample group of about 25 for whom there is firm data, half remained in America permanently.

In the United States, the life of the exiles reflected their middle class and noble backgrounds with the overwhelming number taking professional jobs, mostly as teachers. Only Garibaldi and some companions from the Roman Republic worked with their hands.

It would be even more difficult to ascertain if contact with American democratic institutions changed the political views of any of the refugees. There is definite proof in the case of Antonio Gallenga and undoubtedly many subtle changes took place. Americans on the other hand overwhelmingly viewed with exiles with affection.

Catherine Sedgwick their staunch friend wrote:

These men . . . were exiled in America where they came in close contact with my family. I wish that those who through ignorance speak of Italians with thoughtlessness and disdain would know these men who have learned to endure years of trials and temptation to which human nature is rarely subjected. Can we who honor our fathers for those few years of a difficult life that they had to endure, ever withhold our admiration of these men who have sacrificed forever all that is most dear for the sacred cause of liberty and truth.[34]

AN EFFECTIVE SCHOOL OF PATRIOTISM

Political exile has been termed "an effective school of patriotism,"[35] and the importance of the Italian political emigration to America from 1831 to 1860 is centered in this concept. The significance of the exiles in the spectrum of both Italian and American history is focused on the fact that because of their presence in America, the cause of Italian unity gained in a variety of ways.

Crucial to this conclusion is the fact that the Italian expatriots rarely, if ever, forgot the land of their birth, even when they settled permanently in the United States. They continued to work tirelessly for the cause for which they had fought and suffered in Italy. Through many committees and rallies, they never ceased to publicize the idea of Italian unity. They collected arms, raised funds, conducted benefit concerts, and in the case of some, returned themselves to fight for independence.

In these efforts it should be noted that there was a lessening of regional differences among the exiles, who came from all parts of Italy. The fact of their isolation in a foreign land blurred regional distinctions and caused them to band together, both to help each other in their daily lives and to further the Italian cause. They were all Italians, no longer merely Sardinians, Neapolitans, or Lombards. The same cannot be said completely in regard to political differences.

The earlier years of the exiles' stay in America were characterized by a strong republican-monarchical division in their ranks. The republicans were especially vigorous, and branches of the *Giovine Italia* were formed in American cities. Republican lectures were greeted with enthusiasm and they published their own newspaper briefly in New York to counteract a monarchical paper, which subsequently prevailed.

It is important to note that while political differences were often evident, as events progressed the Italian refugees in America, like most of their compatriots in Italy, gradually accepted the Kingdom of Sardinia as leader in the unification movement. By 1859 many republican exiles in the United States were lecturing to raise funds for Sardinia in the Second War of Independence.

Of this move toward Piedmont, it can at least be said that exile in America did not cause the refugees to become intransigent in their political views, and permitted an accommodation to take place. That the modification of ideas was *caused* by exile in America is a different problem, although the case of Garibaldi and his efforts toward reconciliation begun during his American exile, offer a valid possibility. (See appendix).

Regarding the significance of the Italian political emigration of 1831-1860 for American history, it is of importance that the exiles were assisted by an influential group of American men and women. Individuals like William Cullen Bryant, Andrews Norton, Theodore Sedgwick and his sister, Catherine, George Ticknor and Henry Theodore Tuckerman helped the Italians adjust to American life. More importantly they formed the nucleus of a group of Americans dedicated to Italian independence, which expressed its ideas through public meetings and the press.

Largely because of contact with the exiles, this group publicized the theme of Italian freedom and made it fashionable, especially in literary circles, and meaningful to the American public as a whole. It is interesting to note that most of these Americans were also interested in other social causes, and in many cases the same persons were abolitionists and evangelicals.

The presence and activities of the Italian political refugees exerted an overwhelmingly favorable influence on American public opinion as Marraro argues, and sometimes expressed itself in official policy and in the actions of our diplomats in Italy. Their presence may also have abetted the development of the Young America movement in the Democratic party, which championed the cause of the oppressed peoples of Europe.

The importance of the emigration for Italian history revolves around this theme. Through the sympathy generated by the exiles, Italy gained a supporter of her cause across the Atlantic. Howard Marraro explains this support:

> And though America was not the country which actually accomplished most for Italian freedom and unity, it was the country where passion for that cause was, beyond all comparison, strongest and most disinterested.[36]

Exile in America also provided the Italian patriots with a safe haven to await that time when they could fight again for Italian freedom. Many of the refugees did return to Italy. Foremost among them was Garibaldi. Giuseppe Avezzana fought with him with the *Mille* and later served in Parliament. Gallenga and Filopanti also became Deputies and Gaetano Castillia was made a Senator of the new Kingdom. Whether the ideas of these men who entered public life in Italy or their observations of her democracy changed, remains a matter of speculation. It is very possible, as the case of Antonio Gallenga proves, that their exile in America may have produced a subtle effect on their thoughts and actions while they participated in the public life of the new Kingdom of Italy.

The Italians who emigrated to America from 1831 to 1860 as political refugees came to the United States in search of freedom, and liberty from the political oppression which prevented Italy from becoming one, independent and free. Their exile in the United States proved an effective school of patriotism which helped achieve that goal.

NOTES

1. Alessandro Galante Garrone, "L'emigrazione politica italiana del risorgimento," *Atti del XXXII congresso di storia del risorgimento*, (1954) p. 60.
2. The term *moti*, Italian for movements, designates the insurrections in Italy, organized principally by the secret patriotic sects as the Carbonari, Federati of Milan and later the Giovine Italia.
3. Alessandro Galante Garrone, *op. cit.*, p. 68.
4. Quoted in *Ibid.*, p. 70.
5. Friedrick Kapp, *Immigration and the Commissioners of Emigration of the State of New York.* (New York: 1969) Statistical Table VII, p. 227.
6. Paolo G. Brenna, *Storia dell'emigrazione italiana.* (Roma: 1928) p. 227. This figure compares favorable with that of the State Commissioners of Emigration which sets the number of Italians entering New York, the chief, but not only port of debarkation, at 10,813 for 1831-1860. Friedrick Kapp, *op. cit.* p. 230.

7. H. Nelson Gay, "Il secondo esilio di Garibaldi (1849-1854)" *Nuova Antologia*, Vol. 147 (1910) p. 635.

8. Silvio Pellico, *My Prisons: Memoirs of Silvio Pellico.* (Cambridge: 1836) p. 185.

9. Renzo Montini, *I processi Spielberghiani* and Aldo Zaniboni, ed. *I fogli matricolari dello Spielberg.* (Roma: 1937).

10. Quoted in Angeline Lograsso, "Piero Maroncelli in America," *Rassegna storica del risorgimento.* Anno 15 (1928) p. 920.

11. The Carbonari were members of a secret patriotic society (Carboneria) which gained adherents in Italy from the time of the collapse of the Napoleonic regime thru about the 1830's. It flourished in Southern Italy, Lombardy and Piedmont. Freedom through revolutionary action was its aim, but both monarchists and republicans were included and no clear-cut ideological policy was formed.

12. Quoted in Angeline Lograsso, *op. cit.*, p. 897.

13. Quoted in *Ibid.*, p. 274.

14. *Catalogue of Italian, French and English Books (Many of Them Very Scarce) Composing the Library of the Late Piero Maroncelli*: New York (no date).

15. Quoted in Giuseppe Castelli, *Luigi Tinelli (Da Mazzini a Carlo Alberto).* (Milano: 1949), p. 89-91.

16. Federico Confalonieri, *Memorie e lettere.* Vol. II, p. 372.

17. H. Nelson Gay, *Le relazioni fra gli Stati Uniti e l'Italia negli anni 1847-71.* (Torino-Roma: 1907), p. 84.

18. Howard Marraro, *American Opinion on the Unification of Italy 1846-1871.* (New York: 1969), p. 207.

19. Kent Robert Greenfield, *Economics and Liberalism in the Risorgimento: A Study of Nationalism in Lombardy.* (Baltimore: 1934), p. 152.

20. Federico Confalonieri, *Memorie e lettere*, Vol. II, p. 169.

21. Quoted in S. Eugene Scalia, "Federico Confalonieri in America," *Italy-America Monthly*, (April 15, 1934), p. 15.

22. Federico Confalonieri, *op. cit.* Vol. II, p. 201.

23. Federico Confalonieri, *op. cit.* Vol. I, (Introduction), p. 11.

24. Quoted in Howard Marraro, *op. cit.*, p. 166.

25. Giuseppe Garibaldi, *Le memorie di Garibaldi.* A cura della Reale Commissione. (Bològna: 1932), Vol. I, p. 221.

26. Quoted in H. Nelson Gay, "Il secondo esilio di Garibaldi (1849-1854)", p. 659.

27. Giuseppe Garibaldi to N. Valerio. Letter of September 22, 1853 from Boston. Garibaldi-Meucci Memorial Museum, Staten Island, N.Y. See appendix.

28. J. Doggett, Jr. *New York Business Directory for 1841 and 1842.* (New York: 1841), p. 28.

29. G. F. Secchi de Casali, "Trent'otto anni d'America," *L'Eco d'Italia*, (March 4-5, 1883), p. 1, col. 5.

30. Pietro Orsi, "Antonio Gallenga," *Nuova Antologia.* (March 1, 1932) and Michele Rossi, ed. *Dizionario del risorgimento nazionale.* (Milano: 1930).

31. "Revolution and Parties," *Il Proscritto* (December 25, 1851), p. 81, col. 4.

32. G. F. Secchi de Casali, *"Trent'otto anni d'America,"* L'Eco d'Italia, (June 17-18, 1883), p. 1, col. 4.

33. This history was especially praised by John Adams. Carlo Giuseppe Botta (1766-1837) was a physician and historian who was exiled to France in 1792. His son, Vincenzo Botta, lived in America from 1853 to 1894 and took an active role in the Italian and American communities, but was not technically a refugee since he came to the United States voluntarily and with no political motives as Pietro D'Alessandro.
34. Quoted in Angeline Lograsso, *Piero Maroncelli*, p. 271.
35. H. Nelson Gay, "Il secondo esilio di Garibaldi (1849-1854)", p. 635.
36. Howard Marraro, *op. cit.*, p. 313.

APPENDIX

Unedited letter of Giuseppe Garibaldi to N. Valerio, Consul General of Piedmont. The original is displayed in the Garibaldi-Meucci Memorial Museum, Staten Island, New York.

Boston, 22 settembre 1853

Caro Valerio,

Le tante gentilezze vostre verso di me mi hanno ardito a chiedervi l'incamminamento delle acchiuse, e pregarvi di comandarmi alcuna volta a mio torno.

Circa all'idea manifestarvi di concilizaioni tra gl'Italiani ho scritto a vari di più influenti proponendo per programma: Ranadarsi intorno alla bandiera Italiana del Piemonte qualunque sia stata la convinzione di sistema per il passato e troncamenti; non avendo altra meta che quella di riunir l'Italia a quel Governo, conbattendo tutti gli stranieri che l'opprimono.

Lo pregherò la stessa idea altrove a tutta possa, convinto di far bene. Se vi pare, scrivete a Gavazzi acciò si strova in New York, ove io penso essere tra 7 od 8 giorni e se troverle bene, sazioneremo in una riunione quanto se è detto. (Vostro)

G. Garibaldi

ANDREW ROLLE

The American Italians
Psychological and Social Adjustments

What a world apart America must have seemed to people who came from rocky, remote villages high in the Appenines or from the arid reaches of Calabria—to settle in the crowded Bronx, Brooklyn, and New Haven. For these strangers in the new land, adjustment, like it or not, was a necessity.

Fear of strangers—the Greek xenophobia—reminds us that no animal dares trust an outlander. Whether a human society, too, will countenance foreigners in its midst depends partly upon whether they are viewed as troublesome or not. Before immigrants could qualify as "our kind of people" measurable shades of differentness and visibility had to be reconciled. This involved their very names, language, and appearance. Even skin color and smell were determinants. The annoyance of garlic breath and the odor of rancid Toscano cigars hardly furthered respectability. Newcomers who did not appear capable of absorbing the new culture were, therefore, "bad." Assimilation was a one-way process. Since, for the natives, the "best" values and insights did not come from abroad, immigrants had to adjust old identities to those of the new country.

The term adjustment became a crucial one for immigrants, as the behaviorist Theodor Adorno has explained. Himself foreign-born, he saw the willingness of "persecuted people" to adjust as vital to a nationality like the Jews. They were expected to prove themselves and "not to be so haughty as to insist stubbornly on remaining what they had been before." For the Italians as well as for other minorities, adjustment was complex. Yet the necessity for accommodation is summed up by an Italian maxim: *"Avere la legittimità dalla propria: e il modo con cui si stabilizzano le rivoluzioni e si tengono le donne."* (Make sure accepted customs are on your side: that is the way to settle revolutions or to keep women.)

Even in those early years after the turn of the century disruptive changes were already occurring in American life. These could ravage the authority of the immigrant family unless a father or mother faced up to various crucial challenges. Among these were how to handle the greater personal freedom available to their children, a reduction of the authority of both the father and mother, and an increase in class mobility. These undreamed of liberties exerted a sharp influence upon the newcomers. The stability of the home gave way to a sudden need for plasticity and adaptability.

It was not easy to leave one's past behind. Let us not infer that a Freudian oedipal bond existed between immigrants and their homelands. There is no need to strain for such an explanation of why some tried in vain to cling to clannish and stoic traits. These were partly a holdover from a long history of south Italian repression by foreigners. Now, behind an outer mask, some tried to fuse two markedly different life styles, which led to what the sociologists call role-confusion.

America's demanding culture made it hard to create a personal island in its midst. It calloused over one's capacity to feel sentimental about the past. Immigrants and natives alike were expected to scatter pieces of themselves, figuratively, over the American landscape, to surrender personal values and attitudes to a greater whole. Retreat into the past, except by memory, was impossible. Yet, how anguishing it was for the tender-hearted to keep the people one loved from vanishing forever. Anais Nin (who was not Italian) has described both the wrench of separation from leaving the old world and the callousness of Americans: They "do not reveal themselves, they do not even seem present." It was the newcomer's place to establish himself, not America's.

The major traumas came in the immigrant's earliest years. He was not allowed the more relaxed and slower adjustments that normal individuals enjoy as they move from infancy into adulthood. Young Italians in America, forced to mature rapidly, dressed, talked, and thought like persons a generation or two older than they were. Yet they could not be fully responsive to the enduring values of their fathers. This split caused them to be trapped between destructive hypocricies and contradictions which we will examine more fully later.

As immigrants and their children sought acceptability, several processes were going on at the same time: While the Italian wore down prejudice, the need to do so eroded one's distinctiveness. In the former process a sense of material gain predominated. In the latter a measure of loss—however disguised—occurred. This was partly because timid immigrants dared not risk self-disclosure.

Susceptible also to uncertainties about the future, the more timid were overwhelmed by feelings of insecurity. Knowing themselves to be limited in controlling the new environment, immigrant responses sometimes verged on the irrational. A few attempted to maintain the illusion (fantasy) that they had greater control over their destiny than was warranted by their status in a foreign country. Persons who felt handicapped in fulfilling the requirements of the new culture, nevertheless, craved acceptance by it. What better way than to exhibit those traits of diligence, industry, and sobriety which Americans seemed to reward? Both obsessive and compulsive behavior replaced earlier attitudes, in order to avoid and to overcome distressful feelings about one's ability to cope.

Most immigrants came from peasant backgrounds. Some were genuinely ashamed of their roots. Yet, to sing a song of defensiveness would be unseemly. Instead, they followed "the American way," although unconsciously their feelings may have been rebellious at the necessity for compliance. The cursing of America's woes was summed up in the phrase *Managgia l'America!* (Damn America). Few dared to utter it.

In an age before ethnic activism could be understood, let alone sanctioned, personal frustration sometimes did erupt into violence. Today, some minority groups see violence as a necessary weapon for oppressed peoples. Anarchistically-minded immigrants once participated in industrial strife, but usually alongside non-immigrant workers. Still other foreigners turned toward a life of crime and gangsterism as a means of self-transcendence. Mostly, immigrants yearned for assimilation, wanting to join the "in" group, rather than to rebel against it. But, at least temporarily, the pressures of America's mass culture were not friendly to cosmopolitanism.

The many complicated ways in which immigrants were forced to hide their true feelings are difficult to describe. A masculinity pervaded the dominant American culture, which made it necessary to reject ideas that seemed sentimental, soft, or feminine as somehow unworthy or weak. One simply had to erase memories of fishermen from Sorrento singing *"O Mia Italia Adorata!"* For hard-headed materialism was looked upon as the best means by which to achieve "progress." One was encouraged to cling to those strong, orderly, and efficient Yankee patterns by which farmers and merchants alike were accumulating worldly goods. The Americans obviously valued tough-mindedness over romantic notions about the nature of life.

Furthermore, they had already set up the rules by which the game of American life was played. The majority dictated the terms, conditions, and rewards. At times it looked like none but Anglos could, furthermore, win. The emergence of odd stereotypes, substituted for one's own values, led foreigners into differing degrees of ego impoverishment. Hidden beneath their hurt feelings lay weak self-identifications and repressed frustrations.

A variety of adaptational maneuvers were required to defend against anxiety. The main one was not completely to succumb to the American system, yet to avow—at least superficially—that it was marvelous. Sublimation was another way to overcome pressing anxieties. In the privacy of one's own home it was possible to find solace, particularly when listening to treasured operatic recordings by Enrico Caruso, Beniamino Gigli, or Lucrezia Borgia. Others tuned in their radios, covertly, to the speeches of the Italian dictator Mussolini or to the interpretations of his Fascist apologists such as Giuseppe Cardellini. There was a secret and furtive aspect to these activities that resembled other less adapted psychological displacements, such as over-eating (leading to obesity) and stealing (kleptomania).

Extreme eccentrics, not necessarily disturbed, channeled their anxieties into unique endeavors. One of these, Baldassare Forestiere, came to be known as "the Human Mole." At Fresno, California, this former Boston subway worker dug a series of underground tunnels some twenty acres in area. Beginning in 1904, the dark haunts of Forestiere took thirty-one years to dig. Its sixty-odd galleries, including a kitchen, bedrooms, and even a dance hall, seemed to suggest that Forestiere liked living away from the world he saw above ground.

One mile outside Julesburg, Colorado, another underground tunnel builder, Umberto Gabello, left behind what has become known as "The Italian's Cave." A miner who had made a small fortune in the gold fields at Cripple Creek, Gabello was considered crazy by his neighbors. He lived like a hermit in his house-cavern, avoiding all contact even with persons who lived nearby. Upon his death mysterious underground carvings were found in his cave which seemed to suggest that he considered the place to be his monument to a physical godhead beyond man himself—the sun.

More famous are the Watts Towers of Simone Rodia (Rodilla) at Los Angeles. He fashioned these out of bits of glass, tile, and pieces of junk. Because he had no building permit, Rodia was in constant dispute with city officials over safety. As he erected these tall, odd structures, people thought Rodia crazy. Fastened to the towers by a window-washer's belt, he would sing Italian operatic arias while he cemented tile high above the ground.

Were such immigrant productions a kind of last resort by which neurotic anxieties could be projected and acted out? We would have to know considerably more about Forestiere, Gabello, and Rodia before their artistic eccentricities could be chalked up to alienation or to escape from a squalid world lived on the surface of the earth rather than below or above it. But such hypotheses do hold a certain fascination. In each case these immigrants built enduring monuments to themselves. Rodia's bizarre towers have given pleasure to thousands of visitors; indeed they have been declared an historical monument by the Los Angeles Cultural Heritage Board.

For such immigrants only on its surface did America really seem open and tolerant of foreign ways. Actually the new land swept away one's hereditary pride. The prohibitions and renunciations necessary to control the resultant personal anxiety really suggested that Americans clung to rigid categories of power. All that a novice could do was to bury feelings of inadequacy in the face of the limits set by the commanding society. Rather than acting out inner anxieties, most immigrants grew expert at hiding that wholly natural reaction to coercion—aggressivity. The expression of resentful feelings was simply taboo. To display one's anger was dangerous, and had to be defended against by passivity and conformity, which, in their turn, required denial. Fear too became involved in the repressive process, and it led to isolation of feelings, which produced further resentment.

A morass of conflicted and repressed emotions, therefore, remained locked and festering in the unconscious mind, that illusive and symbolic instrument by which we all obscure our innermost fears and wishes. There is some evidence that occasionally repressed feelings of depression were unconsciously converted into killer diseases, including tuberculosis and asthma. These sometimes broke out when the immigrant did not receive at least average attainable expectations. Those strong enough to overcome adversity were later able to achieve a healthy consolidation of their personality difficulties.

By unconsciously seducing their rage, immigrants superficially warded off the need to be loved—chancy at best in a new environment. This was, of course, one means of avoiding rejection, a form of "playing it safe." But to deflect one's inner hurts involves the use of further defense mechanisms learned in childhood and repeated later in life—among them denial, undoing, and the ritualization of the distasteful aspects of daily life. Yet these behavior patterns are fully understandable. All cultures produce the need to protect individual ego.

In considering the Italian minority's attempts to overcome feelings of inferiority, comparison with the experiences of modern Blacks is useful. America's "Black culture" can point to a considerable store of poetry and literary activity by which Negroes worked through their emotional conflicts. Blacks cultivated patience and even apathy in the face of abuse, aided by music and folklore. Although Europeans seemed to overcome social and economic problems more rapidly than did Negroes, it is difficult to find a large body of first-quality immigrant poetry, novels, or folksongs, especially among the Italians. In the first years following their arrival immigrants were too busy searching for status to write much of anything. Unlike the Blacks they saw a chance for achieving quick upward mobility by embracing new forms of materialism.

Admittedly, then, assimilation for the Italians was easier than for the

Blacks. The process, being non-defiant, went farther and faster. Indeed, its intricacies are in danger of being forgotten. The psychic effects of giving way to the established system, rather than standing up to it, were however great. A man who has to give up his language, his culture and, in some cases, even to change his name, is placed under extreme pressures, both unconsciously, and at the conscious level.

The further inland the Italians settled the greater and quicker the loss of their institutions and folkways. Take cuisine for example. San Francisco, for all the fame of its restaurants, could be said to have an Italian cuisine that is inferior to that available in New York.

The immigrant forgot quickest the language spoken for generations by his forefathers. As immigrant children went to common schools, whether the parents were miners in the Mesabi Range or fruit pickers at San Jose, they read the same books as other schoolmates. Only in certain cities, as in San Francisco, could immigrant children attend a parochial school where they could hear their parent's tongue spoken. Following the passage of a relatively few years, afterschool classes in Italian became harder to find. In the public schools the nationalistic McGuffey *Readers*, Portia's "Speech on Mercy," or Scott's *Ivanhoe*—assigned reading for all—had a part in making immigrants look upon English, not Italian, as their major inheritance. Because some members of the first generation knew only a local dialect, English was the first *common* language immigrants had yet spoken.

One of the surest ways to avoid discrimination was to embrace the language of the new country. "Differentness," particularly in the use of language, was at the heart of intolerance in America. There was hardly anything more pathetic than immigrants who could not speak, read, or write the English language.

They pick up a quasi-English (immigrant American) from Poles on the Lower East Side of New York, from Chinese storekeepers in San Francisco, from Jewish garment workers in Brooklyn. The foreigner's use of language resembled his job situation: he filled in the gaps with work and words far removed from what he was trained to be or say in the old country.

The uneducated transformed words into their own equivalent: *Bum* has an "Italian" plural *bummi*. *Rag, bar* and *car* became *raggo, barro*, and *carro. Job, basket, shop* and *mortar* were changed to *jobba, basketta, shoppa*, and *mata*; *grocery* to *grosseria* and *customer* to *cos-tu-me. Business* is hardly recognizable as *bi-zi-ne*. No one could guess that *Bokeen, stracinosa, sediolo, rai-ro-de*, and *elettricosa* stand for *Hoboken, station house, City Hall, railroad*, and *electric cars*.

H. L. Mencken, whose *American Language* discusses this transposition of words, points out that the "new language" which immigrants created was of real value to them. Many spoke only local dialects, some mutually unintelligible except by persons from the same region who flocked together. Their "American-Italian" jargon usually described terms unfamiliar in the homeland. Among these were *visco* for *whiskey,* *ghenga* for *gang,* *loffari* for *loafers,* *blacco enze* for *blackhand,* *grinoni* for *greenhorns,* *roffu* for *roof,* and *gliarda* for *yard.* The word *fight* they changed into *faitare, faiti, faitava, faito,* and *faitasse.* The Italians of the West used *ranchio* for *ranch,* a word seldom heard in the East. *"You bet"* became *you betcha;* a *son-of-a-gun* was called a *sanemagogna; job* was transformed into *giobba* along with *lynch* into *linciare.* The latter term was one which no immigrant cared to utter loosely.

A major adjustment, virtually required of all immigrants, involved, thus, the learning of a new vocabulary. English, later to become the business language of the entire world, forced itself in upon all foreigners. Ethnic aspirants wishing entry into America's commercial life could not afford nostalgic retreat into *Italianità,* with memories of Neapolitan songs, Bolognese *pasta* or Venetian gondolas. Language and other patterns of behavior, including dress, formed part of an imposed conformity without which "rising to the top" was impossible.

Pressure to change family names by eliminating vowels or shortening names was also considerable. Some anglicized both first and last names. Tomassini became Thomas and Lombardi was changed to Lombard. The Italo-American novelist Lucas Longo shows how the threat of discrimination effected such changes in subtle ways. Longo's *Family on Vendetta Street* gives us the following glimpse of an Italo-American doctor who changed his name from Bentolinardo to Bentley when he received his medical degree:

Doctor Bentolinardo. How many years his father had waited for his son to gain that title. All his life he had worked with one firm, Feliciani & McGinley, building contractors. He used to arrive early on the job, a half hour before, so that the bosses would never find fault, never fire him, and always send him out on the new jobs. He needed the money to pay for his son's medical education. Sacrifice was his daily bread—but he did it willingly, to work to save a few pennies. Some on the job—not Italians—seeing the olive oil seeping through the brown paper bag, called it dago grease. . . .
Bentley. When the old man saw that gold-lettered shingle hanging out off the building on Prospect Park Terrace, his whole being being buckled. Dr. Bentley. He couldn't read English, but that betrayal he could read. All the letters weren't there. . . . He wept like a baby and called his son a traitor. He returned to our street still crying. Some, trying to ease his ache, lied, saying, "The printer is to blame . . . the stupid printer who made that sign is to blame . . . not your boy . . . your boy, the doctor, he loves you . . . but that printer how does he know to spell these long involved Italian names?" During all this time, his son, Dr. Bentley, busy curing so many, never came to see him. One day the

doctor called on a patient who lived on our street. He felt he had to declare himself: "I don't want to hurt my father. But he's unreasonable. I can't explain to him my feelings. . . . I had to change my name to feel right and different. I know he's my father, but I can't live the way he has lived."

He didn't trust anyone any more, that poor old man. He ripped his name out of the mail box. His physical appearance became deplorable. He never opened a window. Missed Mass. Refused to throw out garbage. Did not care what happened to his money. Shut himself off completely.

"Sick I went to work. With fever. I saved. Every penny. For him. My Ralph. And how does the traitor pay me back? With a new name. I am Bentolinardo. This new Bentley—who knows him? God, do you?" Then, overwhelmed by frustration, unable to understand the betrayal, he fell to the ground, where, like a demented fool, he pounded the concrete with both fists. He tore at his clothing. He was about to bang his head against the pavement when friends ran to him, picked him up, carried him home. . . .

Personal stress among immigrants was, thus, more widespread than most historians believe. Furthermore, it is a gigantic cliché to think of the Italian as coping with his anxieties only by dramatic overstatement. Expressiveness and expansiveness are not the unique possession of any one national group. The dissipation of anxiety took place by other means. One of these was introvertive. Personal self-consciousness grew, quite naturally, out of the immigrant's inability to correct abuses for which he felt responsible.

In reacting to involuntary and categorical treatment by persons of more advantaged social status, there occurred a disordering of realities that others took for granted. Personal confusion, even inner chaos, resulted; the prejudicial stereotypes of "dago" and "wop" delayed positive self-esteem. Neurotic patterns of winning approval further inhibited personal growth. Unrelieved social and psychological frustration gave way to anger or apathy. The apathetic turned their unspent aggression inward upon the self or outward toward imagined enemies. In any case, self-hatred was difficult to escape. A child who would not assume that his parents were as good as anyone else's was to begin life with disabilities that non-ethnics find it difficult to understand. And immigrant children made no such assumptions.

To feel uniquely cut off, isolated, and alone, even within one's community, is to court lifelong disorganization, destructive behavior, or feelings of rejection. The minority community numbered among its members persons with such spoiled identities. Devoid of purpose or goal, these seemed unable to participate in the larger society. Yet they were mute and sullen as to the values of the old one. These unstudied immigrants resemble the stuffed and hollow men described by T. S. Eliot's *Wasteland*.

But, not all immigrants gave in to the dominant culture. Some, unlike Dr. Bentolinardo, refused to Anglicize their names or to eliminate their accents. Most could have done so within a few years had they dedicated themselves to the effort. But these stronger egos felt that their original names should accompany their accents. They wished not to hide what they were in order to be successful, although sometimes it was necessary to go against one's own wishes.

Still others denied they were victims of prejudice, at least in the commonly understood sense. They felt that the United States was treating them with a generosity that required reciprocation and loyalty. Not bitter about being underdogs, these accepted their fate. They saw their own dignity as the quality that would live on after they were gone. Believing it was what they contributed to the world that mattered, not what they took out of it, why should they change their names and manner of living?

Looking back on their record it would be easy for the psychohistorian to see these persons as cowed by the demands of American life. We could say that, at least for some, parts of their very souls seemed seared. For a kind of stasis did set in among them. And intimacy posed problems related to identity. Freud's *Civilization and Its Discontents* reminds us that all cultures exact their price of the individual.

If we look at the Germans or the Scandinavians or the Irish experience in America, we see them as having also had difficulty, like the south Europeans, in withstanding the demands of the American life style. The Germans did show a certain brittleness in blunting the tug of "Americanization," however. In Kansas, German Mennonites settled in closed communities and fought to maintain native language schools, customs, and religious systems. In Texas too the Germans resisted change. Whenever cultural patterns they could not respect were thrust upon them, through legislation, or by intimidation or boycott, they resented the situation strongly. The Germans even spurned ideas actually more suited to life in America than were the old ways to which they adhered. Conversely, Italians were rarely critical, aloof, or superior in attitude. What they wanted was acceptance. They felt in no position to push for the dubious benefits of foreign identification as opposed to the orthodoxy of Americanization.

As latecomers, Italians had to bow to the wishes of others. They felt bound to adopt existing values until they had achieved success enough to follow their own way of life. In the process they frequently abandoned their old ways forever. The Italian community achieved wealth and political influence much later than did the Germans, Irish, Scandinavians, or Jews. This prolongation encouraged Americanization.

Abandonment of the original language was, thus, one of the first hallmarks of acculturation. To speak the new language without an accent became an important goal. Yet, the unconscious effects of such denial of the spoken and written past were severe. One could see this in the discomfort which some felt when they encountered a countryman who insisted upon speaking Italian. This was especially evident if the quality of such a person's diction was relatively high. To be reminded that one had given up his original language required a painful, albeit unacknowledged, repression. This might take the form of boasting that the new environment was a superior one, worthy of sacrificing past ties and loyalties. Self-justification meant stressing the material values that Americans so admired —among them better housing, transportation, or clothing.

Italian mutual aid societies, patriotic lodges, and national church groupings were among the first psychological props to be dropped. Each served to demarcate the immigrant's alienism from American society. Gradually there was an unspoken rejection of these vestiges. For some older persons only slowly did the breakdown in *Italianità* occur. These clung to the symbol of Columbus and his discovery of 1492, just as French immigrants basked in the reflected memory of Lafayette's participation in the American Revolution.

A sense of expediency helped Italians realistically to face the competitive American environment. An earnest, straining determination stood them in good stead in so materialistic a society. Foreigners from a country where property was scarce would do almost anything to acquire a plot of land or a small business of their own. In order to feed over-large families they would work nights pressing pants in a nearby town, or dig coal in a mine, or bag cement. Many held down two jobs at once. This outside income made it possible to achieve more rapid propertied status, indispensible for acceptability.

But one had to follow the American "carrot-on-a-stick" mentality. This turned around the lure of abundance, which required the repression of emotion, deferment of gratification, and the sublimation of subsequent stress. By following such a formula one could better himself financially as well as socially. Perhaps he might even cross over the hazy line between blue collar and white collar work. The success ethic, of course, followed the dominant Horatio Alger mythology that a poor boy could rise from rags to riches. The immigrant, thus, learned to hide stress, to disguise anxieties and his sense of helplessness. One was to act as though all such repression was worthwhile—that the American myth was, in fact, reality.

Although Italians showed deference toward the entrenched system, more than a few abhorred its inhumanity. One way to survive and to keep chaos at a distance was by repeating, if only half-heartedly, vestigial old-world rituals designed to preserve one's integrity. Regressive behavior, obsessive and compulsive, aided immigrants in mastering childlike feelings of panic, stirred up and re-created by an inhuman market economy.

A sometimes sterile Victorian code linked morality to community respectability, making strange demands of the Italians. Some immigrants swallowed their pride and temporarily abandoned drinking wine. Others found conformity to the system too big a price to pay for success. These kept on nursing their Zinfandel, California's alternative to Florentine Chianti. Yet, as Merle Curti has pointed out in his study of a Wisconsin county during the late nineteenth century, there was a strong sentiment for temperance in America, and "the immigrant was expected to do things the way the old stock specified." The Prohibition era of the 1920's further darkened the temperance landscape that Italians found almost incomprehensible. In his *The Paesanos*, Jo Pagano has one of his characters say: "By God, what a country! Make a goddam criminal out of you joost to take a glass of healthy wine!"

Few Italians participated in temperance societies, as did Scandinavian and English immigrants. Yet, they stood in sharp contrast to whiskey-imbibing native Americans. In quiet defiance of the Prohibition laws they went on brewing both beer and wine, however. Their youngsters skipped many a Saturday evening bath when the family tub was filled with mysterious fermenting alcoholic beverages. Most Italians kept wine in their cellars throughout the bleak Prohibition era. Under the shade of a grape arbor, they enjoyed the conviviality that accompanied washing down *pasta* with what Americans called "Dago Red." This type of relaxed, harmless drinking seldom led to drunkenness. Alcoholism was, indeed, unusual among these immigrants.

Interest in food was as pronounced as in drink. Italians hounded neighborhood stores that carried Genoese *baccalà, torrone* from Cremona, hard-crusted breads, tuna packed in olive oil from Lucca, Eureka lemons raised from Sicilian seeds, and other regional delicacies. In such establishments one could also find imported Florentine *Chianti* and Milanese *boccie* balls for Saturday afternoon games.

Immigrants held these *bocci* matches on any level plot of ground available. *Bocci* players vociferously wagered money, a shot of *grappa*, or a bottle of wine on the outcome of a match. They fascinated their American neighbors with the intricacies of the game. Each player was allowed two wooden or steel balls, known as *boccies*. The lead-off player rolled a smaller ball, the jack, down the smoothed, dirt-floored alley. Noisy contestants tried to hit this moving target and to knock their opponent's balls away from the jack. The proud winner was the person who came the closest to the jack ball. San Francisco's Bocci Ball Restaurant catered to customers who played the game and to opera buffs who came to hear *"La donna è mobile"* or *"Un bel di"* and to sip *poncino*, coffee laced with brandy.

The *boccie* game was both a symbol of the past and an indication that the immigrant could afford time to relax. Similarly, rich meat courses on Sundays supplanted the *polenta* (corn meal), *pasta*, and chestnut bread of earlier days. Old style or new, there was an integrity about immigrant cooking that was unforgettable, as the son of a native Italian family that lived in Salt Lake City recalled:

The feast was nearly ready. The side dishes had already been heaped upon the kitchen table—platters of tuna and anchovies and pickled olives and mushrooms surrounded by sliced salami and cheese. There were bowls of dried olives, swimming in olive oil and flavored with garlic and orange peel; there was celery, and sweetly aromatic *finnochio*, and wafer thin Italian ham. . . . The roasts and chickens were finishing at the same time; the pastries, heaped on the side table, were flaky and crumbling; the chicken soup was clear yet full-bodied in flavor, the spaghetti sauce was rich and thick.

The whole tenor of immigrant life steadily improved. As with food, clothing too became more abundant. Whereas village women once wore black dresses to avoid laundering, in America their clothing changed to brighter colors. Bare feet took on shiny shoes; soiled clothes gave way to new ones. Each Christmas tons of immigrant-bought rarities, sometimes obtained with money buried in backyard Mason jars, got loaded onto ships bound for Italy.

At week's end a worker who had worn rough laboring clothes was anxious to change into a white shirt with collar, new necktie, and patent leather shoes. He invested in upholstered parlor furniture, carpets, electric lights, and flush toilets—all evidences of his newfound wealth. Yet, the more he indulged in such amenities, the more the immigrant grew similar to his American neighbors.

A study of the social atmosphere in Minnesota's mining towns suggests that the assimilation of immigrants is a theme that should be stressed as well as alienation. Rural colonization was closely entwined in the process by which foreigners achieved acceptance. Although immigrants who settled in the Mesabi and Vermillion ranges encountered small-town "cultural islands" grounded in sentiments of nationality, these rural centers could not withstand "the assimilating effects of shared experience." The small town probably encouraged unity. Traditionally, foreign society assigned women a more sheltered role than males. But immigrant wives in small towns quickly formed friendships with persons of different nationality. There occurred an "astonishingly rapid adjustment of all groups to prevailing American folkways" that extended to school children, civic activities, and recreation. The growing number of immigrants who married outside their national group also exercised "a mediating role among newcomers of the father's nationality." In the small towns of Minnesota, religious life too became markedly inter-ethnic, even in Roman Catholic congregations.

Humbert Nelli's history of the Italians in Chicago tells us that, in that large city, upward mobility occurred at a more rapid rate than we once believed to be so. Business and commerce played a special part in encouraging Americanization. Immigrant businessmen, especially those who formed partnerships with native Americans, acted as "links between two worlds." Whereas city stores operated by immigrants listed their products in both English and Italian, more tradesmen used only English in their advertising.

Although the overseas Italians made adjustments to the environment, some of them demonstrated a type of resilience described by John Horne Burns, an American of Boston Irish stock who was in Naples during World War II: "Unlike the Irish who stayed hurt all their lives, the Italians had a bounce-back in them." This, even when harsh discrimination stared them in the face.

A premise of the melting pot ideal had been to reduce all citizens, regardless of background, outlook, and experience, to a basic sameness. Historians overlooked, even tended to deny, widely differing acculturative patterns. Behavioral experiences in the American environment were never constant. Some immigrants arrived with values similar to those of the American middle class. In Europe there was regional as well as rural-urban variation. To avoid cultural stereotyping we need to remind ourselves of this, and to recall how some immigrants "got stuck" in the process of shifting from one society's set of values to those of another. Discrimination grew partly out of the immigrant's "differentness," for he did not, of course, share the formative background of his American contemporaries.

NICHOLAS JOHN RUSSO

From Mezzogiorno to Metropolis

Brooklyn's New Italian Immigrants
A Sociological, Pastoral, Academic Approach

Immigration history is repeating itself in the New York area. True, the foreboding Ellis Island no longer functions as the processing station for waves of hopeful immigrants arriving on ocean-going vessels of every size, but since the passage of the Immigration Reform Act of October 3, 1965, thousands of newcomers from the eastern and western hemispheres arrive at Kennedy Airport and at the Port of New York. Among them are more than 20,000 Italians a year from *Il Mezzogiorno* (southern Italy and Sicily), most of whom, not unlike the Italians at the turn of the century, settle in the tri-state New York metropolitan area. Each year they come to join their relatives who preceded them, and who assist them to find work, housing and a sense of community. They come, because *Il Mezzogiorno*, despite a fine record of industrialization since World War II, is still underdeveloped. They come because Italy, although slightly larger than the state of Arizona, is overcrowded, having a population of 55 million.

Italians have been migrating for a century in search of labor and opportunity. Since 1876, 20 million people have left Italy, more than half of whom have settled permanently overseas and, of these, almost six million have come to the United States.[1]

Italians will continue to emigrate, because the future holds no hope of employment for thousands of new workers who annually enter the labor market. A study of the Bari-Brindisi-Taranto area in 1968 showed that the Apulian labor market had a surplus of manpower and foresaw 131,000 unemployed workers. This means that the unemployed worker will leave Apulia and settle elsewhere. He soon sends for his wife or fiancée. Similar surveys for Campania, Calabria and Sicily would yield similar results. Seventy percent of the migrants go to northern Italy and to the common market countries of Europe, especially France, Switzerland and Germany, and the rest overseas to the United States, Argentina, Brazil, Canada, Venezuela and Australia (See Table 1).

118

Table 1

Twenty Years of Migration from Southern Italy
to Northern Italy, Europe and Overseas

Provinces and Regions	1951-1961	1961-1971	1951-1971
L'Aquila	−63,412	−48,821	−112,233
Teramo	−38,568	−27,829	−66,397
Pescara	−19,135	−3,223	−22,358
Chieti	−59,324	−50,699	−110,023
ABRUZZI	−180,439	−130,572	−311,011
MOLISE	−84,155	−62,124	−146,279
Caserta	−48,731	−81,380	−130,111
Benevento	−55,617	−58,637	−114,254
Napoli	−26,969	−150,381	−177,350
Avellino	−92,591	−88,727	−181,318
Salerno	−61,909	−91,701	−153,610
CAMPANIA	−285,817	−470,826	−756,643
Foggia	−110,451	−116,096	−226,547
Bari	−126,870	−114,580	−241,450
Taranto	−28,168	−32,231	−60,399
Brindisi	−15,746	−38,491	−54,237
Lecce	−37,207	−84,451	−121,658
PUGLIA	−318,442	−385,849	−704,291
Potenza	−69,767	−90,548	−160,315
Matera	−14,562	−34,053	−48,615
BASILICATA	−84,329	−124,601	−208,930
Cosenza	−108,125	−109,138	−217,263
Catanzaro	−116,096	−142,702	−258,798
Reggio	−125,933	−114,852	−240,785
CALABRIA	−350,154	−366,692	−716,846
Southern Italy	−1,303,336	−1,540,664	−2,844,000
Sicily	−389,189	−624,122	−1,013,311
Sardinia	−79,871	−153,054	−232,925
TOTAL	−1,772,396	−2,317,840	−4,090,236

SOURCE: M. Natale, "Stima retrospettiva della populazione residente provinciale nel periodo 1951-1961," in *Sviluppo della popolazione italiana*, pp. 147-55; ISTAT, *Censimento della popolazione*, 1971, p. 36.

Since the Second World War, more than 430,000 Italians have found a new home in the United States. Seventy-five percent of them, repeating the pattern of the first immigration (1885-1915) settled along the eastern seaboard. Thirty percent of the total number declared that New York City was their destination, with the greatest number going to Brooklyn, then Queens and finally the Bronx. Smaller groups gravitate to Manhattan and Staten Island.

The passage of the Ryan-Rodino Bill (HR 9615) on March 16, 1972, permitted American citizens to send for married brothers and sisters who had previously been prohibited entry into the United States. Italy was the main beneficiary of this bill, receiving 28,000 additional visas, (7,000 new visas a year over a four-year period, in addition to the annual 20,000). This bill and the Immigration Reform Act of 1965, contributed in a significant manner, in atoning for the unjust immigration laws of the 1920's, and in making amends for the Walter-McCarran Act of 1952, which continued the policy of blatant discrimination against southern and eastern Europeans, among others.

The southern Italian and Sicilian of today is very different from the Italian immigrant at the turn of the century. Only 18 per cent are engaged in farming (in the north it is 7 per cent) and 30 per cent work in industry (in the north, 48 per cent).[2] A survey of the Bureau of Employment Security and of the Immigration and Naturalization Service gives the following employment categories on the basis of 75,000 Italians employed in the United States at the end of January, 1965: 30 per cent—industry workers; 25 per cent craftsmen, foremen and kindred workers; 18 per cent operatives and kindred workers; 13 per cent, service workers (except private households) and 4 per cent professional and technical workers.[3]

Vanishing is the peasant, fatalistic culture of the old immigrants and, with it, the myths, codes of honor and the vendettas. The mass media, education, tourism, and returning migrants have opened up the isolated "paese" to the outside world.

However, this "progress" solves only a few problems. The new immigrants to the United States are relatively unprepared for the needs of an urban-industrial environment, where the knowledge of English and formal education are indispensable tools of social mobility. The immigrant has tasted enough of the outside world to be open to change and is willing to bear the many hardships in order to succeed. Being achievement-oriented, he moves swiftly into an acceptance of the urban environment, with all its problems, because he sees in it the vehicle of upward mobility.[4] The price he must pay for this swift progress is dedication to his work and much loneliness due to isolation from a normal social life. The psychological center of interest for the newcomer is his peer group (a male friendship group), the strong, cohesive Italian family (although we notice some reluctance in maintaining the extended family relationships, with the multiple reciprocal obligations, and in some cases, a yearning for the American nuclear family model, with the independence it offers. This happens after the initial reliance on Italian-American relatives comes to an end, and the immigrant family is able to purchase its own home. His Catholic religion is also very important to him. Culturally it differs from American Catholicism, being less dependent on doctrine and external observances, and emphasizing morality, individualism and devotionalism.

The wholly-urban Diocese of Brooklyn, comprising the two New York City counties of Kings and Queens (with a Catholic population of 1,600,000 and an overall population of 4,589,186) is host to the largest number of Italian newcomers, 4,500 annually. In February, 1971, Bishop Francis J. Mugavero established the Brooklyn Diocesan Migration Office, appointing Rev. Anthony J. Bevilacqua as director. Coordinators were chosen for each large group of immigrants settling in the diocese. I was asked to accept the position of coordinator of the Apostolate for the Italian Speaking.

The challenge was enormous and frightening. The 1970 census indicated that there were 151,076 *Italian-born* persons in the boroughs of Kings and Queens and, if the second generation is included, the number totaled 511,425 (see Figure I).

We readily accepted the invitation because we strongly believed that the opportunity of serving Christ by welcoming the stranger into the human and ecclesial communities, of strengthening his faith, and of preaching and witnessing the Gospel on the streets of the ethnic community, would make every risk and every effort worthwhile.

After much consultation, research and thought, we decided to approach the problem from three different angles: (1) Sociological, (2) Pastoral, and (3) Academic.

(1) THE SOCIOLOGICAL APPROACH

My own research indicated that the American church, at the turn of the century, did not integrate the Italians into the ecclesial community. It took three generations for Italian-Americans to "feel at home" in the American church.[5] Today, any newcomer is confused by the sight of large parish or diocesan building complexes. Why not go to the grassroots, seek the aid of the parishes, and use second and third generation Italian-Americans as the "bridge" which would enable the new immigrants to assimilate with less pain?

The immigrant soon finds the Italian baker, pork store and pastry shop.

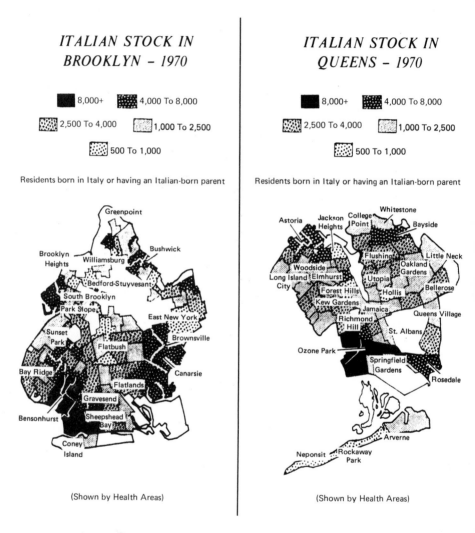

ITALIAN STOCK IN
BROOKLYN – 1970

■ 8,000+   ▨ 4,000 To 8,000

▨ 2,500 To 4,000   ▨ 1,000 To 2,500

▨ 500 To 1,000

Residents born in Italy or having an Italian-born parent

ITALIAN STOCK IN
QUEENS – 1970

■ 8,000+   ▨ 4,000 To 8,000

▨ 2,500 To 4,000   ▨ 1,000 To 2,500

▨ 500 To 1,000

Residents born in Italy or having an Italian-born parent

(Shown by Health Areas)

(Shown by Health Areas)

© 1973 by The New York Times Company. Reprinted by permission.

Figure I

Two Generations of Italians in Brooklyn and Queens—1970

Why not open a series of storefront-migration-offices next door? I visited Father Michael Castrilli, who had opened a storefront in Paterson, New Jersey, as well as a beautiful social and cultural center in the basement of St. Michael's church. His insights were tremendously helpful.

With the approval and encouragement of Bishop Mugavero, five offices were opened over a period of 14 months in precisely those five communities which, according to the census, had the highest concentration of Italian immigrants. I visited politicians, priests, leaders of Italian societies, and the heads of community organizations. With few exceptions, we were greeted with enthusiasm. Only two stores were speedily obtained. The others took months of searching by us and by real estate agents. Each store is modestly adorned with office furniture, typewriter, copying machine and file cabinets. Prints of Italy and of religious themes hang on the walls. It is quite clear to the immigrants that the bishop, priests and people of the Diocese of Brooklyn, in the spirit of love, are making them welcome. The office is called *Centro Cattolico per Emigrati* (Catholic Migration Office) and our gospel-inspired motto is *"Ero Forestiero—E Mi Avete Ospitato"* ("I was a stranger, and you made me welcome").

Absolutely no charge is made for our services. The storefronts are open five days a week, and usually one evening or one Saturday morning. Any immigrant is welcome. Our immigration counselors speak Italian, Spanish and English, one also speaks Portuguese and another speaks French. Once the word spread, we found ourselves assisting Spanish-speaking people from Spain, Central and South America, Haitians, Tunisians, Portuguese, and English-speaking Barbadians, Indians, Irish, Trinidadians and Ghanians.

We publicized the fact that the Christian community of the Diocese of Brooklyn was doing good, by printing 10,000 brochures in Italian and English for each office. These brochures, fully describing our work and our services were mailed to all priests, politicians, Italian social and mutual aid societies, funeral directors, schools, community leaders and welfare offices. Besides many articles in local newspapers, the Catholic press, the Italian press, both in America and Italy, feature articles appeared in the *New York Times* and the *New York News*. I made seven appearances on various New York radio stations (on one I spoke in Italian), and filmed one-half hour interviews for Channel 9 and for R.A.I. (Italian Television). Eyewitness News (Ch. 7) visited our Bensonhurst office in January, 1973.

Who staffs these offices? We did not advertise for workers, but rather sought persons who were college graduates, fluently bi-lingual or tri-lingual, having majored in sociology or social work. We looked for individuals with a sense of commitment and service, who had themselves experienced the immigrant situation so that their knowledge would be experiential and compassionate. Of the nine persons interviewed, only one was a man, and unfortunately he spoke no English. Four of the five women selected were born in Italy and spoke both Italian and English fluently. Several immigration lawyers, Catholic Charities, the U. S. Catholic Conference, and the Italian Consulate, all generously assisted in training the young ladies.

The first office opened on September 1, 1972 in Bensonhurst, Brooklyn, and is located next to a pizza parlor and a pastry shop. This office is annually funded by the Italian Board of Guardians, a Catholic group in Brooklyn, which assists needy Italian children and families. The second office was in operation on February 1, 1973, on Steinway Street, one of the largest shopping areas in all of Queens County. We were forced to take three stores "as is". This meant that much work had to be done. Thanks to the contracting talents of Father Donald Shea of Cathedral Prep., Brooklyn, some students and local workers, painting, wood paneling, flooring and electrical work was done well and with much saving.

Each office keeps a supply of U. S. Immigration forms, citizenship applications, social security, medicare and medicaid literature. A young man named Mario came to us to file for U. S. citizenship. His English was adequate, but he could not understand some of the questions. Our counselor asked him the questions in Italian and typed the answers in English. We also directed him to his local police station, since none of his American neighbors could tell him how to be fingerprinted, a requirement for filing an application for citizenship.

Our immigration counselors often have to accompany immigrants to the immigration department, to utility companies, social agencies and schools. We assist local schools at times of registration, acting as advocates and interpreters. Today there is a grave need for bi-lingual classes for Italian immigrant children in New York City. Their number is estimated at 15,000 and to date the city has done little to alleviate this problem. We have encountered several cases in both public and parochial schools, where the children of immigrants have been classified as "retarded", "obstinate", "emotionally handicapped", and have been placed in special classes. Our counselors must often fight to explain that the chief problem is one of culture and communication, not one of mental deficiency—something which should be quite evident to professional educators. A case in point is that of a 12 year-old girl, Maria, who had a reading score on the second year level. The school was attempting to send her to a class for retarded children. Her peers taunted her. With the cooperation of our counselor and a bi-lingual psychologist over the period of a year, Maria now reads on the eighth year level, and has overcome much of her shyness and the emotional damage done by teachers and classmates who often looked down on her.

The New York City Health Research Council estimates that in one year (1970) 3,335 children were born to Italian *immigrant* mothers.[6] Of these, 1,501 were born in Brooklyn and 925 in Queens. Italian is spoken almost exclusively in these households.

Antonio immigrated to America with two sons and all three are working. Two years ago he filed the necessary applications to bring his wife and daughters to the United States. Nothing happened. Each time he called the government office he was told not to worry, because it takes time. In frustration he came to our migration office and, after several inquiries, our counselor found that the applications had been lost in the New York office. New forms were filed by our office and, in less than three months, the family was reunited.

There are times when we are frustrated by "no exit" situations. One immigrant came from Argentina and was on his way to visit relatives in Italy, via New York City. He changed money in Argentina and was given counterfeit American dollars. He was arrested and is being detained for trial. Since he has no visa, he cannot work. His wife and children are also in New York, with no means of support. Since they are not residents, they are not entitled to welfare.

A student from Italy discovered he has leukemia. He cannot carry the necessary college courses and therefore cannot retain his student visa. He is being assisted medically because of the advanced medical technology available in New York, and does not want to return to his little town in Sicily. There is no immigration procedure to follow in this case.

The third office was opened in South Brooklyn, on Court Street, between Union and President Streets, the area where the first Italian immigrants to Brooklyn settled 90 years ago, and where Mother Cabrini established a school and convent. A list is kept of all doctors, dentists and lawyers who speak Italian, and the immigrant is referred to them. Thanks to the cooperation of the business community and several charitable agencies, we supply information on available jobs and housing, and aid the immigrant in filling out the necessary application. With the help of Italian-American women, who speak Italian, immigrant women are taught to comparison-shop, and are informed of the importance of innoculating their children. It is shocking to learn of the large numbers of black, Spanish-speaking and immigrant children who are not receiving the polio vaccine.

Filomena, an immigrant from Naples, was encouraged to bring her husband and four friends to our center, where they were coached for the citizenship examination, over a period of five weeks. Yes, they all passed.

A sad, young expectant mother, awaiting the birth of her third child, came to one of our offices. She wanted to send for her mother, who intended to remain in America as a permanent resident. A local dabbler in immigration counseling told her it would cost $288 for his work. She could not afford it. We prepared all the forms for her. The cost—nothing for our services, just the payment of the government fee of ten dollars.

Despite the modernization of most of Italy, some "small town" cultural traits are still evident in the southern Italian and Sicilian immigrants. One of our social workers visited a home where the parents were accused of not sending their two daughters, 14 and 13 years old, to school. The parents did not think it was illegal, and they informed the worker that their daughters had had enough schooling and, after all, girls do not need as much education as boys.

Thirteen-year-old Felice was doing poorly in school. His English was good but evidently he was not doing any studying at home. Our worker discovered that, both after school and on weekends, he had to work in his father's pizzeria.

Ozone Park in Queens County was the site of our fourth office, dedicated by Bishop Mugavero on November 3, 1973. Adapting to a different culture takes its toll in the form of neuroses and marginal individuals, especially the children, some of whom must live in an Italian folk society at home, and in a confused, violent, urban atmosphere on the outside. Family counseling and assistance in problems of delinquency, truancy and dope addiction, are among our many services. The Ozone Park office is annually funded by the Ferrini Welfare League, a Catholic group in Queens which administers to the social, emotional and welfare needs of Italian families. Both groups share the same new premises, and this situation concentrates in one location a certified social worker who speaks Italian, an immigration counselor, and an executive secretary.

Young Giovanni informed us that his best friend would be confined to the hospital for four months. The patient was in some difficulty with the U. S. Immigration Department and could not go to the office nor communicate in English. Our worker acted as advocate, visited the hospital several times, and was able to solve the problem to the satisfaction of the Immigration Department.

On November 8th, 1973, the fifth office opened its doors in the Bushwick-Ridgewood area which is on the border of Kings and Queens counties. In the first four days, 27 cases were processed by the immigration worker. Elderly persons from the old and the new immigration often have problems with social security, medicare, food stamps, Italian pensions and, out of a sense of pride and dignity, seldom ask for welfare, even that small supplement to which many are entitled. Our worker's ability to speak Italian, to see or visit the elderly without red tape and on a face-to-face basis, and her willingness to accompany the needy to any government office, has given us much success so far and a great amount of satisfaction.

(2) THE PASTORAL APPROACH

The day is gone when Italian immigrants settle exclusively in the ethnic community, the "little Italys." Today's Italians settle in every section of Brooklyn and Queens[7] (See Table 2).

Pope Pius XII in his *Exul Familia*, August 1952, Pope John XXIII in many letters and addresses, the Vatican Council II in the constitutions and decrees on *The Church Today, The Liturgy, Priestly Formation, On the Bishops*, and *The Missions*; Pope Paul VI in his *Populorum Progressio* and

Table 2

*Distribution of Italian Immigrant Population
in Selected Areas of Brooklyn and Queens, 1970**

Areas	Born In Italy (1st Generation)	Children of Italian-Born Parents (2nd Generation)	Total Italian Foreign Stock (2 Generations only)
Bay Ridge	7,127	18,576	25,703
Bensonhurst	15,087	25,460	40,547
Gravesend—Sheepshead Bay	6,965	13,345	20,310
Sunset Park	3,582	7,536	11,118
South Brooklyn	2,058	4,187	6,245
Canarsie	2,657	6,477	9,134
Bushwick	8,875	8,787	17,662
Ridgewood	2,941	5,746	8,687
Long Island City—Astoria	13,139	19,501	32,640
Corona	4,570	5,875	10,445
Ozone Park—Richmond Hill	7,051	16,965	24,016
Flushing—Bayside	5,142	14,959	20,101

* SOURCES: *U.S. Census Reports, 1970*, and the Center for Migration Studies, Staten Island, N.Y. (These figures do not include an estimated 15,000 Italian immigrants who have settled in Brooklyn and Queens from 1970 to 1974).

his Apostolic letter dealing exclusively with migration, *De Cura Pastoralis Migratorum*, August 22, 1969, all repeatedly emphasize that immigrants are not to be "pressure-cooked" into becoming like the members of the host society, but are to be assisted into *slowly* integrating, never losing respect for their own culture, language and religious practices. Pope Paul VI declared that few new "national" parishes would be established (these were foreign-language parishes, without boundaries, created for those who spoke that tongue within a large area overlapping many American territorial parishes). The Holy Father elaborating on the writings of his predecessors, binds the pastor and the bishop to care for the immigrants, in their own language, no matter where they settle, and to minister to their human, social and spiritual needs. He says:

All the faithful, both clergy and laity, including men or women religious, should be properly admonished to receive immigrant people benevolently and to strive zealously to assist them in the pressing needs which they encounter from the start.

Let them assist other Christians who lack ministers of their church or community; nor are they to deny assistance to non-Christian people.

The spiritual care of all the faithful, and thus of the immigrant people, falls most especially on the shoulders of the pastors of the parishes within which they live. These shall one day give an account to God regarding the fulfillment of their duty.[8]

Provision is even made for the canonical assignment of a priest who speaks the immigrants' language, to serve more than one parish.[9] All papal documents on migration remind bishops, priests and faithful that it is from a position of strength and self-confidence that immigrants will move out to assimilate into their host society, not from the premature disruption of the ethnic group, nor from the destruction of the psychological world of the individual immigrant.

We are still far from meeting the needs, but thanks to the generosity of Italian-speaking priests of the diocese; the Scalabrini Fathers, five of whom celebrate Mass in Italian in Brooklyn and Queens; and some recently-arrived Italian priests, the Eucharist is offered in Italian in thirty-seven parishes each Sunday, and Italian instructions and services are given in seventy-eight parishes out of a diocesan total of 235. Of course, we still encounter "naive" opposition from ethnocentric clergy and laity who simplistically believe that all we have to do is to teach the immigrants English and "make them Americans" and all human, cultural and liturgical problems will vanish.

The Italian Apostolate published a booklet containing the Christian wake service and cemetery prayers, with homilies, and another homily for the Mass of Christian Burial. The Diocesan Cemetery Office offered to publish a folder containing all the cemetery prayers in our booklet, and arranged them for the faithful's participation. These folders were distributed to all funeral directors for use by the people. Father Silvano Tomasi, C.S. and I have co-authored *The Italian Ritual*, of all the sacraments, blessings and selected homilies, arranged for American priests who can read Italian, and this book was published by the Catholic Book Publishing Company of New York in 1974.

A ministerial-apprenticeship program was inaugurated in September, 1973. Every Wednesday, Italian-speaking seminarians from the Seminary of the Immaculate Conception, Huntington, New York, drive to an Italian parish in Brooklyn and Queens, where each one works under the direction and supervision of one of the priests. They visit homes, hospitals, community organizations and learn every phase of parish work among immigrants. They spend three hours every week in one of our five migration offices. I meet with them once a month, discuss the assigned sociological readings, compare each man's experiences and evaluate them. All of us profit from this mutual sharing.

In order that clergy, teachers, seminarians and social workers may respond effectively to the needs of the newcomers we emphasize that cultural patterns and customs are not "trivial" or "strange" but are rooted in the deepest values of life. The immigrant community must not be weakened in an attempt to "force" Americanization because culture is a stabilizing factor and gives identity to the individual. Any breakdown of this culture will cause marginality. The American must help the immigrant preserve a genuine respect for his own ethnicity, culture and customs, as he acquires knowledge and respect for the culture of the United States. Those in a position of leadership and authority are constantly encouraged to bring about opportunities for association with the older residents, especially in the parish. Modern sociologists (Herberg, Eisenstadt, Handlin, M. Gordon, Glazer, Moynihan) strongly affirm that religion plays a central role in a person's life and is the basis for social identification. Finally, those who seek to work with the newcomers are reminded that the process of assimilation is not one but two—cultural assimilation, taking on the ways of the host society (this happens very quickly) and social assimilation which usually takes several generations—entering the organizations, the cliques and the total social system of America.

(3) THE ACADEMIC APPROACH

The priests of the Diocese of Brooklyn were quick to see the need for learning the Italian language. Thirty-one priests enrolled in the first conversational Italian courses which were begun in the fall of 1972. One class met for two and a half hours a week in Brooklyn and the other in Queens. The St. Cloud audio-visual method was used. This program, using film strips, tape recorders, picture books and records, takes a carefully selected and graded variety of true-to-life experiences out of the contemporary life of Italy and organizes them into skillfully planned units. The student makes gradual progression from the simple to the complex, and is immersed into the sight and sound of his Italian environment, as each verbal signal he hears is associated with specially drawn pictures on the filmstrip, showing essential details which evoke the meaning expressed in speech.

Italian is also taught on three levels in Cathedral College-Seminary and on two levels in the theologate at Huntington. Bishop Mugavero gave strong impetus to language study, by insisting that each seminarian become fluent in a second language. Spanish and Italian are the languages most-studied. With the whole-hearted support and inspiration of the bishop and the episcopal vicars, the Diocesan School of Languages was established and from June 11, 1973 until July 20th, "total-immersion" courses were given in Spanish and Italian. The seminarians and priests lived at Cathedral College from Monday to Friday evening. There was one professor for every five students, and despite the long hours of work (13 hours a day) both teachers and students were elated by the results. The courses missed nothing —the spoken language, the culture, history, food, music and liturgy of the people, were all thoroughly exposed. Once a week the entire class and professors would visit a Spanish or Italian community, celebrate Mass in the foreign language, and then have coffee and cake with the immigrants, speaking with them in their own language. The enthusiastic welcome given the group and the immigrants' expressions of gratitude and affection, were enough reward to make every sacrifice and every effort during a hot six weeks, very much worthwhile. This same program was offered again in the summer of 1974.

These wonderfully rewarding experiences have taught most of us who are engaged in this apostolate that the newcomers to our diocese are seeking to achieve the same things that we or our parents sought before them. Hostile reaction on the part of the host society, is based on the fear that the immigrant threatens "to take something away" from the "Americans." Charity and openness on both sides will enable both groups to become aware of a higher loyalty, a greater solidarity in which both can participate to effect a common achievement—the establishment of a truly Christian community in the Diocese of Brooklyn which for more than a century has been for the Irish, Germans, Italians, Poles, Lithuanians and Spanish-speaking newcomers, the "Diocese of Immigrants."

NOTES

1. Francesco Barbagallo, *Lavoro ed Esodo nel Sud, 1861-1971* (Naples: Guida Editori, 1973).
2. G. Lucrezio Monticelli—L. Favero, "Un quarto di secolo di emigrazione italiana", *Studi Emigrazione*, Anno IX, n. 25-26 (March-June 1972), p. 32.
3. United States Department of Justice, Immigration and Naturalization Service, *Annual Report, 1967*, (Washington, D.C.; U.S. Government Printing Office, 1968), p. 127.
4. Sylvan Tomasi, *Post-War Italian Immigration to the United States: Volume and Social Characteristics*. Paper (mimeographed) delivered at annual meeting of American-Italian Historical Society, Fall 1969.
5. Nicholas J. Russo, "The Religious Acculturation of the Italians in New York City." Unpublished doctoral dissertation, Department of Sociology and Anthropology, St. John's University, N.Y., 1968.
6. New York City Health Research Council, "Table I—Estimated Number of Live Births to White Foreign Born Mothers by Country of Origin", New York City, 1970. (Typewritten report of an estimated 20% systematic sample of all births to white, foreign born women) October 1973.
7. We took a random sample of 500 cases (100 cases from each office) from a total of more than 3,000 immigrants served, in order to learn the place of origin of the new Italian immigrants. Results: 54 per cent came from Sicily (Palermo, Trapani, Catania, Messina and Agrigento), 23 per cent are from Naples (Avellino, Salerno and Ischia), 11 per cent from Le Puglie (chiefly Bari), 7 per cent from Calabria and 5 per cent from the rest of Italy.
8. Pope Paul VI, *Instruction on the Pastoral Care of the People Who Migrate*, (Pastoralis migratorum), August 22, 1969, (Washington, D.C., U.S. Catholic Conference Press, 1969), nos. 29-30, secs. 1-3, p. 21.
9. Italians throughout the centuries have been accustomed to many dioceses, abundant parishes and a large proportion of priests. In 1973 there were in Italy and the islands of Sicily and Sardinia, 282 dioceses, 27,550 parishes and 65,001 priests. Source: Giuseppe Lucrezio Monticelli, "Radiografia Anagrafico-Ecclesiale Delle Regioni di Immigrazione", *Servizio Migranti*, Anno X, no. 2-3, Feb.-Mar., 1974, p. 56.

JEAN ANN SCARPACI

Immigrants in the New South

Italians in Louisiana's Sugar Parishes, 1880-1910*

Louisiana's sugar cane fields represent one of that state's leading industries. During the 19th century most of the sugar raised in the continental United States grew in the southeast and south central areas of Louisiana. The sugar Parishes encircled the city of New Orleans. They picturesquely line the Mississippi River from its mouth, northward to the city of Baton Rouge; they extended westward into the region surrounding Bayou Lafourche and Bayou Teche as illustrated in the map of Louisiana.[1] The cultivation of sugar cane required a large labor force of skilled and unskilled workers. During the period of cultivation from February through July 15 "hoe gangs" fought the advance of weeds into the rows of cane and kept the drainage ditches clear. During the harvesting or grinding period, from October through January, cane cutters and loaders supplied the sugar mill with a steady amount of cane.[2]

Each fall during the late 19th century, the harvest season or *zuccarata*, as they called it, attracted thousands of Italian laborers to Louisiana's fields of sugar cane. These immigrants responded to the chronic scarcity of labor on the sugar plantations, but they were a migratory or temporary part of the state's foreign-born population. The number of Italians in the labor force of the plantation rose and fell in relation to the cultivating season and to the existence of higher paying jobs elsewhere in the United States.

At the turn of the century, Italians constituted the largest immigrant group in Louisiana. Census totals recorded an increase in Italian foreign-born from 2,527 in 1880 to 20,233 in 1910.[3] Yet, these official figures did not reflect the seasonal influx of immigrant labor. Estimates of this floating foreign population ranged from 30,000 to 80,000.[4] After 1905, the totals drastically decreased. Italian migration to the sugar parishes, illustrated

---

* Originally presented at meeting, American Historical Association, New Orleans (December, 1972), and published in *Labor History* (Summer, 1974). Reprinted with permission.

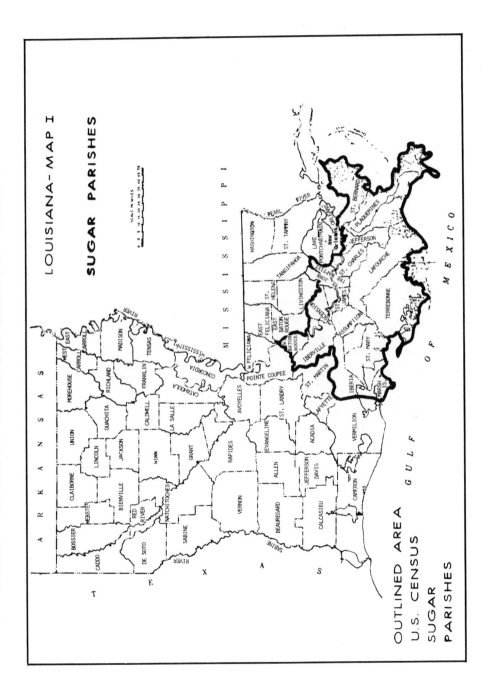

in Census Chart I only faintly suggests this pattern of the increase in the foreign-born population between 1880-1900 and the decline in 1910.[5]

Census Chart II illustrates the overall view of the distributions of the Italian population in the state.[6]

While on the plantation, the immigrants adjusted to the routine of work. They shared the social status and wage scale of their Afro-American co-

Census Chart I

Italians and Native Whites of Italian Parentage In
Louisiana's Sugar Parishes 1880-1910 (5 or more recorded)

Parishes	1880*	1890*	1900*	1910**	1910***
Ascension	27	529	1,332	578	1,206
Assumption	9	270	770	460	926
Iberia	15	41	355	275	549
Iberville	13	645	886	865	1,701
Jefferson	139	380	1,012	1,209	2,455
Lafourche	6	149	830	343	626
Plaquemines	143	324	362	135	265
St. Bernard	2	15	123	238	524
St. Charles	4	323	626	254	615
St. James	8	317	1,218	699	1,225
St. John	3	249	450	144	293
St. Mary	17	207	1,639	1,246	2,363
Terrebonne	6	17	550	294	537
W. Baton Rouge	5	199	120	210	296

* Only foreign-born reported in 1880-1900 census
** Foreign-born
*** Native whites of Italian parentage

Census Chart II

Italians Residing in the Sugar Parishes
and in the State of Louisiana 1880-1910

	Sugar Parishes Foreign-Born	Total*	Entire State Foreign-Born	Total*
1880	397		2,527	
1890	3,665		7,767	11,076
1900	10,273		17,577	26,621
1910	6,940	13,681	20,233	42,911

* The total indicates the Italian foreign-born and the native whites, one or both of whose parents were born in Italy.

workers. Italians adapted to the new work experience and new environment, yet they retained their old world traditions. The continuous link with their native culture provided a group cohesiveness during their lives on the plantation, a cohesiveness which remained with those immigrants who moved out of the class of laborers into the role of entrepreneur. In this paper I shall focus on the main economic and social patterns of the Italian agricultural laborers on the sugar plantations of Louisiana.

Throughout the period of Reconstruction and well into the 1880's, both cotton and sugar planters had been complaining about what they termed the "unreliability" and "inefficiency" of the black Americans who comprised their labor force season after season. The planters failed in their attempts to regiment these workers. The agricultural laborers preferred other fields of work; they did not respond to the planters' demands, and especially sought employment in the towns and cities. Those who did remain in the labor pool on the plantations produced less than the planters expected.[7]

According to many planters' accounts of the post war period, blacks quickly began to demonstrate their desire for economic independence. From 1865 through the 1880's white planters considered the black worker an unpredictable factor in Southern agricultural labor. The blacks seemed dissatisfied with their unchanging existence as they worked for the plantation owner for daily or monthly wages. And so they sometimes accepted jobs as laborers on a particular plantation, worked for a short time, then picked up and left. Planters attributed this behavior to their refusal to grant advances in pay, or their refusal to pay on a weekly instead of monthly or seasonal basis. Another cause of discontent was related to the amount of wages offered. Groups of black laborers struck for higher wages during periods of the year crucial to the cultivation of the sugar crop. Occasionally, laborers left one plantation for another which offered higher wages. This seeking for better conditions of employment extended over a wide regional and interstate area as many blacks moved between Louisiana and Mississippi.[8] After the Civil War, wages tended to move upward until the depression of 1873, when groups of planters agreed to reduce wages and their black employees refused to make contracts on such a basis. The black workers continued to be discontented, decidedly unsatisfied with the schedule of operation and work imposed by the sugar planters.[9]

The planters resented this "Ishmael" tendency of the black Southerners. Those native whites who depended upon native black workers viewed the latter's economic behavior as irresponsible and unreliable. The spector of labor trouble loomed large in the eyes of the planters. They felt trapped, unable to replace what they labeled as an inadequate and insufficient labor force with another. Hence, some planters banded together to meet this challenge to their economic survival. *Ad hoc* associations were formed which provided an united front in the face of the demands for better wages voiced by the black labor force. Members agreed to pay a standard wage, in order to end the uncertain situation in the sugar region. Planters formed a solid front and attempted to convince workers of the foolhardiness of their efforts to pit one planter against another or to incite regional rivalry. Some planters used extreme measures to restrain blacks, such as having them arrested as "debtors" or breakers of contracts. To forestall the migration of the workers, other planters effectively controlled the landing areas for boats, and employed river patrols to prevent the disembarkation of workers.[10]

The "Negro Exodus" aroused serious concern among those agricultural entrepreneurs who had counted on a permanent black labor force. Benjamin Singleton, one of the movement's major advocates, likened the human stream to the exodus of Moses and the people of Israel.[11] Many blacks moved to cities, both in the North and in the South; others migrated North to work as farm laborers. Regions, such as Kansas, where sugar beets were produced, attracted laborers who sought better wages. The year 1878 marked the peak of this veritable "Kansas fever." No accurate data as yet is available to enumerate with precision those Afro-Americans who left the South. The largest migration did occur in 1878-79; it originated from Mississippi and Louisiana. Estimates ranged from 5,000 to 10,000.[12] The constant invocation to migrate was potentially ruinous to southern agriculture.

The strikes of workers in the early 1880's heightened the pessimism of the planters regarding their efforts to keep the blacks on the plantation or to control their attitudes toward working there. On April 19, 1881, strikes and riots broke out in St. Bernard Parish at cane planting time.

> . . . the strike assumed more serious proportions, verging into a riot. It is stated that about three or four hundred negroes banded together under the leadership of some of the Spaniards or "islang," and went from plantation to plantation, compelling the laborers to stop work until the planters consent to pay the wages demanded . . . Finding it necessary to quell the turbulent disturbers a committee of planters called at the Governor's office and asked for the authorities of the State to assist them as the parish authorities are powerless.[13]

By April 21st, Governer Louis Wiltz had instructed the sheriff in St. Bernard Parish to stop the "rioters" or call upon the militia to help.[14] Instead of questioning their harsh system which failed to attract a sufficient and competent labor force, planters criticized the workers' response. They condemned the blacks for what they termed "deserting" the plantations; they condemned the blacks for demanding higher wages, and for failing to meet the planters' quota of production.

A large supply of labor remained a necessary economic factor for the sugar industry. The shortage of labor that had haunted the sugar industry in the post Civil War period continued into the 1880's. Since the planters became convinced they could not control a black work force, they sought workers from other quarters. One enterprising planter summed up the situation succinctly: "The only draw back I fear is want of reliable labour. Old darkies good but dieing [sic] out. Young ones about good for nothing. Have sent to Portugal for 25 laborers and their families."[15]

Closer at hand was an established colony of Italians in New Orleans. Between Louisiana and Sicily trade routes long had existed, and as early as the antebellum period, a colony of Italians, mainly merchants and those in related occupations, had resided in New Orleans. In 1850, 915 Italians lived in Louisiana; by 1870, the number had increased to 1,884.[16] Approximately 97% of the Italians in the state were Sicilians. They had come from the north central, central, and western sections of Sicily. Those who had emigrated directly had followed the citrus trade routes from Palermo and Messina to New Orleans.[17]

The connection between trade routes and emigration of people from the Mediterranean stirred the imagination of many white southerners after the Civil War. Expanded commercial ties could serve two purposes. The first benefit lay in increased profits and greater economic activity. The second advantage related to the need for laborers to develop the South's agricultural and industrial potential. In 1867, a conference called to discuss the problem of Southern commerce led to a request that the Federal Government, through mail contracts, provide subsidies to a steamship line plying between Southern ports and ports on the Mediterranean. The delegates to the commercial convention suggested that there would be a "natural" balance of trade:

. . . considering that we grow cereals and they grow fruits—that we can export cotton, tobacco, rice and petroleum to them, and receive fruits, olive oil, wines, sardines and works of art in return. . . .[18]

This trade route also might supply laborers directly to the South.

We have to glance the eye over the map to see from whence these new supplies must come. The northern shores of the Mediterranean embracing Spain, Italy, Sicily and Sardinia, with Greece, are teeming with a population of fifty millions. The climate is the same as that of the Southern States. Their farmers, fruit growers and laborers would be at home in the sunny fields of the South. The climate which the Northern emigrant shuns they are accustomed to. While readily acquiring a knowledge of the course of agriculture now existing here, they would bring with them, and introduce, the modes of producing their various fruits and wines. The waste fields, now deserted, would, under their patient labor, become fruitful with the grape, the olive, the fig, the orange, the lemon and kindred products. . . .[19]

Other sources similarly acknowledged a connection between trade routes and European immigration. James C. Kathman, Chief of the Bureau of Immigration for the State of Louisiana, compared the climate and fertility of Sicily with that of Louisiana.[20] Both Kathman and General P. T. Beauregard spoke to this point in the issues of *De Bow's Review* which appeared in the 1860's. Beauregard also served as president of an Immigration and Homestead Association formed in 1873 to encourage foreigners to come to Louisiana.[21]

As a matter of fact, Mediterranean ports often appeared as destinations on Louisiana shipping lists. The location of New Orleans and its position as a center of distribution for the Midwest obviously was a factor in the development of such trade. Markets for specific commodities reflected the needs and resources of this middle region of America. Shipments of American cotton and of wheat crossed the ocean for European ports which in turn offered fresh fruit and other agricultural products for the American market.[22]

The citrus fruit trade centered in Sicily, hence there was a long tradition of commercial transactions between that island and New Orleans. In addition to this history of trade with Mediterranean ports, the ethnic make-up of the New Orleans business community began to reflect this contact,[23] as may be seen from names taken from business directories and names of individuals mentioned in newspaper reports. The substantial Italian colony which grew in this city before the Civil War centered around the fruit trade. Italians not only imported and distributed the citrus fruit, but they also unloaded the ships and peddled the fruit through the city and surrounding suburbs.[24]

Immigration to Louisiana continued to follow the citrus trade routes already established. During the late 19th century most of the ships bringing Italian immigrants and products to New Orleans left from Palermo. For example, in 1880 the British Steamship *Scuida* sailed from Palermo to New Orleans with 210 immigrants and a cargo of lemons from Messina and Palermo.[25] The S. S. *Elysia* in 1887 sailed from Palermo to New Orleans with 613 Italian immigrants and a cargo of lemons and Mediterranean fruits.[26] The S. S. *Utopia* with 796 Italians from Piana dei Greci, Sicily sailed from Palermo to New Orleans in 1888.[27] Sugar planters welcomed this convenient link between commerce, immigration, and a potential labor force for their plantations. In 1881, the Louisiana Sugar Planters' Association created a Committee for Italian immigration which, from 1881 through 1908, in concert with the State Bureau of Agriculture and Immigration, supported efforts to recruit such immigrants.[28]

The majority of the Italians still clustered around the city, but some individuals sought economic opportunities outside New Orleans itself. The first sugar planter to hire an Italian laborer was John Dymond. In 1870, Dymond of Plaquemines Parish, located south of New Orleans, employed one Sicilian. During the next decade, Dymon and his neighbors offered jobs to other immigrants.[29] The census figures for Plaquemines Parish record this scattering of Italians in the sugar parishes; by 1880, 143 Italians were in Plaquemines.[30]

This influx of Italian laborers to the cane fields was largely seasonal. The Italians who came directly from Italy to the cane fields travelled at grinding time (October through December), and returned across the ocean immediately after the crop was harvested. These migrants in fact were following the pattern of agricultural nomadism that long had been a way of life in Italy for the peasant.[31] Augusto Miceli, a New Orleans attorney who came to America in the 1920's, reported that tramp steamers between New Orleans and Palermo would carry Italian "birds of passage" to Louisiana, expressly for the grinding season.[32] Charles Cangelosi of Baton Rouge, Louisiana noted that ships carrying immigrants for the plantations sometimes came directly up river to Baton Rouge.[33]

Similarly on a seasonal basis, during the 1890's and early 1900's, other Italian laborers began to pour into the sugar region from Chicago and New York, and Italians residing in New Oreans and in other Louisiana towns outside the sugar region often temporarily supplemented the labor force. This annual hegira of Italian immigrants usually began in October and tapered off by March. Those from Chicago and New York had the added attraction of being able to avoid the cold Northern winters. One sugar planter observed:

> You see, our Dagos have a way of going to Chicago for the summer months. They work in the sugar fields until May 1 or May 10, and then put out for Chicago where they work in shops, in mines and on railroads until winter sets in when they pack up and come to the sugar belt. Their fuel bills would be more than the railroad fares, and they make money on the deal.[34]

It is clear that much of the annual migration of Italians to Louisiana was internal as well as seasonal.

On the plantation, the Italian laborer had to adjust to the firmly established work routine. Planters continued to welcome the foreign laborer as a replacement for the black American worker, although the immigrant at best merely supplemented the native labor force. Most of the foreign workers filled the unskilled, low paying jobs that were essential to the cultivation and harvesting of sugar cane, for the planters did not change the jobs or the wages as the ethnic composition of the labor force changed.

From the pay rolls and time books,[35] can be gleaned the wage rates. Ordinary labor received 75 cents a day during the cultivation season. For grinding, teamsters and cane loaders received $1.40 per day, and cane cutters received $1.25 per day. Only the best workers earned positions as teamsters and loaders. And only first rate cane cutters received $1.25. The other workers—old men, women, and boys were paid less, from 75 to $1.20 per day, depending upon the amount of work they could do. The wages of old men, women, and boys for cultivating the crops ranged from 25 to 60 cents. Whatever was the seasonal chore, the work days lasted from sun up to sun down.[36]

In addition to his wages, the plantation laborer was given a house and a garden patch of about one-quarter acre; there he grew corn, peas, and sweet potatoes, aided by the plantation mules and plows furnished free of charge. He also received free fuel and hauled it to his house by using the plantation team which was provided for this purpose.[37]

Vincent Brocato who came to Raceland, Louisiana in 1895 at age 22 from Cefalu, Sicily described the housing for families as tenement-like buildings of one story divided into apartments. The single men lived in dormitory dwellings. All the houses were built crudely and like most rural dwellings of that period, lacked indoor plumbing. Wood stoves and open fireplaces provided both heating and cooking facilities. Kerosene lamps lighted the dwellings.[38]

The plantation tasks requiring little skill, such as hoeing and ditching, accrued to the Italians. When Donelson Caffery of St. Mary's Parish wrote to his son from Washington, D. C. in 1897, he noted: "Some few hundred Dagoes will be required to ditch the swamp land."[39] This kind of work was necessary to keep the land dry. As hoe men and briar hook handlers, Italians were considered "superior" to other laborers. This belief of the planters helped to secure a "monopoly" or preference for the Italians in the cane fields.[40]

Some Italian immigrants believed that the wages on the plantation meant "plenty money" in comparison with the economic conditions they had endured in Sicily,[41] where poverty and misery had surrounded them. In Louisiana, the habits shaped during their years of impoverishment in Sicily enabled ambitious and frugal laborers to survive, and in some cases, to get ahead under the wage system of the plantation. An Italian, A. Piaggio, who visited Donaldsonville, Louisiana in 1895, a time of depression in the sugar industry, explained how an immigrant family could achieve subsistence or better in the plantation setting:

A family of five Italians, the father, the mother and three children, arriving on a cane plantation from Italy all set to work. Even in a depressed labor market, the father by working three watches of six hours each, at 50 cents a watch, could earn $1.50 a day. The mother could earn $1, and the children, even if only 5 years old manage as a rule to earn 10 cents a day. So that the aggregate of such an average family's work per day was about $3. . . .[42]

It is difficult to understand how these laborers could *save* money on wages ranging from 50 cents to 75 cents per day, even with the whole family working, and even though during the depression years the wages did not compare unfavorably with those received by industrial workers.[43] One old Sicilian said he saved money because he "ate nothing but *pane e cutadro* [bread and knife].[44] Ridley Le Blanc who had worked at Raceland Plantation in Louisiana expanded on the old Sicilian's account. Le Blanc described Italian laborers as:

very good workers in the fields . . . They were good gardeners, raised goats, made and baked their own bread, made and formed their spaghetti, made cheese and made their clothes. They were self supporting and saved nearly all of their small earnings and quickly went into their own successful business.[45]

Gaetano Mistretta, the son of an Italian merchant in Assumption Parish, reinforced Le Blanc's observation. Mistretta recalled that his father's store accounts indicated that the laborers purchased very little. The immigrant workers either made or grew everything they needed; they were accustomed to subsist on a piece of bread and cheese for an entire working day.[46]

The presence of the immigrants, therefore, neither altered the kinds of jobs available on the plantation nor increased the status of the jobs held on the plantation. In fact, it was the Italian who adjusted to the long established work routine, and the wages and living conditions did not vary with the ethnic composition of the labor force.

Although their contemporaries predicted that the Italian would soon replace the black American in the sugar region, the latter continued to dominate the labor force between 1880 and 1910. For the Italian, direct contact with blacks as co-workers was a new experience. Thus the foreigner faced a double adjustment, the first one to the work routine, the second one to the native American socio-economic structure. Since Italian and native American black laborers shared the same position in the plantation system, they also shared the low occupation status of agricultural workers.

The particular composition of the work force prompted comparisons between the two groups. Most of the studies, conducted by native whites, concluded that the foreigners were more productive than the blacks. In this competitive setting, hostility might have developed between the two groups, but the immigrants seemed unperturbed. Eliot Lord reviewed the work situation on the South's farmlands and noted that

They [Italians] have no rooted prejudice to competition with negro labor. Intermixture with negro labor can usually be obviated by the division of employment on plantations and any necessary association of the Italian whites with the blacks is not precluded by any race animosity.[47]

Walter Fleming, the Louisiana State University political scientist, observed that when blacks and Italians filled the work force, as they did at Sunnyside Plantation in Arkansas, "there is no friction between Italian and black; but there is no race mixture."[48] One Louisiana planter affirmed that the forty families of Italian laborers on his plantation did not quarrel among themselves or with the other workers. The Italians, he stated, kept separate from the blacks in social relations and in fact, the immigrants tended to keep their own counsel in all matters.[49]

Some individuals reported that all plantation workers, Italians, Afro-Americans, and those of French ancestry ate and lived together without any hostility. One informant said it was not unusual to have a black family living next door to an Italian family. In the fields, work squads contained both immigrant and black American laborers and when a black served as hoe gang boss, he did not encounter resentment from the Italian workers in the crew.[50] One might conjecture that the black American served as an on-the-job trainer for the newcomers.

Although both conflict and violence did characterize some Italian-black American relationships, the press did not report a persistent hostility. Immediate events precipitated the instances of conflict rather than "racial" or national confrontation. And it was significant that the press did not evaluate as "racial" provocations the fights, shootings, and thefts which occurred from 1880 to 1910 between Italians and the black southerners. Certainly, the Anglo-American society of Louisiana considered both these groups as violence prone, and native white southerners were very sensitive to any evidence of "race" incompatibility. In fact, much of the crime committed by Italians and black Americans occurred within their own ethnic communities. And white Americans only became alarmed when they were personally affected.[51]

It thus appeared that Italians and the black Americans created a framework of tolerance in their associations; neutrality was the keynote. The immigrants' attitude of tolerance or acceptance of persons so unlike themselves in appearance, religion, language and specific customs, *i.e.*, their black co-workers, may be explained by the Sicilians' general indifference to the world outside their town. *Campanilismo*, or provincialism, characterized the South Italians' identification with their village existence, as Charlotte Chapman's study of Milocca, Sicily illustrated. In Milocca, settlers from other Sicilian towns always retained their *furasteri* or refugee quality. These identities even were inherited by *furasteri* children born in Milocca. And such identities followed the emigrants to America. For Miloccese, these human bridges led to Pittston, Pennsylvania and Birmingham, Alabama. In addition, Chapman observed that the individual's willingness to interact with groups or entities *within* the village varied according to his feeling of identification. Hence, the Sicilian placed himself, his family, and his town as the prime interests within his frame of reference. All else for him was secondary. In Louisiana, the indifference with which the Sicilian regarded the black American reflected this scale of immediate priorities and led to a minimum of interaction.[52]

When describing intergroup relations between the immigrants and the native blacks, Mistretta and others claimed that Italian immigrants initially bore no ill-will against their black co-workers. They had no reason to dislike the blacks and regarded them with curiosity. However, once the newcomers realized that they shared the socio-economic position of the blacks who were relegated to the lowest position in Southern white society, the foreigners decided to avoid further association with the black Americans. The avoidance of identification with them was one factor in the Italians' decision to leave the cane fields.[53]

An interview with Italians who had moved from sugar plantation work to farming in Independence, Louisiana provided a more detailed explanation of this sociological phenomenon.

> One Italian informant . . . said he and his family had been badly mistreated by a French plantation owner near New Roads. When asked how he had been mistreated, he stated that he and his family were made to live among the Negroes and were treated in the same manner. At first he did not mind because he did not know any difference, but when he learned the position that Negroes occupied in this country, he demanded that his family be moved to a different house and be given better treatment.[54]

In fact, much of the criticism levelled at conditions on the plantation originated from the observation that blacks occupied an inferior position in the South's social hierarchy. Representatives of the Italian government repeatedly stated its wish that the Italian settle in the South on a par with the native Anglo-Saxon and not compete with the native black for his title of agricultural proletariat.[55]

Thus, the Italian immigrant's exposure to the prejudices of Southern white Americans ultimately influenced his attitude toward the black Americans. The newcomer realized that treatment equal to that of the black was inferior treatment. And much of the conflict that developed between the groups paralleled the movement of Italians up the socio-economic ladder from laborer to tenant to farmer or businessman.

Their economic competition always had threatened to create an environment of hostility between Italians and black Americans on the plantation. The conclusions drawn from comparative studies made during those decades by Alfred Holt Stone and others influenced some of the planters to continue to seek Italian workers. Stone, for example, emphasized that Italians worked harder, produced greater yields per acre, worked in all weather, and sacrificed everything to accumulate savings, and implied that the black Americans did not match these achievements.[56] One would expect to find that the combination of an increase in the number of Italian workers on the plantation force and their reputation for high productivity would have aroused resentment and hostility among the blacks. The blacks might well have regarded the immigrant as a depressant to wages because of his high rate of productivity.

In fact, many Italians, rather than accepting lower wages when the depression hit the sugar industry, left the cane fields altogether. They did so, for example, when the repeal of the McKinley Tariff affected the market by removing the protection of the domestic industry.[57] Perhaps the proximity of New Orleans and the relative ease of movement in and out of the sugar parishes into industrial centers acted as a "safety valve" for these foreign laborers. Moreover, many of the Italians viewed plantation work as merely temporary, as a means to accumulate savings in order to embark on a career of agricultural or business entrepreneurship.

All evidence indicated that instead of tightening the competition for jobs, the increase of Italians in the plantation labor force had been a direct response to an endemic scarcity of labor. Although the concerted exodus of black Americans from the South had declined during the 1880's, planters continued to record a decrease in the annual migration of black laborers within the south, from the harvesting of cotton to the grinding of sugar. Yet this movement of black workers from the rural areas into the lumber mill regions and to the southern towns and cities did not remove them entirely from the labor force of the plantations. Throughout the 19th century, the planters still depended primarily on black labor.[58]

Later, as the rate of immigration to Louisiana fell and as the Italian sugar workers already in Louisiana responded to better economic conditions elsewhere in the United States, planters again began to recruit Southern blacks and whites from the cotton region. Obviously, the previous flow to Louisiana of Italians had not forced black laborers from the plantations as the literature of the period seemed to predict it would. Immigrant workers on the plantations had increased in number until the turn of the century; planters always seemed anxious to employ more each year, but the immigrant labor force apparently never was sufficient to meet the needs of the sugar industry. As blacks left the fields, Italians had been recruited to fill their places. When Italian migration slackened, blacks again were courted. The general pool of plantation labor continued to remain insufficient.[59]

As indicated, the Louisiana sugar plantation exposed the Italian immigrant to many new conditions and experiences. The cycle of cane cultivation, the process of sugar refining, the English speaking population, and the particular presence of black American co-workers, all demanded his attention. Nothing in his past had prepared him for these experiences and he had to adapt them to his own frame of reference. But his frame of reference was the strong cohesive group identity which was carried almost undiluted from Italy to America. Although this gradually was redefined in America, the basic pattern of values involving close ties with family, fellow villagers (*paesani*), and co-nationals, remained. This provided a familiar setting which more than counterbalanced the unfamiliar aspects of American life.

Rather than these day-to-day patterns within the Italian American community, the native American press mainly documented the most "sensational" or "colorful" events. Press accounts focused on incidents of conflict or violence, celebrations, and participation in contemporary events. On the plantations most of the reported violence stemmed from disagreements over money or work assignments and the conflicts were generally among family members and friends. In most cases of violence among Italians, the press assumed that the motives had been personal and that all the witnesses would remain silent. (In such newspaper accounts the stereotyping of Italians as violence prone was typical.) When an Italian fruit peddler, Luca Rizzo, shot his brother-in-law, Vito Corenno on the Glenn Orange Plantation near Morgan City, the *Thibodaux Sentinel* noted

. . . these same parties had a cutting affair about two years ago, and the usual dense ignorance of the shooting is shown by those who presumably know all about it, including the wounded man.[60]

This code of silence and determination to remain apart also was a direct carry-over from Italy as has been documented by Danilo Dolci. Dolci who has worked among the people of western and central Sicily, characterized these attitudes by referring to the proverbs: "The man who goes his own road can never go wrong," and "The man who plays alone never loses." As one Sicilian emigrant explained:

If a man goes alone, he needn't get involved in any trouble. He goes his own way. He does whatever he pleases, he goes his own road. With other people one says one thing, another says something else, and they can't agree.[61]

This self imposed isolation implies not the isolation of the individual but of his particular extended family group.

The identification with the family group that was typical of life in Sicily and was carried over to America led laborers to save money in order to bring their wives to America. The arrival of every ship in New Orleans set the scene for family reunions.[62] This tradition of close family ties also included private reprisals for dishonor to family. An Italian laborer in Lafourche Parish carried out this private code when he shot and killed the prospective husband of his sixteen year old sister. Some observers hypothesized that the brother had learned that his sister's fiancé already was married to a woman in Italy.[63] At any rate, it seems clear that the code of honor that encircled the family, making each member of the family responsible for the other's behavior, still functioned in Louisiana.

The group cohesiveness that persisted in America impressed Count Gerolamo Moroni, Italian consul at New Orleans. In 1912, Count Moroni observed that Italians preferred to work on the sugar plantations because they were situated near villages and cities in which a merchant co-national resided. The merchant offered not only familiar commodities, but also sociability to the settlers.[64] In addition, workers lived in close proximity on plantations, and in effect, formed small villages. In fact, the Italians' retention of their group cohesiveness, though thousands of miles from their native Sicily, probably played an important role in attracting Sicilians to Louisiana. Most Sicilians had lived in towns, more aptly termed "rural cities," with populations ranging from 2,000 to tens of thousands. Life in America's isolated rural communities would not readily appeal to peasants who were accustomed to residential clusters.[65] Certainly, the proximity of a large Italian colony in New Orleans which was easily reached by train and boat, helped the immigrant feel that the environment was more familiar.

Mutual benefit or benevolent societies which were common in Sicily and had served as a reinforcement of *campanilismo* in the Old Country, served similarly in America. Including fraternal as well as welfare functions, they provided health benefits and burial costs, and they sponsored social functions such as anniversary celebrations, religious observances, and commemorations of American holidays, like Columbus Day. Many of these societies reflected the old world emphasis upon town and regional loyalties.[66] This was evident in Louisiana. Six mutual benefit societies were listed for the sugar parishes in the Italian consul's report of 1910. Two other societies were recorded in the American press.[67] Indeed, the very names of some societies demonstrated their regional orientation. In addition to town and regional identities, Sicilian saints such as Santa Lucia and Santa Rosalia, and the Immaculate Conception, particularly revered by Sicilians, also provided names for societies.[68] Whenever these societies staged a celebration, dignitaries representing the native American community participated. In 1907, when the Duca D'Aosta Association of Franklin sponsored a celebration, both Senator Murphy J. Foster and Lieutenant Governor J. Y. Sanders addressed the gathering.[69] Such official attention to the Italian Americans who had become citizens, encouraged them to support these politicians.

We have seen that those Italians who remained in Louisiana as entrepreneurs continued to express a group cohesiveness which preserved their ethnic identity. And, as the immigrant moved out of the agricultural laborer class, he placed a wider distance between himself and his former black American co-worker. The Italian entrepreneurs soon acquired the race prejudice manifested by Southern whites. This was the price paid in exchange for social acceptance.

From available statistical data, it is difficult to determine precisely how many Italians actually worked on sugar plantations. Neither United States Census figures, nor the yearly reports of the arrivals of immigrants in Louisiana reflect the volume and impact of this migration. In fact, the temporary nature of work in the *zuccarata* which caused a rapid turnover in the labor force led to more of an internal migratory pattern. Workers from Chicago, Kansas City, St. Louis, New Orleans, and New York, as well as from Sicily, flooded the sugar regions each year seeking employment.

Towards the end of the 1910's we know that fewer Italians came to work in the cane fields. Instead, some of them climbed out of the status of wage earner and stepped up to positions of economic self-sufficiency. They achieved their goal through frugality and single-minded concentration upon saving money. Wages on the sugar plantations permitted ambitious immigrants to move into tenantry, share cropping, and eventually land ownership.

Yet, as we have seen, most of the temporary or seasonal migration did not remain in the state. The majority of the immigrants originally had followed the call of the annual *zuccarata* because the wages and the conditions of work had seemed more favorable than wages in other areas of employment. The situation soon changed, and by 1908 an Italian Government official noted that an immigrant laborer could save one-fifth more during eight months of construction work than he could save during twelve months of farm labor.[70]

In addition, the social climate within Louisiana influenced some immigrants to leave the State. As agricultural wage earners, Italians shared with their native black co-workers the low status assigned to this occupation. White Americans considered this work dirty and undesirable. Therefore, they placed a stamp of inferiority upon those who were laborers on the plantation. The attitude was partly social, a contempt for manual labor; and partly racial, the undesirable jobs were only for groups rated inferior by the native white community.

For economic gain, Italian laborers might have been willing to tolerate these attitudes, but clearly they would not when they could obtain the higher wages elsewhere in America. Other factors such as peonage, yellow fever, lynchings of immigrants, and the white community's intolerance of some of the customs of the Italians, prompted many immigrants to quit Louisiana altogether. With the original attraction of high agricultural wages canceled by better economic opportunities elseewhere, Italian immigrants no longer responded to the call of labor in the annual *zuccarata*.[71]

NOTES

* This essay benefitted from the incisive questions and comments offered by my colleagues Perra S. Bell and John G. Van Osdell.

1. J. Carlyle Sitterson, *Sugar Country: The Cane Sugar Industry in the South, 1753-1950* (Lexington: University of Kentucky Press, 1953), p. 267. Louisiana Map is compiled from United States Department of Commerce, Bureau of the Census, *Eleventh Census, 1890: Statistics of Agriculture*, pp. 68, 394-395, 405, and Thomas Lynn Smith, "Depopulation of Louisiana's Sugar Bowl," *Journal of Farm Economics*, XX (August, 1938), 503-509.

2. "Facts Concerning Domestic Cane Sugar Production: furnished in a letter to the New York Press by Walter Suthon, a planter of Houma, Louisiana," *Sugar Planters' Journal*, XXXII (April 19, 1902), 428-429. (Hereafter *SPJ*.)

3. *Tenth Census, 1880: Population*, 511-512 and *Thirteenth Census, 1910: Population*, 778-788.

4. For estimates of floating population see Editorial, "Italian Immigration," *Daily Picayune*, August 12, 1904, p. 6 and Italy, Ministero Degli Affari Esteri, Commissariato Dell' Emigrazione, *Bollettino Dell' Emigrazione, Anno 1904* (Roma, 1905), A. Ravaioli, "La Colonizzazione Agricola Negli Stati Uniti," p. 32.

5. Chart I was compiled from the following: *Tenth Census, 1880: Population*, 511-512; *Eleventh Census, 1890: Population*, I, 630-631; *Twelfth Consus, 1900: Statistics of Population*, 757-58; *Thirteenth Census, 1910: Population*, 778-788.

6. Census Chart II was compiled from statistics in Census Chart I, *op. cit.* plus *Eleventh Census*, pp. clxvii, 608, 685, 687, 689. *Twelfth Census*, pp. 813-817, and *Thirteenth Census*, p. 773.

7. Roger W. Shugg, *Origins of Class Struggle in Louisiana, A Social History of White Farmers and Laborers during Slavery and After, 1840-1875* (Baton Rouge: Louisiana State University Press, 1939), p. 258, Sitterson, *Sugar Country*, pp. 243-245.

8. Sitterson, *Sugar Country*, p. 243. For more than a decade after the war Negroes moved at the end of the year from one plantation to another, and during the first two weeks of each year the roads of the sugar region were lined with carts piled high with all their belongings. Although conditions at their new places were rarely better, many Negroes continued to hope, and even with hope they liked to exercise their rights as freedmen to change their employers.

9. *Ibid.*, pp. 243-245.

10. Morgan Dewey Peoples, "Negro Migration From the Lower Mississippi Valley to Kansas, 1879-1880," (unpublished Master's Thesis, Louisiana State University, 1950), p. 45.

11. Walter L. Fleming, "Pap Singleton, The Moses of the Colored Exodus," *American Journal of Sociology*, XV, no. 1 (1909), 61-78, and Peoples, "Negro Migration," p. 11. Benjamin Singleton was responsible for founding 11 colonies in Kansas between 1873 and 1874, after an unsuccessful effort in 1870 with the Tennessee Real Estate and Homestead Association. By 1879 the movement had become a flood. Singleton wrote pamphlets on Sunny Kansas but "educated" Negroes scorned his plans. By the end of 1879 he claimed to have brought 7,432 Negroes to Kansas.

12. Roy Garvin, "Benjamin, or Pap Singleton and His Followers," *Journal of Negro History*, XXXIII (January, 1948), pp. 7, 11.

13. "Riot in St. Bernard," *Daily Picayune*, April 19, 1881, p. 1.

14. *Louisiana Capitolian* (Baton Rouge), April 21, 1881, p. 2. Strikes also occurred in St. John's parish during the spring of 1880 as reported in "Here and There," *Le Louisianais* (Convent, La.), April 17, 1880, p. 1.

15. Sitterson, *Sugar Country*, p. 315. Sitterson cites a letter from Daniel Thompson to Cyrus Woodman, August 1, 1880 in C. L. Marquette (ed.), "Letters of a Yankee Sugar Planter," *Journal of Southern History*, VI (1940), 533.

16. *Seventh Census*, 1850, p. 506 and *Ninth Census*, 1870, pp. 340-341.

17. Cavalier Guido Rossati and R. Enotenico, "Gl' Italiani nell' Agricoltura degli Stati Uniti D'America," in *Gli Italiani Negli Stati D'America* (New York: Italian American Directory Company, 1906), p. 37; Italy, Ministero Degli Affari Esteri, Commissariato Generale Dell'Emigrazione, *Emigrazione E Colonie: Raccolta Di Rapporti Dell R.R. Agenti Diplomatici E Consolari*, III, *America* (Roma, 1909), pp. 202-221; interview and letter from Gaetano Mistretta, Donaldsonville, Louisiana, February and November, 1966.

18. *Remarks on the Importance to the Nation in View of the Condition of the Southern States and the Prostration of Commerce, of Establishing Steamship Intercourse with the Nations of the Mediterranean Sea* (New York, 1867), p. 9.

19. *Ibid.*, p. 8.

20. "Department of Immigration and Labor," *De Bow's Review*, IV n.s. (November, 1867), p. 474.

21. *Address of the People in Behalf of the Louisiana Immigration and Homestead Company*, Louisiana State University Archives, Baton Rouge. P. T. Beauregard Papers.

22. *Daily Picayune* (New Orleans), December 16, 1880, p. 1 notes the arrival of the British S. S. *Sciuda* from Palermo with 210 immigrants and a cargo of lemons. The *Daily Picayune*, December 8, 1887, p. 8 notes the arrival of the British S. S. *Elysia* with 613 Italians and a cargo of lemons and Meriterranean fruits to be shipped north and west by the Illinois Central Railroad. William Harris, State Commissioner of Agriculture and Immigration, in a pamphlet, *Louisiana Products, Resources and Attractions with a Sketch of the Parishes* (New Orleans, 1881), recorded exports of grain from New Orleans to the ports of Leghorn, Venice and Naples and exports of tobacco to Italy. This relationship between trade routes and immigrant traffic across the Atlantic receives attention in Marcus Lee Hansen, *Atlantic Migration*, Chapter VIII, "Commerce Bridges the Atlantic" (Cambridge, Mass.: Harvard University Press, 1951), pp. 172-198.

23. This debt was acknowledged even at the height of reaction to the 1890 murder in New Orleans of the Police Chief which was attributed to the Italian element. Editorial, "The Obligation Due the Italians," *Daily Picayune*, November 12, 1890, p. 4.
   . . . We of New Orleans owe to the Italians a vastly larger obligation than New York owns to. It is mainly through Italian enterprise and capital that the importation of foreign fruits at this port has been developed from a mere peddling business conducted in a few sailing schooners, to the dignity and proportions of a great commercial interest employing a score and more of steamships and hundreds of thousands of dollars of capital. New Orleans today through the efforts of native citizens of Italian parentage and of Italian born adopted citizens has in a dozen years past become a leading market for the importation and distribution of tropical and foreign fruits of all descriptions.

24. Alcee Fortier, *Louisiana, Comprising Sketches of Parishes, Towns, Events, Institutions and Persons Arranged in Cyclopedic Form* (4 vols. Madison Wis.: Century Historical Association, 1914), III, 742-743, discusses one of New Orleans' leading Italian businessmen partnerships, the Vaccaro Brothers. Stefano Vaccaro, born in Contessa Entellina, Sicily, came to New Orleans in 1860 and in 1862 engaged in the fruit and produce business which he followed until 1893, when his sons, Felix, Luca, and Joseph took over. The Vaccaro Brothers first engaged in the fruit and produce business at Decatur and North Peters Streets, being wholesale dealers until 1898, when they began importing bananas and coconuts from Spanish Honduras to New Orleans whence they were shipped to all parts of the country.

25. *Daily Picayune*, December 16, 1880, p. 1.

26. *Daily Picayune*, December 8, 1887, p. 8. The article notes that most of the passengers originated from Sicily and Southern Italy.

27. *Weekly Times Democrat* (New Orleans), October 20, 1888, p. 3. Many of the passengers brought with them small cargoes of Sicilian lemons and the occupation of fruit grower and vendor predominated.

28. "Cane and Corn," *Daily Picayune*, June 11, 1881, p. 1 and Minutes, May 12 and June 9, 1881, Louisiana State University Archives, Louisiana Sugar Planters' Association Papers. William Harris, State Commissioner of Agriculture and Immigration, in a pamphlet, *Louisiana: Products, Resources and Attractions with a Sketch of the Parishes* (New Orleans, 1881), recorded exports of grain from New Orleans to the ports of Leghorn, Venice, and Naples and exports of tobacco to Italy.

29. "Italian Immigration," *Louisiana Planter and Sugar Manufacturer* (New Orleans), XXXVIII (September 22, 1906), 179-180. (Hereafter LPSM.) The Sicilian, Antonio Musacha was sent by a labor agent in New Orleans to Dymond's Belair Plantation.

30. *Tenth Census, 1880: Population*, 511-512.

31. Grazia Dore, "Some Social and Historical Aspects of Italian Emigration to America," Trans., by Andrea Martontty, *Journal of Social History*, II, no. 2 (1968), 110.

32. Augusto Miceli, interview in New Orleans, Louisiana, November 10, 1965. Mr. Luigi Scala, former Italian Consul at Independence, Louisiana noted

that steamship companies encouraged "birds of passage." Interview in Providence, Rhode Island, October, 1966.

33. Letter from Mr. Charles Cangelosi, Baton Rouge, Louisiana, September 26, 1965.
34. "Importation of Porto [sic] Rican Sugar and Exportation of Italians: Interview with Hon. W. E. Howell of Lafourche Parish," *SPJ*, XXXI (August 31, 1901), 722-723.
35. Payroll for Dunboyne Plantation, January to December, 1897, Louisiana State University Archives, Edward J. Gay and Family Papers; Time Books 1898-1901 and 1905-1908, *Ibid.*, Uncle Sam Plantation Papers.
36. "Facts Concerning Domestic Cane Sugar," *op. cit.*
37. *Ibid.*
38. Interview with Mrs. Vincent Brocato, Raceland, Louisiana, November 14, 1965. Mrs. Brocato came to Raceland with her family in 1895. There her family joined her father who had emigrated in 1894. Mrs. Brocato conveyed information from her own life and from her husband's experiences. Mr. Brocato was alive in 1965, but unable to provide an interview. Also see interview with Mistretta.
39. Letter dated March 3, 1897, Letter Book 1866-1906, Louisiana State University Archives, Donelson Caffery and Family Papers.
40. Hall Clipper, "Special Correspondent," *LPSM*, XXIV (June 9, 1900), 359.
41. Letter from John V. Baiamonti, Jr., Tickfaw, Louisiana, December 8, 1970. Mr. Baiamonte interviewed Sicilian immigrants and their children in Tangipahoa Parish during the course of his research on the Italians in Tangipahoa Parish.
42. "Italians Returning to their Fatherland," *Daily Picayune*, December 21, 1895, p. 9.
43. Henry Marshall Booker notes in his study "Efforts of the South to Attract Immigrants, 1860-1900," (unpublished Ph.D. dissertation, University of Virginia, 1965), 54, that the Southern States paying the highest wages for farm labor with board for the period 1866 to 1899 were Texas, Florida, and Louisiana.
44. Letter from Mr. George Piazza, a New Orleans attorney, September 29, 1965.
45. Letter from Mr. Ridley Le Blanc, December 1965. He was formerly connected with the Godchaux Company in Raceland, Louisiana.
46. Mistretta letter and interview, *op. cit.*
47. Eliot Lord, *The Italian in America* (New York: B. F. Buck Company, 1905), p. 184.
48. Walter Fleming, "Immigration to the Southern States," *Political Science Quarterly*, XX (June, 1905), 297.
49. Lee J. Langely, "To Build Up Louisiana: Needed Outside Capital and Labor will be Welcomed," *Manufacturers' Record* (Baltimore), XLV (April 14, 1904), 276-277.
50. Brocato interview and letter from Le Blanc, *op. cit.*
51. *L'Italia* (Chicago), August 15-16, 1896.
52. Charlotte Gower Chapman, *Milocca: A Sicilian Village* (Cambridge, Mass.: Schenkman Publishing Company, Inc., 1971), pp. 151-157. Chapman collected her data on Milocca in 1928.

53. Mistretta interview.
54. Luther Williams, "The People of Tangipahoa Parish: A Sociological Comparison of Two Ethnic Groups," (Unpublished Masters' thesis, Louisiana State University, 1951), p. 85.
55. "Baron Des Planches and Italian Immigration," *LPSM*, XXXIV (April 21, 1906), 246.
56. Alfred Holt Stone, "Italian Cotton Growers in Arkansas," *American Monthly Review of Reviews*, XXXV (February, 1907), 209-213.
57. "The Plantation Labor Problem," *LPSM*, XVII (December 5, 1896), 362.
58. Sitterson, *Sugar Country*, pp. 315-317. David Hellwig's study of the attitude of the Afro-Americans to immigration considered their reaction to the South's attempt to recruit Italian labor. He noted that the blacks displayed their displeasure against the recruiters not their protégés. Hellwig found no massive conflict between the two groups. The blacks contrasted the virtues of a traditional labor source against the potential threat of "the Italian as corrupt, violent, anarchistic, prone to join unions and in general a threat to both the American and Southern way of life." Letter dated September 30, 1973, St. Cloud, Minnesota.
59. *Ibid.*
60. "Italian Killed," *Thibodaux Sentinel*, May 29, 1909, p. 1.
61. Danilo Dolci, *The Man who Plays Alone*, trans. by Antonio Cowan (Garden City, N. Y.: Doubleday and Co., Inc., 1970), p. 4.
62. Chapman, *Milocca*, p. 73 and "Southern States Items," *Daily Picayune*, August 30, 1894, p. 11.
63. "Italian Murdered," Weekly *Thibodaux Sentinel*, October 13, 1900, p. 1.
64. *Bollettino Dell' Emigrazione, Anno 1913*, Gerolamo Moroni, "La Louisiana e L'immigrazione Italiana," pp. 51-53.
65. Rudolph Vecoli, "Contadini in Chicago: A Critique of the Uprooted," *Journal of American History*, LIV (December, 1964), 404-405.
66. Ibid., p. 413 and Chapman, *Milocca*, pp. 172-173.
67. *Bollettino Dell' Emigrazione, Anno 1910*, Moroni, "Società Italiane Nel Distretto Consolare di New Orleans," pp. 1118-1193. "Over the State—Patterson," *Kentwood Commercial*, June 18, 1895, p. 4. "Latest News in Louisiana," *Daily Picayune*, October 16, 1906, p. 16 and "Latest News in Louisiana," *Ibid.*, July 27, 1910, p. 14.
68. *Bollettino Dell' Emigrazione, 1910*, Moroni, "Società Italiane . . . ," "Latest News in All Louisiana—Kenner," *Daily Picayune*, August 30, 1903, p. 14.
69. "A Gala Day in Franklin," *St. Mary Banner* (Franklin), May 11, 1907, pp. 3-4.
70. Robert Foerster, *The Italian Emmigration of Our Times* (New York: Arno Press and the New York Times, 1969. Originally published by Harvard University Press in 1919), p. 369. Foerster cites "Memorandum degl' instituti italiani di patronate per gli emigranti in sulle cause che ostacolano L'avviamento all' agricoltura degl' immigranti italiani negli Stati Uniti in the *Bollettino Dell' Emigrazione, Anno 1909*, p. 9.
71. The factors contributing to the decline of immigration to Louisiana are discussed in Chapters V and VI of Jean Ann Scarpaci, "Italian Immigrants in Louisiana's Sugar Parishes: Recruitment, Conditions of Labor, and Community Relations, 1880-1910" (unpublished Ph.D. dissertation, Rutgers University, 1972).

CLEMENT LAWRENCE VALLETTA

Family Life

The Question of Independence

To speak of Italian American life is also to speak of the family. Whether one considers Italian national character or social change, one inevitably reflects upon the possibilities of family coherence in the throes of Americanization. This is true of every immigrant group, but the earlier immigrations have been more influenced by mobility, intermarriage, occupational varieties and the cumulative changes in life style. That inexorable pull toward a middle class existence has distorted our attitudes toward the family. Reactions by "nativists" toward the most recent immigrants, reactions by "Americanized" generations toward their own ancestors, studies by social scientists of behavioral characteristics all focus (with varying degrees of sophistication) upon such externals as: cleanliness and smell or the amount of indoor plumbing, statistically measurable indices (occupation, educational level, residence, income level, religion) especially in comparison to one's parents; facility with the English language especially the hyperstandard variety; and a patriotism associated with institutional definitions by the public school system, the corporations, and the Veterans' associations. The significance of family life for each immigration has been attenuated, it appears, by this process of middle classism (otherwise known as bureaucratization, much of Americanization, and industrialization). The spirit of "progress" has extended efforts by our society to overcome limitations of disease, poverty, and ignorance; but at the same time the process of indiscriminate change has resulted in a breakdown of tradition most evidenced in the breakdown of the family.[1]

This discussion will consider Old and New World conditions of family life as related to the American concern with independence. I assume that each immigrant group has had in mind a model life style concerning both these concerns which involve on the one hand maintaining a way of life that in the Old World had become improbable of having, and on the other hand achieving distinction (in Old and New World terms) especially for one's progeny. The latter attraction is complicated by nativist (or composite

153

ethnic American) modes of independence; e.g., squire, yeoman farmer, master craftsman, self-made businessman, orator, professional. The former mode involves regional and village variations, time of immigration, and the intangible forms of world view. It is difficult but necessary to consider these questions particularly from the vision of the Southern Italian peasant (who comprised the majority Italian immigration). He probably had a hierarchical sense of social organization with Lords and bourgeoisie above him (about 15 per cent of the population) and *cafoni* (lower lower, or 5 per cent) beneath him. His sense of independence in *his* terms involved the level of *civiltà* (a civilized way of life, genteel, courteous behavior with time to enjoy what life may offer) and such lesser but significant aspects of deference as occupation, instruction, and family name.[2]

Those impressions formed the basis for apprehending New World opportunities. Tensions between the style of the *famiglia* in terms of social deference and the opportunity for individual and family "progress" in the New World were and still are descriptive of generational change and adaptation. It is clear, for example, that a value of the American educational system—development for each child to the maximum of his/her desires and abilities—was not necessarily desirable to many immigrants, Italian and non-Italian, who often expected children to leave school at an early age as in the Old Country and contribute to the needs of all the family.[3] In some ways American experience reinforced this pattern because of the necessity to acquire and maintain a residence without the help of parents as in Italy. But the Old World model involved much more than economic independence.

The immigrant remembered and tried to live in the cyclical rhythm of the seasonal and church calendar. Individual independence was in actuality family participation in those activities sanctioned by traditions of the village and church as well as the social and economic system. To the immigrant, repetition was not necessarily to be avoided as boring or unproductive; on the contrary, he lived for the celebrations of Christmas Eve dinner, Christmas, Carnevale, Easter, the annual feast in honor of the patron divinity, and the christenings and weddings of family and *paesani*. Such times included the nuclear family as expanded with grandparents, sisters and brothers, and on occasion *compari* and *comari* and *paesani*. Even in the New World, the immigrant proletariat in the construction or garment industries lived to celebrate in these traditional ways.

The concept of time as compared to a current view is more cyclical and irrational than linear and rational. Although the immigrant, and even his offspring, may plan carefully, even cunningly, they realize that fate and the unexpected may have more to do with the future than anything that can be done, nor does this mean that a fatalistic or *carpe diem* attitude prevailed. Not to do anything or to degenerate morally was to invite, indeed beg, for divine retribution. But to be too ambitious, to place self ahead of family, to work too hard was also an undesirable way to live. From this viewpoint it would be the career-oriented, acquisitive, solitary individual who would be regarded as irrational. Hence the sayings, "Who has no one is truly forsaken," or the description of the ambitious, money-grubbing person as one who has, "a sickness."

Independence has involved to the immigrant, then, some point of resolution among such Old (or remembered) and New World tensions as loneliness, helplessness before fate, and what appears to be social and religious chaos as defined by the disregard for interrelatedness (or what to a modern view is dependence). To the first generation some connection with the soil was maintained if only with small garden plots or preparation of purchased foodstuffs that recalled peasant usages. This was to some extent more possible in the city with the great food markets than in the country. The rural experience offered greater opportunities for extensive gardening, canning, wine-making, and the raising of livestock. Family relatedness was the dominant configuration of culture, extending to ceremonial and even prestigious levels.[4] Reasons included the settled nature of village and urban life, as distinct from the mobile life style of other cultures; the high death rate which explained in part the imminent sense of fate; the increasingly hard land tenure conditions meaning exorbitant taxation and merciless exploitation exacerbating the already extensive suffering.[5] Furthermore the larger Italian society was also familial—either as extension or support—inasmuch as the large landowner and the nobility were associated with a family name of royalty if not power. The Church reinforced the aesthetic as well as religious forms of The Holy Family. The patron saint or Blessed Mother was regarded, in a sense, as a powerful person or parent who could intercede with God on behalf of one's own family needs. In America *la miseria*, echoed by the expression *porca miseria*, reinforced the need for a strong family relationship in both divine and human shape particularly in lieu of the bureaucratic forms of social aid and even after their enactment of effective regard for poor people.

If one means by independence freedom to do one's own thing, one would be judged by the first generation as puerile, if not mad. But the modern lives in a world interlaced with technological and bureaucratic organization in which an individual existence depends less directly upon the soil, relatives, and faith than upon income, peers at work, and capacity to adopt to changes in occupation:

> For several thousand years the families of much of Europe lived in . . . a household economy. The family was . . . an institution of power; and this power affected the other functions of protection, recreation, et cetera.
> With the techniques of production improving and with transportation becom-

ing better, communities were increasing in size, trade was growing, and some economic functions were being specialized outside the average family. . . .

The inventions of the steam engine and steelmaking gave a great impetus to the growth of large size communities, and these increased enormously the shift of functions from the family to other organizations.[6]

The implications of this historical pattern are worth pursuing by considering the relationship in the older household economy as the mutual obligations of food acquisition given for food preparation, of teaching children in exchange for obedience, etc. Hence the question as recently posed: "What happens to the contract between the parents when the x and y of their exchange are nearly the same, and when in fact they do not exchange them with each other, but with impersonal bureaucracies outside the family?"[7] The answers of course have been the stuff of Americanization. (Recent aspects of popular culture—movies like *The Godfather* and television programs like *All in the Family*—are vicarious satisfactions perhaps of a personal need to obtain "justice" and emotional release in an increasingly impersonal world.) The degrees of industrial and bureaucratic organization at the time of immigration may serve to explain patterns among the old and new immigrations and for each group. Although Oscar Handlin has demonstrated the fallacious distinction between "old" and "new" groups, the disparagement of the recent groups was a function and a fictional one at that of middle class notions derived from the bureaucratic organization and the attendant "values" of industrial progress and worth. This latter pattern ran in the experience of British and German groups, to a lesser extent with Middle European groups and Northern Italian groups, and to an even lesser extent among Southern Italian immigrants. Indeed, the relative isolation of village life in Southern Italy, the successive invasions of the cities by foreign powers, (although not as repressive as the experience of Polonians, Ukrainians, Slovaks), and the collusion between those powers with the large landowners even after national independence all meant that the Italian continued to maintain family independence in economic and general cultural forms. While to a Polonian or Slovak, independence may have been synonymous with statehood, to the Italian national sovereignty even when attained in the late nineteenth century meant not only continued but intensified exploitation.[8]

The Italian immigrant came with an extraordinary sense of independence because he had experienced many dimensions of history: He had not the preoccupation with bureaucracy of other nationalities but he understood the interworking of organizational structure and its personal dimension in the family, the village, and the church; he had won national status but he was even worse off, finding it more necessary to emigrate; he came to America at the zenith of its industrial need for manual labor which he offered in exchange for a relative degree of family integrity; and given his historical position he realized the shallow alternatives offered by bureaucratization and in a persistent way he fought to maintain the familiar and essential familial design. The battle was not decisive; the American process changed him and his heirs. Each generation faced an identity crisis, if they had the time for it. Hard choices were made over whether family or personal—often sees as altruistic—desires should take precedent. The growing influence of the media as agent of a consumer ethos became especially noticeable in the changing role of the second generation wife, who whether she worked or not demanded more comforts and privileges than her mother had known. And for the male there were also the attractions of a better existence at least better than his father had known. His children might realize a life of *civiltà* or professionalism of some kind. The experiences of The Great Depression and Second World War slowed this process, but the period of the last twenty years accelerated it. The second generation wife increased her influence during the fifties and sixties as the economy improved. Children could continue their education, and with changes in life style fewer children meant greater freedom for wives to work and plan for their offspring and their advancement. The negative reactions associated with the Vietnam War dramatized the growing differences between educated children and well-meaning parents. The ambivalence was intensified: on the one hand the new immigrants wanted to prove themselves (to have their children be a credit to their nationality), but on the other hand they refused to admit failure of self or society because to them family and society became one in America. Especially was this the case for the second generation who had fought or lived through World War II; the old (often first generation) suspicious notions about political power had been forgotten. If the second generation felt inferior before the War in terms of class, wealth, language, residence, etc., they learned during and after the War that their situation was national, that when the externals were put aside in time of crisis people were truly the same; and what is more they discovered that they were as good and brave a group as any other. No wonder they looked with shock at youngsters burning college buildings—which in some cases they, the veterans, had built with their own hands. If they felt more at peace with themselves but still concerned about doing better for their children, no wonder the reaction there was (and is) to civil rights legislation requiring quota representation in occupations and education. This was exasperated by the influx of Black and Hispanic Americans into the northern cities, and into the old ethnic neighborhoods. That point of resolution of tension worked out by the second generation was now threatened. Ethnicity was not only reinforced, it was intensified especially as Blacks claimed verbally a kind of social independence from the rest of society. If it was not only all right but in terms of the civil rights movement even quite legitimate and effective to be Black, then white ethnics believed *a fortiori* that proving themselves American in middle class ways was perhaps not required. It was furthermore an immense relief to be Hungarian, Polonian, Italian . . . as well as American— especially as more people began to suspect that the American Dream was not working out: high levels of drug and alcohol abuse at all age levels but particularly among young people, mental breakdown and tension-related physical disorders even among the ethnic upper middle class, and the chaotic results to the neighborhood of forced integration, ill-conceived highway construction and urban renewal that tore down abruptly but built up poorly if at all. Hence the current reactions evidenced by the creation of the National Center for Urban Ethnic Affairs, the recognition by ACTION of the importance of ethnic communities, the passage and funding by Congress of Senator Schweiker's (Pennsylvania) Bill to develop ethnic curriculum materials for the schools, and the continuing rise of so-called ethnic political power.[9] Although these changes appear worthwhile, the important experiences of the past may still be ignored and relegated even by the so-called new ethnic consciousness.

To understand and act upon tradition is in a sense to develop and extend insights into the presentness of the past. Each generation maintained a sense of family independence that has increasingly involved extrafamilial forms. To the first generation the family was the *sine qua non* of life. There arose in the second generation an ambivalence which has resulted in certain adaptations. To the third and fourth generation self-conception also has meant the realization that what was lost in the past might if regained prove more valuable than assimilation into an anomaly of upper class. The perspectives of world view were cyclical and emphatically traditional within the seasonal and religious year. Millions of immigrants sharing that experience readily accepted hardships in America if they could retain that life here or for many upon their expected return. That ostensible passivity had the literal boundaries of the ethnic community and the intangible sense of pride in family tradition. The question of family and independence is crucial to the understanding of not only the Italian American experience but of the course of modern civilization. There were and are many answers, and as many stories as possible must be recounted from the many regions in America and abroad. I will illustrate a few of the responses discovered in the Wilkes-Barre, Pennsylvania, region.[10]

A very successful individual of Northern Italian extraction and of the second generation indicated that he was able to attend law school because of the success of his parents' grocery store in a small community near Wilkes-Barre. Fluent in both Italian and English (as his mother was, as well) he soon became a very successful lawyer among Italian Americans. After conducting title searches for prospective property owners, he found that "the banks had their own lawyers, so [he said] I had to start my own bank." He raised $150,000 in ten days with five Italian-Americans and one each of Irish, Jewish, Lithuanian, and WASP descent. He called it appropriately enough, The Liberty National Bank, and catered to those recent immigrants who needed mortgage loans. His experience and that of others like Amedeo Obici who founded the "Planters Peanuts" corporation began as a small family business and gradually expanded.[11] This was somewhat different from the experience of the self-made American millionaire who associated with an already extant corporate enterprise. Even the larger Italian-American run corporations were composites of several relatively small enterprises. This was the experience of the lawyer's enterprises and of other companies such as one in the area that appears to be only in construction but which in actuality has included a chain of small hotels, farmlands, an electrical contracting firm for the utilities, and even a small (relative to Bell) telephone utility.

It is significant that the Italian-American lawyer became a prominent member of the American Legion and quite influential in local and state and through his friendships national politics. He has had little patience or understanding—as might be expected—for those who were critical of their country. He would rather praise what he calls the "Italian genius," the capacity for hard work and progress. To illustrate his point he refers to the several local millionaires of Italian extraction, to a relative who is a full vice-president of The Bank of America, and he indicates how less advanced are those other groups (who emigrated at the same time as the Italian) in the fields of law and medicine.

During the early years, 1890-1930, there were many small ethnic areas called patches or names like Brookside, Irishtown where the Russians lived, Polander Hill, Scotch Hill, Welsh Hill, Hilldale, where the Italians lived. Each area or neighborhood, even a few within city limits, revealed a dual life style, urban-rural, industrial-agrarian, cyclical-linear. Many families had tiny farms in their backyards providing eggs, fruit, vegetables and in some instances milk and beef. Cows were grazed in fields during the day, tended by a man paid by several families. The miner's lot was extremely hard, but as labor conditions improved he was able to work fewer than eight hours if he and his laborers filled their quota of railroad cars. Gradually he won the right to have his quota checked by his union representative as well as the company "docking boss" who determined the worth of a car of coal after a certain percentage for slate or rock was discounted. Informants tell how well the first and older second generations maintained group solidarity with other ethnic groups before management that had theretofore

(1902) manipulated the various groups, continually tried to intimidate immigrant voting, and black-balled certain men from ever finding work in the anthracite fields. Family solidarity necessitated unionization and membership in benevolent organizations which, until the advent of social security benefits, provided help for the widowed family. Individuals still recall the Roma band playing a dirge during a funeral procession for one of its members.

At least five separate Italian groups in the area formed cooperatives into which members paid a sum of money as stock and then bought food at wholesale prices. Members took turns working behind the counters. There were elaborate by-laws printed in Italian which detailed the rights and duties of members and officers. (These organizations deserve separate study, illustrating a democratic tradition informed by a desire for a secure family and therefore communal structure.) These organizations built halls to house the cooperatives, provided a large dance floor for wedding receptions and the yearly banquets, and usually established a men's club. Once a year they had a pig roast: "a dozen sucklings" baked to tender perfection. Each member worked only three or four hours so that "everybody worked and everybody enjoyed." During the summer months groups played a game known as the Wheel which was won by the team that made the fewest tosses of wooden wheels between designated points spaced well over a mile. Losers feted winners with baked chicken, wine, and salad. It should be noted that the coops worked well until some five years ago when "nobody wanted to work and everybody wanted the best cuts of meat." The second generation appears more interested in rotary type organizations— such as UNICO—which promote a "better image" of Italian Americans.

These examples illustrate the generational patterns associated with becoming American at first to remain Italian and then with becoming externally American to gain acceptance from others especially by the younger second and older third generations. At any rate, these examples may be multiplied to suggest that the question of independence was resolved, in general, by a degree of extrafamilial organization necessary to maintain family solidarity and gradually group image. Moreover, the Italians like other groups of their American migration had meagre capital for investment, and diminishing opportunities for starting even smaller businesses, if not well into the first generation to serve immigrant needs, certainly into the second and third generations as the process of trust and conglomerate formation increased and accelerated the process of middle classism. While Italians were effective at the shop and local level in the I.L.G.W.U. and U.M.W. other nationalities (Jewish and Irish) controlled the leadership with tight fists.

Yet there persists the almost universal emphasis by Italians upon the family and neighborhood as integral with at least a semblance of cyclical world view. It appears that the latest generations are realizing a modicum of opportunity at the top echelons of industry, government, and education. The problems of prejudice are of course not extinct. The old ambivalence of identity (inferiority and pride) seems recurrent if only in that larger description of Americanization with its perennial irony. By seeking self and family fulfillment, by doing credit to name and nationality, one diminished that heritage and with it insight and renewal, the human possibilities, that the larger society had misunderstood and relegated from the start. Like their ancestors, the newest generation would participate as they saw fit. The challenge was not merely to return to the roots, but to understand and perhaps live the implications of cyclical world view, family life (albeit modified), independence, the neighborhood, and those forms of group and institutional association that are centuries old, and that first integrated Western Civilization: this during what appears to many as a breakdown of tradition without even a sensible commitment to what may be learned from experience. Thus the most recent generation may realize that their ancestors and their stories bear certain painful and enlightening truths: that the oral tradition now revived with media usage reemphasizes the history and character of those stories; that ethnic neighborhoods form viable and quite self-sufficient settlements in what appear to many to be disintegrating cities; that certain urban problems may have been intensified by planning which did not account for the proximate diversities and basic needs and values of the various groups; that the history and meaning of the Republic has thrived when national needs were balanced with local realities and when family, neighborhood, and regional integrity is a basic value; that the diversities of language and culture in America constitute a living resource for self and social understanding, both nationally and internationally.

We have had fortunately the benefits and visions of men like Leonard Covello who have revealed the universality of the particular experience when thoroughly understood and lived.

NOTES

1. For a discussion of family "demoralization" and "remoralization," and for a good historical overview, see Carle C. Zimmerman, "The Future of the Family in America," *J. of Marriage and the Family*, 34:323-333, 1972; a recent survey of literature on the Italian American family is contained in F. Ivan Nye and Felix M. Berando, *The Family: Its Structure and Interaction* (New York: Macmillan, 1973) especially pp. 72-88. For a revealing collection of source materials, see Francesco Cordasco and

Eugene Bucchioni, *The Italians: Social Backgrounds of an American Group* (Clifton, N. J.: Augustus M. Kelley, 1974). It is only recently that scholars are beginning to realize that ethnicity exists as "the source of events," (p. 310) even though those same authors qualify that observation elsewhere (p. 302)—Nathan Glazer and Daniel Moynihan, *Beyond the Melting Pot* (Cambridge: M.I.T. Press, 1963). For a recent study of ethnic influence see John L. Shover, "Ethnicity and Religion in Philadelphia Politics, 1924-40," *American Quarterly*, 25:499-515, 1973. Studies of national character written during the 1950's tended to ignore ethnic influences, e.g., David M. Potter, *Plenty of Plenty*, 1954; David Riesman, *The Lonely Crowd*, 1950; studies of the sixties tended to consider such influence: *Beyond the Melting Pot*, Milton Gordon, *Assimilation in American Life*, 1964, Stanley Lieberson, *Ethnic Patterns in American Cities*, 1963. The emphasis upon ethnic studies may also involve greater consideration of family life indicated by the increasing interest in such works as Stuart A. Queen and Robert W. Habenstein, *The Family in Various Cultures*, 3d ed. (Philadelphia, J. B. Lippincott, 1967).

2. See Leonard W. Moss and Stephen C. Cappannari, "Estate and Class in a South Italian Hill Village," *American Anthropologist*, 64:287-300, 1962.

3. The significant study of the interpenetration of Old and New World experience is, of course, Leonard Covello, "The Social Background of the Italo-American School Child: A Study of the Southern Italian Family Mores and their Effect on the School Situation in Italy and America," Ph.D. dissertation, New York University, 1944.

4. Silverman, Sydel F., "An Ethnographic Approach to Social Stratification: Prestige in a Central Italian Community," *American Anthropologist*, 68: 899-921, 1966. See also, my "Friendship and Games in Italian-American Life," *Keystone Folklore Quarterly*, 15:174-187, 1970.

5. Banfield, Edward C., *The Moral Basis of a Backward Society* (New York: The Free Press, 1958). See also, E. J. Kunkel and Walter Goldschmidt, "The Structure of the Peasant Family," *American Anthropologist*, 73: 1058-1078, 1971.

6. W. F. Ogburn and W. F. Nimkoff, *Technology and the Changing Family* (Cambridge: Houghton Mifflin Company, 1955), p. 141. The influence of technology upon American society has been exceptional and perhaps extensive: "Instead of being affected very long by the power of the land and the climate, they would affect the land and the climate by their power," John Burchard and Albert Bush-Brown, *The Architecture of America* (Boston, Little Brown and Company, 1961), p. 8.

7. C. Christian Beels, "Whatever Happened to Father,' *New York Times Magazine*, Aug. 25, 1974, p. 52.

8. Grazia Dore, "Some Social and Historical Aspects of Italian Emigration to America," reprinted in Cordasco, *The Italians*, pp. 7-32. See also, Denis Mack Smith, *Italy, a Modern History* (Ann Arbor: University of Michigan Press, 1959) pp. 214-15. The reverse effect of emigration of returned prosperity (which suggests the problem with generalization) is discussed by Benedetto Croce, *A History of Italy, 1871-1915*, trans. Cecilia M. Ady (New York, Russell & Russell, 1963), p. 229.

9. Michael Novak, *The Rise of the Unmeltable Ethnics: Politics and Culture in the Seventies* (New York: Macmillan, 1971).

10. Several informants in the region were interviewed during sabbatical leave in the fall of 1971 and up to the present.
11. For a discussion of the "Planters Peanut and Chocolate Company," see *Fortune* (17:78-85, 1938) which describes it as "paternalistic" and "a small closely held corporation" with "65 per cent of it owned by Mr. Obici, Mr. Peruzzi, and their families," p. 78-79. Certainly the experiences of Obici and the others should not be regarded as either indigenous to Northeastern Pennsylvania nor as widespread among Italian Americans. (The generalizations presented are quite tentative, given the research that still has to be done.)

RICHARD A. VARBERO

The Politics of Ethnicity
Philadelphia's Italians in the 1920's

While the 1920s marked a leap forward in the political acculturation of Italian immigrants in metropolitan America, Philadelphia's important colony lagged behind comparable cities in political self-definition. Philadelphia's Italian leadership failed to attain the key posts or prominence that fellow immigrants had captured in New York or Chicago, or even in such cities as New Haven, San Francisco, and New Orleans.[1] And while anonymous Italian workers threaded their way into the ward networks, they often experienced frustration in their quest for more important political roles. Although the Philadelphia story of ethnic group political adjustment is complex, part of it can be explained by the social character of late nineteenth and early twentieth century immigration. Equally important was the role played by the special nature of Philadelphia's Republican-dominated political system in adapting Italians to urban politics. Both factors together served to make Italian political development a gradual rather than a dynamic episode in the city. In retrospect, the importance of the 1920s for Italians in Philadelphia lies more in the issues which stimulated their political participation. Much less did a pattern of electoral triumphs and magnetic group leadership emerge. The realization of Italian political aspirations lay in the future.

The account of immigrant political adjustment is by now a familiar one. The majority of the post-1880 Italian migrants to America were unskilled workers from *Mezzogiorno* provinces. Unlike those from middle class backgrounds, the laborers brought with them limited political experience, little of which was readily adaptable to the sophisticated party systems found in American cities.[2] Because their immediate concerns were economic rather than political, the peasant laborers appeared disinterested at first in the issues which informed more acculturated immigrants and native Americans, and the workers frequently surrendered their votes to machine organizations. Traditional *Mezzogiorno* cynicism toward existing power networks also frustrated attempts to interest naturalized workers in intensive political activity, especially when peasant distrust was confirmed by initial contacts with *padroni*, American ward heelers, and officialdom in the industrial cities. Sensitive to the plight of the immigrant *contadini*, and aware that collective action was essential to group advancement, the Italian intelligentsia seized every opportunity to explain and vindicate American political ideas and to goad naturalized Italo-Americans to exercise their political rights more selectively on behalf of *paesani*.[3]

Though always more skeptical and less concerned about American political activity than the Italian middle class and intelligentsia, even relative newcomers from obscure *contadini* backgrounds could respond to such news as Fiorello H. LaGuardia's election to Congress and his accession in 1919 to the presidency of New York's Board of Aldermen. LaGuardia's triumph and comparable achievements by other Italians illuminated for the transplanted peasant the contrast between the relatively static *Mezzogiorno* social order and the more dynamic American environment. Despite the recognized obstacles to meaningful political participation, interposed by the existing, and often corrupt, party machinery, and the newcomers' inexperience and gullibility, it became clear that organized political activity added a vital new dimension to the ethnic group's quest for status and recognition.

While the 1920s in general revealed considerable progress, by no means had Italo-Americans been politically quiescent prior to this time. Italians in Chicago, New Haven, Philadelphia, and elsewhere had, like their New York counterparts, begun to assert themselves in the urban political framework.[4] Chicago's Italians, for example, were both "proud and envious" when they learned of LaGuardia's success in New York, but by then Bernard Baressa had already obtained a judgeship in their own city.[5] In other cities, Italian immigrants and their children were experiencing the arduous transition from passivity to activism by increasing their claims on the existing party structures, while already successful politicians were insisting upon defining and clarifying important issues such as immigration restriction and prohibition. Other politicians began to reject token rewards and menial jobs as the customary price for voter support. Wherever immigrant colonies developed in sufficient concentrations to make organization feasible, the political aspirations of ethnic group spokesmen rose accordingly, for American politics was recognized as a viable means of individual as well as group attainment.

As a whole, the era of the nineteen twenties served as a rich spawning ground for a succession of Italian politicians and political brokers, including some unsavory figures like Chicago's Alphonse Capone.[6] But less flamboyant and respected political activists such as Ferdinand Pecora, Michael DiSalle, the controversial Vito Marcantonio, and future New York mayor Vincent Impelletieri also cut their political teeth in the period, and were but a few of those men who rose from immigrant Italian backgrounds to serve as leaders and models for ethnic group political behavior.[7] All the ethnic group spokesmen had responded to the dynamics of pluralistic group politics, and, toward the end of the decade, the "critical election" of 1928 confirmed that the time had arrived in American life when men of immigrant stock, and Catholic beliefs, could compete in a national forum or at least in a broader metropolitan framework. Even if the urban ethnic groups could not command victory in the pivotal contest of 1928, that election signified that they had nevertheless reached a new political plateau from which there would be no descent.[8]

Although Italian immigrants and their children increasingly participated in American political life, not all of the various Italian ethnic colonies in American cities were uniformly successful or productive in political terms. Philadelphia's contribution to the enlarged roster of important Italian political figures dating from the 1920s was limited, even though the group made significant advances in registration and voting behavior.[9] Philadelphia's Italians should have had more clout, for although the city was less an immigrant city than New York, Chicago, or even Detroit, it nevertheless ranked high among those which contained large numbers of foreign-born Italians and those of Italian stock.

Table 1
Italian-Born Population in Major American Cities, 1930

City Rank	Number of Immigrant Italians	Percentage of Immigrant Population	Total All Immigrants
New York	440,250	18.7	2,358,686
Chicago	73,960	8.6	859,409
Philadelphia	68,156	18.3	372,078
(Camden)*	(5,508)	(29.4)	(18,716)
Boston	36,724	15.5	233,687
Detroit	28,581	7.0	405,882
San Francisco	27,311	15.9	171,641
Cleveland	23,524	10.2	230,946
Los Angeles	12,685	5.1	247,135

* Despite the separation of the Delaware River, Philadelphia and Camden were linked by family and regional connections: the *paesani*.

SOURCE: U. S., Department of Commerce, Bureau of the Census, *Fifteenth Census of the United States, 1930: Population*, Vol. III, 248-249.

In 1930, the percentage of Philadelphia's Italian stock slightly exceeded that of Chicago and was surpassed only by that of New York. Moreover, Philadelphia's immigrant stock was contained in significantly high concentrations in the politically important South Philadelphia areas.[10]

Table 2

Percentage of Italian Stock in Major Cities, 1930

City Rank	Number of Italians	Percentage of Population
New York	1,070,355	21.0
Philadelphia	182,368	18.0
Chicago	181,861	8.4
Boston	90,819	16.3
Detroit	61,968	6.9
Cleveland	56,317	9.6

SOURCE: U. S., Bureau of the Census, *Fifteenth Census of the United States, 1930: Population*, Vol. III, 316

Despite the heavy concentration of *Mezzogiorno* Italians in selected wards in south Philadelphia, Italian political development in the city, measured in terms of group recognition and the elevation of spokesmen within party organizations was disappointingly low. In the 1930s an Italian complained that

the Italians of Philadelphia have been civic-minded (but) Italians of other parts of the country have shown considerably more activity and success than we have. . . . (Our) inability to make our voices heard in Congress is an indication of poor citizenship. The spectacle of a district predominantly Italian, being time and again represented by an Irishman, Jew, or German, may be entertaining to some, but to us should be a cause for shame. *We* are to blame.[11]

The indictment was justified. The political progress of the Italian bloc in Philadelphia seemed less dynamic than that of other important cities. *Cognoscenti* might argue, on the other hand, that Philadelphia's Italians did achieve recognition on a scale comparable to Italians in other cities, and the names of C. C. A. Baldi, A. Giuseppe and Giovanni DiSilvestro, and judges Eugene V. Alessadroni and Adrian Bonnelly may be summoned to characterize the Philadelphia contribution to ethnic group political activity. But a realistic assessment of the importance of these group spokesmen would indicate that seldom were they recognized outside the sphere of their local perimeters or beyond their connection with the Italian fraternal organizations; nor do their names have the familiar resonances of those cited earlier.[12] Moreover, in related areas, none of these

Philadelphians attained the stature of New Yorkers Edward Corsi, Leonard Covello, or Angelo Patri to symbolize the social correlative of ethnic group political power. As a stage in acculturation, however, the 1920s were important to the Italians in Philadelphia because the political experiences of the group during the period helped shape the city's ethnic politics then and in succeeding decades.

In order to grasp the essential features of Philadelphia's ethnic politics during the twenties, three elements may be isolated: (1) the single-party Republican machine dominance and control; (2) the relative lack of unitary and first-rate political leadership within the ethnic bloc; (3) the relatively gradual political adjustment of a peasant group to the political imperatives of an industrialized urban society. The limitation of space permits an elaboration of the third element only, but the first two can be summarized.

Philadelphia's reputation throughout the late nineteenth century and through the 1930s as a machine and "ring" dominated city has been well-documented elsewhere, and needs only to be briefly reaffirmed.[13] One can update Lincoln Steffens' barb about Philadelphia: the "boss rule" of the city's twentieth century Republican machine was indeed "corrupt," but not at all "contented." Boss William S. Vare, by 1922 the sole survivor of the family triumvirate which dominated the Republican party machine in the city, spared no effort to expand his political and economic power. He did this mainly by suppressing the Democratic party as a "kept minority" and systematically crushing or frustrating Republican reformers and insurgents at the polls with the ethnic bloc votes he commanded with the time-honored techniques of jobs and favors.[14] Although the hegemony of this aggressive Republican machine subsequently was damaged by Vare's rejection by the United States Senate in 1927, and the revolt of Catholic ethnic blocs in the Al Smith election, one-party dominance was not effectively destroyed until the early 1930s, when a revitalized Democratic party successfully competed in former Republican strongholds.

The effects of single-party machine dominance were pronounced and lingering, however, because the lack of party competition thwarted political choices available to groups in other cities. Lacking significant multiple-party selection in Philadelphia, the city's ethnic groups had little leverage in demanding recognition for political loyalty; nor could they threaten mass defections, given their lack of organization. When the prevailing system began to disintegrate by the late 1920s, Philadelphia ethnic groups, the Italians among them, forged ahead politically, but by no means as rapidly as those in other immigrant cities.

A second factor, and one which bore heavily upon the Italians, was the quality of its leadership. Political roles within the sub-community were shaped by a spokesman who was allied with the dominant Republican machine—the "great charismatic leader" C. C. A. Baldi.[15] By all American standards, Baldi was the immigrant upraised, an acknowledged achiever. His career traversed the ethnic community—from huckster to *padrone*, coalyard owner, immigrant banker, real estate dealer, undertaker, and owner of *L'Opinione*, Philadelphia's only Italian immigrant daily. His services to the immigrants, many of whom were located nearby in Baldi's downtown Second Ward headquarters, dovetailed with his political and social ambitions. Baldi's success, however, also rested on the alignment he had made with the established Vare machine; in fact, the immigrant boss and the American politico shared common backgrounds in Philadelphia's streets as hucksters and street cleaners, and perhaps also shared the cynicism such experiences perfected.

Like William S. Vare, and the dons of his native Abruzze, C. C. A. Baldi employed his power to realize familial aspirations; the Italian leader's sons consolidated the family's success in both politics and the professions. Ironically, however, Baldi's extensive personal achievements illuminated the Italians' marginal performance as an ethnic bloc. While Baldi's individual political and social successes rested on undeviating immigrant voter support, the Italian-Americans as a group continued to struggle for recognition and meaningful patronage. One measure of the elder Baldi's personalized style is that his political muscle failed to survive him in the Republican camp after his death in 1930, although the Italians had matured as a political bloc. Despite the rise to prominence of Italian-born Eugene V. Alessandroni as a judge in 1927, and nominally as political successor to Baldi, the Italians were left essentially directionless and faction-ridden at the old man's death. Baldi had joined the city's Republican machine and prospered by it; but he had not changed that party's local principles of organization and control to accommodate the Italians.

A third and important factor entails the nature of group adjustment to American political culture. Even a slice of ethnic group life in the early 1920s reveals significant information about the variety of issues which stimulated political acculturation. Although seemingly thwarted by the prevailing system, members of the immigrant bloc consistently sought a political identity larger than that granted to them by the regular Republicans. Since only the Baldi family held key posts within the regular structure, aspiring young Italians such as Joseph Bartilucci and Eugene Alessandroni allied themselves with the reform movements like the one headed by J. Hampton Moore, an independent Republican who ran for mayor in 1919. When Moore, a former Congressman, won a surprising but narrow primary victory and later the election, he rewarded both men, Bartilucci with the post of Chief Clerk of Municipal Court and Alessandroni with that of Assistant District Attorney.[16] Alessandroni was the first Italian so honored. Almost immediately, the two appointees were attacked for their "political activity" by the downtown leader of the Fourth Ward, State Senator Samuel W. Salus.[17] In fact, that Vare henchman recognized the dangerous precedent of anti-organization leaders among the usually reliable Italians.

Moreover, Bartilucci and Alessandroni represented the rising generation of Italian activists drawn in the main from the expanding constituency of *Mezzogiorno* immigrants. For a considerable period the recognized community spokesmen had been northern Italians whose families had preceded the great *Mezzogiorno* migrations. The northerners John Queroli (Genoese, born in Washington, D.C., 1856) and E. V. H. Nardi (Tuscan, born in Philadelphia, 1861), for example, were instrumental in establishing the politically influential fraternal societies in Philadelphia.[18] Queroli founded the *Società di Unione e Fratellanza* in 1867 and Nardi the *Italia Unità Legione Umberto* at about the same time. By 1900, however, the fraternal orders reflected changing immigration patterns; southern groups predominated. C. C. A. Baldi quickly appropriated the nominal leadership of groups such as the *Società di Mutuo Soccorso Maria Santissima della Grazia di Acqua-Villa-Cilento, Federazione Italiana di Filadelfia*, and others. Baldi's fraternal connections served his political interests in the same way as did his newspaper, *L'Opinione*.

Elsewhere, those with southern origins, such as attorneys Michael Goglia and James Todaro, as well as Bartilucci and Alessandroni, supplanted northerners like Aladino A. Autilio, one of the first Italians admitted to the Philadelphia Bar.[19] Despite differences in backgrounds, however, a common goal of all the acculturated Italian-Americans, northern and southern, was to link Italian immigrants to the American political process. The organizational programs of many of the fraternal societies were exploited for this purpose. Before mixed audiences of Italian and American dignitaries, Italian leaders emphasized Italian-American unity at the festive Columbus Day rallies held in Fairmount Park. Joseph Bartilucci underscored a typical theme:

> We Italians have contributed to the glory of the United States. Our *Mayflower* came long before the Pilgrims' *Mayflower*. We have done our part and shall continue to do so.[20]

Memorial Day exercises brought out politicians like J. Hampton Moore, who addressed an estimated 10,000 Italians at the Sons of Italy Hall at Seventh and Christian Streets. Agreeing with the Italian ambassador, Vittorio Rolando Ricci, that "Italian-American and native American all fight for the same flag . . . the same ideal of democracy," Moore urged the assemblage to "be good Italians and better Americans" by studying American traditions.[21] A representative contingent of the Italian elite, headed by C. C. A. Baldi, Frank Travescio, Joseph DiNilcestro, Dr. G. V. Ciccone, and Constantin Constantini, endorséd the theme of Italian-American unity:

> The Italian has been tested and found of the metal that quickly emerges from the "melting pot" into the moulds of good citizenship, and Ambassador Ricci's visit directs attention to the distinction of the local leaders who were his hosts, and the patriotic quality of their Americanized countrymen.[22]

The patriotic overtures were well-received in post-World War I Philadelphia, especially as the Americanization campaign increased in tempo. But the majority of Philadelphia's Italians in the 1920s were not as politically sophisticated nor as well-regarded by the external society as were Bartilucci, Alessandroni, and the elite contingent. The average Italian voter was not as concerned with "good citizenship" as had been asserted in *The Evening Bulletin*. Nor did the immigrant wards join the independent movement supporting J. Hampton Moore in his surprising primary victory, although Moore's platform attracted middle class Italians, led by the publishers of *La Libera Parola*, A. Giuseppe DiSilvestro and his brother Giovanni, a local attorney active in the Sons of Italy. The DiSilvestro brothers illustrate the Italian political dilemma. They were politically sophisticated and opposed to both Vare and Baldi, yet appreciated the obstacles to organizing the Italian voters. Their paper continued to come out strongly against the system, urging support of J. Hampton Moore for mayor, reasoning that

> Our city has had the disgrace and continues to have it, of being almost always administered by a Common Council composed for the most part of Councilmen who have tended to their private interests rather than those of the masses of citizens from whom they received the vote.[23]

But the average Italian voter was unexcited by such pleas for reform, and the workers in the downtown wards saw little reason to reject the machine, especially since it still held the patronage power, and, equally as important, the streetcleaning jobs. Even the DiSilvestros recognized that a reform executive alone could not ensure changes in the patterns of "contractor" government. Former clean government mayors like John T. Weaver and Rudolph Blankenburg had failed to eliminate bossism, although they had stressed civic purpose in their administrations. *La Libera Parola* praised the former mayors without losing touch with reality. Despite the good intentions of reformers, the city was immobilized by the Vare combine. "No one is able to doubt that our Councilmen . . . care only for the business of two or three dishonest contractors."[24] Thus, Moore's

Italian supporters were encouraged when he reasserted his campaign promises in his inaugural address. The new mayor urged support for a new city charter; the Italian community leaders responded warmly to the plea for a more responsible municipal government. Mayor Moore's intention to divorce police and firemen from political control and to end political assessments especially pleased those Italians who wished to eliminate the Republican machine's leverage. Joseph Bartilucci, the Moore supporter, organized an Italian Citizens' Committee in the heavily Italian populated Second, Third, and Fourth Wards. The committee hoped to dramatize local health and safety conditions to the new mayor, and called upon James T. Cortelyou, the Director of Public Safety, and Eugene V. Alessandroni to "expose the crimes . . . committed in the lower city to the injury of the poor people and with the acquiescence of the agents of the Public Security."[25] But the committee and campaign were led by middle class and educated Italians whose perceptions of political life varied sharply from that of the ordinary laborers who continued to support the machine.[26]

While possessing a more practical view of politics than the middle class, increasing numbers of Italian workers nevertheless responded to its attractions. Despite their subordinate, unheralded status, small groups of politically-conscious Italians made inroads into the established Republican organization. These men, and some women, worked at the elemental level of Philadelphia politics: the division (precinct). For example, by extensive campaigning in West Philadelphia's 34th Ward, the Italians were able to select six committeemen in divisions where Italians predominated. Bartolomeo Mansolino, a community pioneer and leader of the 34th Ward Italian-American Club, achieved a more notable victory. Despite heavy opposition from native Americans, Mansolino won a committeeman's post in the 18th Division of the 34th Ward, where there existed no more than six Italian voters. La Libera Parola interpreted this minor triumph as an endorsement of capable Italians by Americans. Ever sensitive to the immigration question, the editorialists exaggerated the result by further interpreting Mansolino's victory as a rejection of the restrictionist position by the American electorate.[27] Albeit scattered and trivial, such political developments in the tightly-knit peripheral communities were encouraging to Italian activists, because they disclosed increasing political interests on the part of ordinarily indifferent Italians.

However, resistance to Italian independent political development was more formidable in the heavily-populated downtown wards. Here existed the classic illustration of voter ignorance and boss control. Despite these obstacles to independency, middle class Italians proceeded to organise small groups. The Good Government League, for example, was created to "inform the Italians of their interests and to show that there exists among

American citizens, native and Italian born, the same political rights as other citizens."[28] Giovanni DiSilvestro headed the group, and included among his supporters the Reverends T. Della Cipolla and Angelo Di-Domenica, the Protestant leader, and professionals such as Dr. Andrea Lippi, Henry DiBernadino, Samuel Belsito, and Frank Bove. The group was highly enthusiastic but poorly equipped to compete in downtown politics. The League endorsed Henry DiBernadino for magistrate in the primary race of 1921. The locale was the Second Ward, the political territory commanded by the Baldi family. DiBernadino received a smattering of votes, even fewer than those received by a Negro candidate, Amos Scott, a Vare adherent. The League, speaking through DiSilvestro's *La Libera Parola*, held Carmine Baldi responsible for the result. "Do you have so little power," the paper taunted, "that you boycotted your co-national in favor of a Negro?"[29] The unfavorable outcome for independents and the bitter exchanges were reminders of the Vare power to inflict overwhelming defeat at the polls. Italian Democrats fared no better than Independents. In the mayoralty election of 1923 the democratic candidate for City Council from the First District, Richard Del Bello, ran an ignominious last of six candidates in the Italian wards.[30]

Most of the recent immigrants, and the Italian *manovali*, or day-laborers, were unmoved by middle class appeals. Long-ingrained political attitudes —the cultural factor—were not easily changed. A suggestion of the cultural imperatives governing Italian voters was the attempt to register Italian women. Few Italian women could be induced to register in the early 1920s, even by established neighborhood Italian residents. For example, two educated and politically active women, Concetta Lippi and Anna Russo, played "suffragette" roles, hoping to enlist other Italian women in the cause.[31] The results were discouraging. One registrar, Fiorentino Donato, registered four women in one division of the Third Ward; all were Americans. No women appeared at all at another polling place in the Second Ward; however, in that ward's 21st Division seven women did register—six Italians and one Jewess—Republican.[32]

A group of Italian registrars organized to help the Italian women shed their old-country ideas. The responses of the women were similar: "*É mio marito chi deve votare e non io*" ("It is my husband who must vote and not I."[33] Most Italian males opposed the female vote. Ernest Ayella, a Second Ward registrar, was typical: "Women should cook, wash, and have children," he maintained. Ayella registered four women, two Italians and two Negroes, and observed that none was married. "What good are they?" he inquired.[34] Ingrained cultural tradition thus militated against the *professionisti*'s attempts to encourage the Italians to use their voting rights more selectively and to expand the franchise to Italian women.

In general, however, increasing numbers of Italo-Americans were expressing political interests and investing time in office-seeking. Many ran for the prestigious, if tainted, office of magistrate.[35] Italian voters were compelled to be more selective, also, in choosing between the warring factions of the Vare machine. For example, when magistrate Francis X. O'Connor contested Vare's leadership in the 1925 election, Italians like Charles DeTolla joined with the insurgent O'Connor.[36] In an effort to prevent a Vare "steamroller in the 39th Ward, DeTolla was arrested six times for protesting illegal voter assistance by Vare men. Another O'Connor supporter, Severio Ruggieri, was refused permission to register and his naturalization papers were forcibly taken from him.[37] The Vare power was pervasive. When corner loungers in South Philadelphia were arrested and brought before Vare appointee Joseph M. Perri, the magistrate promptly established their political affiliations. Unlucky O'Connor supporters were jailed; the Vare men were released. Such was the nature of the politics in which immigrants were schooled.[38]

Not all political activity was confined to vote-getting. The connection of political group power and the amenities of urban life was not hard to discover. Italian groups mustered support for increased recreational space in the crowded quarters of Little Italy. Forty-two Italian societies organized jointly as the Columbus Day Committee, and, headed by John M. Queroli and Giuseppe Modestino, petitioned City Council for the conversion of a cemetery for recreational purposes in an area "where the population is almost entirely of foreign extraction and where need and poverty prevail on all sides."[39] A small cinder-covered playground was subsequently erected on the cemetery lot. Pressures were also exerted to protect the Italian (and Jewish) curbstone merchants from restrictive legislation.[40] A proposal was introduced in City Council to restrict "licensing" of such merchants to American citizens. If enacted, this restriction would have created havoc in the open markets of South Ninth Street, where most Italians shopped, and for the Italian hucksters of the city. In these instances, the power of the Vare organization to oppose and defeat such measures on behalf of Italian pressure groups was tangible evidence of the Republican machine's good intentions to the Italian voters.

Some of the issues that awakened Italian voter interest tied the ethnic bloc securely to the Republican party. In 1920, for example, the question before the voters concerned the policies of Woodrow Wilson, the Versailles Treaty, and Fiume. Italian sentiment was vigorously anti-Wilson.[41] *La Libera Parola* announced to its readers that "Your duty is clear, to reject Wilson and support Warren Harding."[42] There was no significant dissent from this theme in Republican Philadelphia. The national Republican ticket was strongly supported by the Italians in 1920, and again in 1924 for Calvin Coolidge.

The question of immigration restriction, however, was more troublesome and more enduring to the Republicans in terms of ethnic political alignment. Immigration was an issue that transcended local concerns and persistently agitated Italians of all educational and social levels. Consequently, voter interest focused on the attitude of politicians toward immigration. Many Italians had a personal stake in the outcome of the legislative debates on restriction. Spokesmen became increasingly defensive. For example, in 1920 many Italians believed that the proposed literacy tests were aimed directly at the illiterate workers. Yet, as *La Libera Parola* pointed out, the tests would not exclude the generally literate anarchists and Bolshevists; rather, it would restrict the "honest illiterate worker" instead.[43] The conclusion was clear, according to the weekly: The United States must "reform the laws to freely admit the poor, honest worker of every nation."[44] On the other hand, the paper was less sympathetic to the "educated Hebrews that [*sic*] come to America to spread terror and to make Bolshevist propaganda. . . ."[45] Made self-conscious by the national debates, the Italians were enjoined to "do your duty . . . show to our detractors the glories and the splendor of our past that still exist in the atavistic psyche of our race."[46] The Italian leadership was able to suppress its factional differences to lobby together before important legislative groups on the question of hostile immigration laws.

One group of concerned Philadelphia Italians, the American Committee Against Racial Discrimination, journeyed to Washington in 1924 to call on Pennsylvania Senators George Wharton Pepper and the ardent pro-restrictionist David A. Reed. Visits were also paid to Congressmen Ransley and Welsh, and the leader William S. Vare. Italian spokesmen included the Independents Joseph Bartilucci and Dr. Leopold Vaccaro, as well as their political antagonist, C. C. A. Baldi. Other group members were the (then) Independent Republican Eugene V. Alessandroni, Dr. Joseph Pasceri, and Constantin Constantini.[47] The diverse makeup of the Committee confirmed that there was Italian unity on the immigration issue. Several days later, at the Philadelphia Academy of Music, the Italians enthusiastically introduced New York Representative Fiorello H. LaGuardia. Before an assemblage which included William S. Vare and State Senator Samuel W. Salus, LaGuardia exclaimed that it was no secret that the Johnson Bill was "aimed against the Italians and Jews."[48] Rallying the audience, LaGuardia enjoined them to "fight together . . . and compare the exemption of Italians versus those of English extraction." Alessandroni and Vare made similar pleas; the Assistant District Attorney attacked the "bigotry" and "intolerance" implicit in the bill, while Vare judiciously noted that "our great national products [sic] of road building, construction of homes and public buildings, subways and railroad lines depend on the immigrant."[49] On this issue Vare stuck his neck out for the Italians. He was predictably attacked by the Patriotic Order Sons of America for representing "foreign votes" and for selling out "his fellow brethren" in a "cheap political way."[50] But Vare had little choice. No Philadelphia politician who desired the Italian vote could afford to ignore the immigration question. It was the theme which unified the diverse factions of the Italian political community.

Italian professionals hammered back stridently when native Americans spoke of the harmful consequences of unrestricted immigration. When, after evaluating Grand Jury indictments, Criminal Court Judge Edwin O. Lewis suggested raising barriers against both Negroes and those "from the belts of least education in European countries," so that Philadelphia would remain a "fit place to live," Assistant United States Attorney Claude Lanciano quickly responded to what he believed to be a slap at the Italians.[51] Men like Judge Lewis, Lanciano asserted, "know nothing of the Italians or other nationalities of which they speak." The only time Judge Lewis or men like him "ever have any contact with the culture of Italy is when they go to an Italian restaurant. . . ."[52] Lanciano understated the case when he observed that Italians resented the "one-sided views of American gentlemen." Italian resentment on the immigration issue was an integral component of the Al Smith revolution in 1928.

Some issues had ostensibly little bearing on American political alignments, but were necessarily important in articulating Italian political responses. One such issue was the emergence of the Fascists in Italy. Fascism exacerbated existing Italo-American community tensions; it also added another element to the immigrants' political adjustment. Most immigrant Italians looked with pride upon Mussolini's accomplishments, especially as Il Duce received wide and often favorable press coverage in the United States. But Mussolini's political and ideological opponents in Philadelphia responded bitterly and often violently against his sympathizers. The local Italian leadership strongly and publicly supported the dictator and certain figures became the targets of bombings. In April, 1923, C. C. A. Baldi's home was bombed; in May, the business establishment of M. Maggio was similarly attacked. The police attributed the latter bombing to "Fascist agitation in the neighborhood," and a link was established with the Baldi episode.[53] Two Italians were subsequently arrested. Later, when the Italian and Spanish consulates were bombed, the Italian consul, Luigi Siletti, accused Italian anarchists and anti-Fascists. The real targets, he claimed, were the Italian Bank, located in the same building as the consulate in South Philadelphia, and the reputedly Fascist sympathizers C. C. A. Baldi and John DiSilvestro. The latter had warned of "Bolsheviks insiduously at work." When DiSilvestro's home was bombed in 1927, the anti-Fascists were blamed; DiSilvestro, an attorney, announced: "I am a close personal friend and admirer of Benito Mussolini, *Il Duce*. There are many people who do not like Mussolini."[54] DiSilvestro pointed out that politics was at the root of the whole affair, and he launched a diatribe at the anti-Fascist historian Gaetano Salvemini, who was then publicizing his views.

Fascist ideologues exploited sensitive situations, local issues which were bound to capture attention. Baldi Aquilano, writing in *La Libera Parola*, cautioned Italian union members in the garment trades that impending restrictionist legislation was justifiably aimed at them.

The truth is that the Italian unions to which our co-nationals belong in good faith are controlled by the most subversive rabble that tries to transform the locals into revolutionary and anti-Italian nests. Anarchists and communists in these organizations are insinuating a slow poison against Italy and its government.[55]

Aquilano went on to point out that the United States government felt legitimately threatened by revolutionaries of Jewish and Italian origins. Patently, this was a dual-sided brief, appealing to both the Fascist sympathizers and the American anti-labor union sentiment prevalent in Philadelphia. The significance of such appeals lay in the attempt by propagandists to equate Fascist doctrine with Americanism. Most of the immigrant workers, however, were not attuned to the doctrinal subtleties of ideology.

It is clear that Fascism abetted the nationality consciousness of Italo-Americans; by doing so it helped to shore up the loosely-constructed membership of the provincial factions, especially among the leadership and intelligentsia. By creating a nationalist identity, the potency of group voting was increased. But it must also be kept in mind that Fascism was an emotional, not an ideological, theme for the bloc vote in the 1920s.[56]

Through a variety of avenues, local and national, the Italian voter became aware of the political complexity of American society. The immigrant and local press, the activity of reformers, ward heelers, and special pleaders, combined to stimulate political interest in the voter. As the Italian immigrant, and later his children, became more sensitive to the potency of issues, he regarded his ballot, and the role it opened to him, more carefully. Conversely, the established political forces had to respond to increasing voter sophistication by broadening the traditional patterns of jobs and offices. But throughout the 1920s the Italian immigrants and their children were still acquiring and honing the skills associated with the democratic process. Because these skills were as yet unperfected, and inspirational Italian leadership had failed to emerge to clarify issues and assert the true voting strength of the group, the Italians delayed their entry as a potent force in the mainstream of Philadelphia political life.

NOTES

* This essay is drawn in part from my doctoral dissertation, "Urbanization and Assimilation: A Study of Philadelphia's Italians, 1918-1932" (Temple University, 1974).

1. Andrew F. Rolle, *The American Italians, Their History and Culture* (Belmont, Cal.: Wadsworth Publishing Company, 1972), pp. 85-90; Theodore J. Lowi, *At the Pleasure of the Mayor: Patronage and Power in New York City, 1898-1958* (New York: The Free Press of Glencoe, 1964), *passim.* Varied accounts of Italian political development can be found in Joseph Lopreato, *Italian Americans* (New York: Random House, 1970), pp. 113-117. Lopreato places the "coming of age in the 1930s," but the intensive political acculturation of the varied urban communities seems to have occurred in the 1920s. Luciano J. Iorizzo and Salvatore Mondello, *The Italian Americans* (New York: Twayne, 1971); Humbert S. Nelli, *The Italians in Chicago 1880-1930: A Study in Ethnic Mobility* (New York: Oxford University Press, 1970), pp. 88-112; John M. Allswang, *A House for All Peoples: Ethnic Politics in Chicago 1890-1936* (Lexington: University Press of Kentucky, 1971); Lawrence Frank Pisani, *The Italian in America* (New York: Exposition Press, 1957); Robert Dahl, *Who Governs? Democracy and Power in an American City* (New Haven: Yale University Press, 1961).

2. Joseph Lopreato, *Peasants No More: Social Class and Social Change in an Underdeveloped Society* (Scranton: Chandler Press, 1967), pp. 1-28.

3. Alexander DeConde, *Half Bitter, Half Sweet: An Excursion into Italian-American History* (New York: Scribner, 1971), pp. 172-173.

4. Nelli, *The Italians*, pp. 88-112; Dahl, *Who Govern?*, pp. 42-43; Hugo V. Maiale, *The Italian Vote in Philadelphia from 1928 to 1946* (Philadelphia: College Offset Press, 1950), pp. 146-152.

5. Nelli, *The Italians*, p. 120.

6. *Ibid.*, p. 212.

7. DeConde, *Half Bitter, Half Sweet*, p. 338; Rolle, *The American Italians*, pp. 88-89.

8. Samuel Lubell, *The Future of American Politics* (New York: Anchor Press, 1952); V. O. Key, Jr., "A Theory of Critical Elections," *Journal of Politics*, 17 (Feb., 1955), 3-19; Allswang, *A House for All Peoples*; John L. Shover, "The Emergence of a Two-Party System in Republican Philadelphia, 1924-1936," *Journal of American History*, LX (Mar., 1974), 985-1002.

9. Note Rolle's listing of Anthony Caminetti, Robert S. Maestri, Angelo Rossi, John Pastore, and Albert Rosselini as representatives of political achievement; *The American Italians*, pp. 85-90.

10. In the downtown Wards 1, 2, 3, 4, 26, 36, 39, 48 were over seventy per cent of the city's Italians.
11. *Romanica*, Vol. I (Dec., 1936), p. 10.
12. Pisani mentions Judge Eugene V. Alessandroni and Americo V. Cortese, but in connection with their Sons of Italy activity; *The American Italians*, p. 127.
13. Lincoln Steffens, *The Shame of the Cities* (New York, 1904). John T. Salter, *Boss Rule: Portraits in City Politics* (New York: McGraw-Hill, 1955), pp. 15-71, 75-86, and "The End of Vare," *Political Science Quarterly*, 50 (June, 1935), 214-235; Clinton Rogers Woodruff, "Progress in Philadelphia," *American Journal of Sociology* (1920), 323-324.
14. Shover, "The Emergence of a Two-Party System"; Irwin F. Greenberg, "Philadelphia Democrats Get a New Deal: The Election of 1933," *Pennsylvania Magazine of History and Biography* (April, 1973), 210-232.
15. This characterization was provided by Arturo Cortese, a former employee of Baldi's newspaper, *L'Opinione*. The following sketch is drawn from Cortese's recollections, the *Philadelphia Inquirer*, Dec. 29, 1930; *Public Ledger*, Dec. 30, 1930; *La Ragione*, July 24, 1917; *La Libera Parola*, June 29, 1918, Jan. 3, 1931. Not all interviewees were as favorably disposed to Baldi as Cortese.
16. *Philadelphia Inquirer*, May 19, 1920; *The Evening Bulletin*, May 3, 1966.
17. *The Evening Bulletin*, Jan. 14, 1920.
18. *Ibid.*, Aug. 31, 1932; *La Libera Parola*, Sept. 3, 1932; Ernest L. Biagi, *The Italians of Philadelphia* (New York: Carlton Press, 1967), pp. 206-210.
19. *La Libera Parola*, Oct. 8, 1932; *The Evening Bulletin*, July 23, 1920. Alessadroni had emigrated as a boy from Abruzzi, Todaro from Messina, Sicily.
20. *The Evening Bulletin*, Oct. 12, 1920.
21. *Ibid.*, May 30, 1921.
22. *Ibid.*, May 31, 1921.
23. *La Libera Parola*, Aug. 14, 1921.
24. *Ibid.*
25. *Ibid.*, Jan. 18, 1920.
26. See Nelli's observation in *The Italians in Chicago* that the middle class "seemed unable to recognize or accept the realities of core area and group politics," p. 91.
27. *La Libera Parola*, May 22, 1921; May 10, 1924.
28. *Ibid.*, Aug. 7, 1921.
29. *Ibid.*, Oct. 1, 1921.
30. *The Evening Bulletin*, Nov. 7, 1923.
31. Personal interview, Concetta Lippi and family; and Anna Russo, July 12, 1972.
32. *The Evening Bulletin*, Sept. 3, 1920.
33. *Ibid.*
34. *Ibid.*
35. On the Philadelphia judicial system see D. H. Kurtzman, *Methods of Controlling Votes in Philadelphia* (Philadelphia: University of Pennsylvania Press, 1935), pp. 83-114. An apt description of the system was provided by former District Attorney Charles Fox: The Magistrate Courts were "centers of political activity." Candidates were picked for political purposes

and the minor judiciary was placed in the hands of men of "tender mercies who were also plumbers, undertakers, salesmen or professional politicians . . . unintelligent and in some cases corrupt." *The Evening Bulletin*, Jan. 21, 1928.

36. *Ibid.*, Sept. 15, 1925.
37. *Ibid.*, Sept. 5, 1925.
38. *Ibid.*, Sept. 15, 1925.
39. *Journal of City Council* (Philadelphia, 1922), Vol. II, p. 205.
40. *The Evening Bulletin*, Jan. 17, 1925.
41. Lewis Gerson, *The Hyphenate in Recent American Politics and Diplomacy* (Lawrence, Kansas, n.p., 1964), esp. foreword. Wesley M. Bagley, *The Road to Normalcy* (Baltimore: Johns Hopkins Press, 1962), p. 155; Allswang, *A House for All Peoples*, pp. 116-117.
42. *La Libera Parola*, Oct. 31, 1920.
43. *Ibid.*, May 2, 1920.
44. *Ibid.*
45. *Ibid.*, June 7, 1924.
46. *Ibid.*
47. *The Evening Bulletin*, Feb. 21, 1924.
48. *Ibid.*, Feb. 25, 1924.
49. *Ibid.*
50. *Ibid.*, April 29, 1924.
51. *Ibid.*, Nov. 5, 1927.
52. *Ibid.*
53. *Ibid.*, May 10, 1923; Nov. 24, 26, 1923.
54. *Ibid.*, Mar. 9, 1927. For an account of the admiration of the DiSilvestro family and some Americans for Mussolini see *ibid.*, Oct. 26, 1927. Reverend Edward J. Lyng, pastor of St. Rita's Church, delivered the eulogy for Giuseppe DiSilvestro, and in it praised Mussolini for "doing more than any other individual to stimulate respect for Italy. . . . He sees the value of religion for Italy." Also see *La Libera Parola*, Nov. 5, 1927, which relates how DiSilvestro "strenuously supported Fascism" as a "tangible expression of his philosophical system." Giovanni DiSilvestro's pro-Fascist views got him into deep trouble with the Sons of Italy when he aligned the order with the Italian League (*Lega Italiana*). Other Italian-Americans immediately saw the danger of alignment with an exclusively nationalist group oriented toward Fascism, and protested. Anti-Fascists attacked the organization for political reasons. Ultimately the pact died from inaction, but DiSilvestro was haunted throughout his career by his opponents. Ernest L. Biagi, *The Purple Aster: A History of the Sons of Italy*.
55. *La Libera Parola*, May 19, 1924.
56. This assertion is supported by discussion with Italians from all walks of life. Ernest L. Biagi, the historian of the Sons of Italy, writes: "We have sustained the thesis that the members of the Order Sons of Italy have never been fascists in the sense that they thoroughly understood the philosophy and theories of fascism"; *The Purple Aster*, p. 28. Cav. Biagi reaffirmed this thesis in many hours of discussion on Philadelphia's Italians. In one session, Galleano Nelli, a form militant union leader and radical socialist, participated; he endorsed Biagi's interpretation. Nelli's unhappy conclusion was that many of the immigrants did not appreciate socialism,

either. . . . Also see John P. Diggins, "Flirtation with Fascism: American Pragmatic Liberals and Mussolini's Italy," *American Historical Review*, LXXI (Jan., 1966), 487-506; Alan Cassells, "Fascism for Export: Italy and the United States in the Twenties," *ibid.*, LXIX (Apr., 1964), 707-712; Pellegrino Nazzaro, "The Manifesto of the North American Anti-Fascist Alliance," *Labor History*, 13 (Summer 1972), 418-427.

JOSEPH VELIKONJA

The Identity and Functional Networks of the Italian Immigrant

The one century of intensive Italian migration provided a major demographic, cultural and social contribution to the growth and prosperity of the United States. The statistical identity of millions of immigrants of Italian origin, normally based on the place of birth, does not take into account those immigrants of Italian origin, who came from territories which at the time of the surveys were not under the Italian control. For the pre-1918 period this includes the Italians from Trentino, Venezia Giulia and Istria, Dalmatia, and for the post-1945 period the Italians from Dodecanese and from former Italian possessions in Africa. Unfortunately the American statistics permit only occasional glimpses of the numerical consistency of these people.

The American statistics furthermore fail to provide any reliable information about the repeated arrivals of immigrants, and do not offer adequate information about the departing emigrants.

The problem remains, how to identify the immigrants, how to count those identified, and what contributes either to the retention of their "italianità" or what accounts to its subsidence.

The estimates of demographic consistency, the enumeration of the totality of biological descendents do not reveal the personal identification of counted individuals. It seems more appropriate to estimate the number of those who in some way identify themselves as Italians in the United States and discount the numerous descendents of immigrants who through time assumed and accepted the non-Italian identity. The 1970 Census provides a glimpse to this phenomenon. Of the 4,144,315 permanent residents in the United States with the Italian mother tongue, 1,025,994 were foreign born (first generation), 2,512,696 American born with foreign born parents (second generation), and 605,625 American born from American born parents (third or fourth generation). These figures indicate that the language is retained beyond the second generation, and at the same time

719,550 second generation Italians did not declare Italian as their mother tongue.

Only one half percent of the Italian speaking is classified as rural-farm population. All the others are either concentrated in central cities, in urban fringes or on neighboring rural non-farm areas. The urban preference of the Italians is greater that it is for the United States population as a whole: 73% of the Americans live in urban areas, while the percentage for the Italian-Americans is over 92 percent.

On this general scale only general conclusions can be formulated. The concentration in urban centers combined with the numerical size of the Italian communities accounts in part for the persistence of the Italian character. The immigrants aggregate in selected neighborhoods; the retention of these clusters was often considered essential for the survival of cultural and ethnic groups. The technological modernization, however, reduced the imperative of spatial proximity and enabled the creation of "communities without propinquity's."

The presence of the Italian immigrant in the United States and Canada is substantially similar to the existence of other socio-cultural groups in the complex political and social environment of an advanced societal system. Even after decades of life and work in the new country, the identity of the Italian individuals and groups is still noticeable. The long process of merger with the host society is slow to yield a complete absorption and with it a disappearance of any trace of the Italian character of individuals or groups, or evidences of material manifestation of their former existence.

The search for identity of the Italian immigrant focuses on two principal avenues: the identity within the society and the identity in the area. Although often disassociated, the two views represent two facets of one cohesive personal or collective image. Both aspects are subjected to the process of transformation, though the rate of change is not the same for both: the spatial identity is changed immediately with the arrival of immigrant into a new area. The new area becomes his new home. While the immigrant is physically present at a new location, his association with the "old country" and the "old home" is not completely replaced by new ties. The consequence is the dichotomy between the physical existence at one location, and psychological linkage with the "old places." The slow replacement process gradually reduces the number and intensity of linkages with the "past" and substitutes them with the growth of new active locational associations. Normally the substitution process is not done in a planned and consistent manner; it operates as a response to new needs and to new spatial demands. A significant factor in these processes is the clustering of the people of the same regional or even local origin. If the immigrant group is clustered and also if the group is sufficiently large to provide an adequate chance for communication and exchange, the link with the new location is easily established and the "new home" in a short period replaces the "old ties."

The Italian system is culturally defined: it exists in Italy and in those territories outside Italy where the concentration of the Italians is sufficiently large to enable inter-group communication: clusters of the Italians in France and West Germany, groups of immigrants in Great Britain, and in overseas countries: Australia, Canada, United States, and in Latin America. These clusters, spatially separated from the main core are nevertheless active portions of the "national body" as long as they retain their functional linkages which enable the exchange flows. The existence, therefore, of the Italian clusters in Western Europe, in North and South America, in Australia, is a demonstration of a territorially dispersed, operationally inter-linked cultural system, which is identified by its operational activity rather than by the territorial contiguity.

The Italian immigrant is an element in the total system of the Italian existence in the world: physically separated from the contiguous territory of modern Italy, he remains an active component of the Italian world as long as he retains either active or latent links with the core of the Italian socio-cultural world. The links enable functional flows to operate between the territorially discrete and separated places and people, where the distance can be bridged by modern communication media.

The transition from the home rural setting to the new country's urban existence combines two processes, which are seldom analyzed separately or even identified as distinct: the process of rural-urban transition and the process of migrant's adjustment. The first process of rural-urban transition exists in a homogeneous cultural area, within similar cultural, social, and political systems. The other exists as a process of adjustment from the socio-economic system in one cultural and political area to a new system in a different cultural and political area. The peasant from Chiociaria in Central Italy who migrates to Rome is an example of the first (Gross, 1973); the Italian industrial worker from Torino who moves to Detroit is an example of the other. For most migrants from Italy, however, both processes of transformation are combined since they depart from rural and small town environment in Italy to the urban centers in the United States.

In our analysis, the process of changing identification and the modification of operating network is reviewed in the light of this total transformation process. It has been stated that "urbanization implies the transition from an old to a newer way of life. Underlying the changes . . . is a radical transformation of the methods of organizing work and everyday life. This transformation has been described as a transition from a way of life with vertical to one of horizontal linkages." (Törnquist, 1970:16).

The Italians brought along the socio-cultural traits of their home region. They cannot retain them unaltered. The new and modified physical environment, the social norms and legal regulations, the economic system in operation, provides an unavoidable frame for their new existence. The adjustment process starts immediately. It is neither good or bad, it is an aspect of the irreversible process, in which the time is the most significant varying criterion: how long it takes to substitute the original components of the cultural complex with new ones, step-wise addition first of new elements, then substitution, and progressive abandonment of previously held properties.

The cultural elements, part of the total complex of the individual or group make-up, only in part stay on the way to economic, social and political integration. It is feasible, and the research proves it, to have multi-cultural functional relationships: one language and culture at home, another outside of the home. The comprehensive studies of Joshua Fishman (1972) revealed the existence and the persistence of the dichotomy in bi-lingualism.

The geographical component of the system is the identification of the immigrant groups with specific locality, namely street, neighborhood, parish, town, not, in general, with the larger community in which they are economically integrated or administratively incorporated. The population aggregate of cohabiting families identifies itself not only by the ethnic ties, but even more by the territorial identity, which in its actual or assumed significance becomes part of the group iconography, not measurable directly by the share numbers of the group but rather indirectly evident in the defensive attitude for the preservation of their entity in the original place.

The spatial activity pattern is generated by social interaction. The common language is the medium used in this interaction process. The aspirations of the participant can be met by the use of the langauge in his activities. The immigrant and the aggregate of immigrants develop a network of preferred places, interaction spaces, safe and dangerous locales, frequented and avoided paths (Buttimer, 1972:286). "Individuals and groups feel their way through a city in activity space orbits with the nature and extent of circulation patterns generating an influencing image and establishing affective relationships with particular places, routes, and nodes" (Buttimer, 1972:286).

The economic integration and social adjustment of immigrant groups often obscures the existence and preservation of the mosaic-type "national character" of the American immigrant society, seldom evident distinctly, but nevertheless existing. The immigrants are not atomistic elements to be incorporated into society as untied entities, but rather distinct identifiable pieces of functional systems which interpenetrate other functional ties, although they escape the coverage of the census takers or interviewers due to their unchanneled and unexpected form. The Italians, therefore, with the disappearance of their particular characteristics, are not melted into the American or Canadian society as such; instead, they retain modified aspects, distinct from the surrounding social and cultural environment for some generations.

Each individual is a carrier of the social, cultural, economic network of which he is the center. For his survival, an isolated individual has to adjust totally his network linkages to the host environment, his links with the home society and culture are retained for the time being as remnants of the past experiences. For contemporary functional linkages he depends on the alien host environment. If he likes it or not, he is forced to integrate functionally. A group of immigrants, however, even if only a family, does not need to make such a drastic change: internal links could remain almost unaltered, while the external links are being modified. The level of satisfaction which the individual member of the family achieves depends on the balance between the internal links within the family and the newly established external links of the home which substitutes the network of his region. It is often evident, that the immigrant family retreats more into this closed circle of the family, although the forced and compulsory education of children does not permit the total isolation. The children are more prone to develop their new contacts and establish an increasingly ramified communication network; in their case the establishment of new links is not painful substitution of precedents from the home country. As the children grow and expand their horizons they expand them within the new world.

The sociological analysis of the Italian immigrants in the United States have referred to the Italians as the "urban villagers" (Gans, 1962). In fact, it is not the "village" aspect which is the most relevant, but the set of linkages which are retained. If we consider the set as being part of the village existence, then it could be properly labeled as an "urban village." On the other hand, the essence is the preservation of a segment of linkages which enables the individual to function in his dual role: as a member of the in-group in his family and his closed community, and concurrently as a member of the socio-economic complex of his surrounding, more anonymous, alienated, and atomized. The conflict exists primarily if the external pressure tends to disrupt the inter-group linkages without a clear benefit.

The survival of the Italian communities is a response to two sets of motives which affect the migration processes in general: the search for benefits and avoidance of stress (Wolpert, 1965, 1966; Golant, 1971). The clustering and segregation guarantees substantial benefits to the community participants. Although most of these benefits cannot be measured in economic terms, they nevertheless provide subjective gratification of indispensable value. At the same time, the clustering of an immigrant community at any location triggers the mechanism of protection. The affective relationship with particular places, neighborhood, routes and centers (Buttimer, 1972) stimulates the symbolic significance of the territorial space and supports its permanence even at an economic cost. The process is documented for urban communities (Gans, 1962) as well as for rural villages of the Italian immigrants (Velikonja, 1972).

The avoidance of stress (Wolpert, 1966) stimulates the beginning of migration flows. The process, however, continues also at the new location: the aggregation of Italian immigrants in close proximity in urban neighborhoods reduces the stress of personal and aggregate inadequacy in the host environment. The communication system functions with the use of the Italian language; the alien habits and customs are accepted and not despised. The stress to conform to the host society, particularly to the unknown norms of such a society, is therefore avoided. The necessity in a long run becomes a virtue: the isolation and separation in the early stage a necessity, becomes a symbol of exaggerated dimensions at the time when it is not functionally essential. The transformation and transition from necessity to a symbol is gradual and can last for generations. The clearest evidence is the retention of the Italian language in the third or fourth generation in areas where the use of language is limited to the family and where all the external communications are done with the use of English. The territorial identification process is greatly assisted by the social group identity, where smaller effort is placed on spatial contiguity and closeness of residential locations, and greater on a-spatial intergroup relations. Everybody needs numerous ties for his survival. The complete isolation and alienation is only theoretically possible. The tying together of individuals and groups is, therefore, a matter of degree rather than of dichotomy: the extremes of complete isolation, and the extreme of full integration do not appear in the empirical reality.

The clustering of the emigrants is triggered by the trend to secure an adequate level of satisfaction with communications and contacts with other people, by either sharing the means of interaction, especially the language, or by sharing the content of communication, regardless of the language used. The distinction between the two sets of aspects even when they exist and change concurrently, enables nevertheless to discern and separate the more easily observable aspect of language maintenance or decline and the substitution process of the Italian cultural components with those of the new society. It is, therefore, feasible to have immigrants who retain their language competence while achieving substantive socio-cultural assimilation of the non-Italian content of the host society, or on the other hand the immigrants, who retain the cultural content while losing their language ability. The language in this sense serves as the means rather than as the content character of the Italian existence.

The bilingualism is, therefore, an evidence of needs for functional linkages with two communication systems; both can serve the same functional needs, but more likely they are functionally distinct and separated: one language and communication system at home, the other outside home (Alvar, 1972; Fishman, 1972). Very seldom do both systems operate as interchangeable, where either one could serve the same purpose. The immigrant-newcomer carries with him the potentially integrated communication system of language, signs, gestures, and is willing to utilize it in the new environment if given the chance. The alien symbols of the new society are not being recognized. The slow process of symbol recognition, the satisfaction of learning, recognizing, and then using these previously unknown symbols of communication; this process expands, and slowly substitutes either partially or completely the earlier system. For an immigrant the substitution is partial and is functionally separated: the outside world forces him to adopt new symbols in order to communicate, to break away from the initial isolation. This process is not restricted to foreign immigrants; it is a normal process of migrant's adjustment to a new location. The principal difference is that the different idioms used by a foreign immigrant make the process more evident.

The creation of a new network is a painful process. First the realization that the potential network brought along is either useless or of limited value, then the gradual, slow, induced process of substitution. The acceptance of functional inadequacy of previously cherished networks and symbols is more difficult than the adoption of new linkages. At least for a time being the dual system of networks exists: the former one, and the newly developing one. The relative significance of them changes through time and is affected by the individual and group characteristics. The principal difference is the rate of substitution and the time lag in survival of the former network.

The size of the community is relevant to the preservation of the group and the individual's identity. Not the size alone, but the size in relation to self-sufficiency and degree of satisfaction achieved within the group. Too large an aggregation could be disfunctional for the face-to-face relationship links and lead to fractioning. The experience of rural village communities of the Italians numbering between 200 and 250 people provides an indication of the size demand. Larger groups separated and departed, smaller groups could not survive alone. The agriculture-rural entity, therefore, has the optimal size level at which the volume of external contacts is the minimum and therefore the exposure and demand for external links, which lead toward modification of group identity, is minimized (Velikonja, 1972).

The external linkages are determined functionally; they are, in part, substitutes for previous ethnically labeled contacts, in part new ethnically neutral links. It is, therefore, feasible to have the economic ties (anonymous and ethnically neutral) which do not interfere with the internal ethnically colored links. The coordination of this duality is present in numerous community related settlements in the United States. The loss of ethnic identity begins with the substitutions of ethnically related contacts with new ones: the schools for children, the church service done in other languages, the radio and television. The language is the essential vehicle of ethnic communication, it gives the color and label to existing transformation processes.

The immigrant utilizes different, functionally defined, though separate networks. He coordinates them and integrates them, though when observed from the outside they are frequently perceived as being in conflict.

The economic integration proceeds at a fast rate. Although the Italian immigrant retains some culturally colored preferences in employment—some jobs are more attractive than the others regardless of pay—they are nevertheless soon integrated into the economic system of the host society. A substantive evidence of this is revealed in the comparative studies of Italian immigrants who settled in Montreal (Boissevain, 1970) as compared to those who came to New York (Glazer-Moynihan, 1963); although originating from the same regions in Italy, they acquire different economic behavior with equal ease without major difficulties. The size of the Italian neighborhood and the variety of community services affects the degree by which they depart from the "expected behavior" of non-Italian urbanite.

The economic network system is not substantially different from the rest of the population. It has, however, often smaller spatial extent, with greater stress to find satisfaction within the neighborhood. The interaction and exchange is greatly facilitated by the use of the Italian, especially in the earlier stages of immigrant's adjustment. The cushion of the familiar, be it the language or the kind of service, the availability of merchandise or the association with friends, favors more intense short distance links; as the time runs on the extension and ramification of the network connections penetrates further and further, and by consequence the density and intensity of network linkages subsides. The relocation, the migration is considered as such, for a time being retains an active link with the home environment of the native area, and expands only a short distance from the place of landing into the surrounding. In the later stage, the link with the "home country or place" is weakened and the loss is compensated by the extended network in the new area of existence.

The cultural and social networks and their modifications operate differently. The migration is a relocation of an aggregate, most frequently of a family. The immigrant can retain a great deal of his close ties with the members of his family and old friends, the communication flow is not only actively retained, it also provides a cushion against the "alien outside world" and is often more intensified. The newcomer, if he is with his family, tends to cultivate the inter-family relationships, and tends to strengthen the inter-family ties with people who share similar cultural and social aspirations and goals. Spatially, the network is highly concentrated in the immediate area of existence, linked with connections with similar highly concentrated networks of other families with similar cultural preferences, normally same language and traditions. The language as an index of this network existence, encourages the bi-lingualism: the Italian is used at home and with friends, English is used with the outside world. The fluency in English is related to the need to acquire it: if for economic reasons of employment, economic interaction, the acquisition of English is not essential, the mastery remains weak and rudimentary. In this light there is a direct correlation between the ability to use the Italian as the language of communication and the need to master it in order to derive social, cultural and economic satisfactions.

Language in this sense is a communication medium and reflects the need. As an element of cultural identity, it is not essential: the values which could be defined as "Italian" could be transmitted in languages other than Italian. On the other hand, the use of the Italian does not guarantee that the content of information transmital can be identified as Italian. This reasoning becomes of utmost importance for the analysis of the existence of alien cultural groups, separated from the home country.

The communication is a response to a need to communicate. If the need can be met locally, the communication is limited to the people in the local area. The pattern of speech is contained in a restricted region, there is no urgency to align it to external demands, as long as these external demands play only a minor role. In the agricultural society, with limited range of communication demand, the areas of distinct languages, dialects, isoglosses are small. The economic interaction and political interference created the need for communication beyond the perimeter of the original region. The demand also forced the alignment of the regional speech pattern to the patterns of the wider area. The subsidence of dialects and the converging trend in languages is the evidence of these processes. The dialect or language is a utilitarian tool which acquires cultural connotation only at a later stage. Originally it is only a vehicle to transfer information.

When applying these notions to immigrant communities, it becomes evident, that the need forces the adjustments: the native language of the immigrant is adequate vehicle of communication within his home and possibly his neighborhood. The communication demand beyond the direct perimeter requires that acquiring of a new communication medium. The persistence of native language and the speed by which the new language is acquired is therefore unrelated to the presumed hierarchy of languages, one being better than another, but is a direct response to communication demand.

The Italian immigrant, like any other immigrant is a complex, cohesive, integrated carrier of a variety of properties, at the same coordinated respondent to multiplicity of stimuli, continuously adjusting to the stresses and demands of the interlinked surroundings, and constantly searching for the optimal—benefit yielding—subsystem responses. In our analysis we are concerned primarily with the spatial constraints of these subsystems, and leave aside the assessment of the coherency or conflicts, integration or separation.

Each subsystem has its own spatial dimensions, its own degree of intensity and relative significance. The objective measure of these variables, however, is more illusory than real. Whatever norm is established, it is a subjective approximation of predetermined magnitude, an average or norm of a sort. The expected territorial spread of superimposed subsystems is nevertheless peculiar to the Italians: the nucleated family, the family ties, the regional consciousness, contribute to the intense, though spatially restricted socio-cultural subsystem, in which the frequency of exchange flows, and the intensity of interaction is very high, though territorially restricted. The territorially defined neighborhood is more comprehensive and more "benefit-yielding" than is true for the "normal" American neighborhood. If, however, the neighborhood is ethnically mixed, and the proportion of the Italians in the area small, the behavior of the Indians is not different than that of other populations; it is therefore aligned along the principles of an alienated society (Packard, 1972).

The unanswered question is: to what extent has a more intense recent immigration flow of the Italians altered the general picture? Are the processes today substantially different than those identified and analyzed in previous decades.

One fundamental difference is the result of the 1965 Immigration Act which substituted the national origin quotas with a new set of preferences to family reunion, helping immigrants join relatives who are already in the

U.S. Remaining preferences are given to people of certain occupations and professions that would not displace indigenous laborers. Large proportions of recent immigrants are relatives of American citizens and permanent residents.

The character of Italian immigrants of the new wave is therefore aligned with the family relationship, reinforcing the existing Italian communities, and strengthening the network linkages by introducing into the system new active members, who through renewed communication needs reactivate the exchanges even with people whose communicative ability was declining: the effort of older immigrants to communicate with the newcomer reactivates their memories, brushes up their language and therefore reshapes their field of social communication.

The melting pot mechanism is still operating. The principal criticism of the concept is that it requires a much longer time to complete its course; furthermore it does not necessarily destroy all the components which are being aggregated into a new entity. The persistence of the identifiable ethnic communities is only an indication that the course has not been completed yet. It is not achieved in one or in two generations. The value judgment related to the idea obscures the essence of the concept: new assemblages of people and their cultural properties, their goals and aspirations will become patrimony of new people of subsequent generations. Their awareness span will not include the original components of the culture complex, only the derivatives, transformed through the passing of time and process of alterations. Even if identified as distinct and different than the total cultural complex of the host society, it would be considerably removed from the original culture complex, from which it is derived.

The need is the principal force which generates the changes: the need to expand the communication horizon in order to benefit from the totality of the cultural and social complex of the larger society. In the Italian peasant system of existence, the size of the territorial complex was limited and there was no need to expand it beyond the immediate horizon. In modern society of anonymous contacts, the spread of communication is considerably wider though less intense. The need to be linked into a system, in which the exchange flows would be possible without major impediments, gives a priority value to the communication medium which is recognizable (complementary) by the outside society, which means the adoption of the language of the host country. When the first step is taken, the process continues: after the symbols (words), the adoption of concepts, values, and slowly of the total system. The adopted system is not identical to the genuine original system as it existed before adoption, it is slightly modified by its extension to embrace the new elements: the Italians as components of the American society. This means, that the society is not any more a firm and established assemblage of static components, but is a continous aggregating of new, varied, compatible and conflicting components, which all together form the socio-cultural complex, different at any given time since it is subject to continous modifications. The assimilation process therefore is a process of assemblage and aggregation, and less process of adoption or rejection, where the substitution of elements by new elements is the essential transformation process.

The new Italian immigrants even those who arrive from the rural area of Italy, are not comparable to the peasants who entered the North American continent at the turn of the century. They are not part and cannot form their world of isolation within larger society, since they did not exist in such isolated community complexes in their home territories. They were exposed to modern electronic communication media, through which they were exposed to manifestation of the Italian culture (Gross, 1971, Cronin, 1970). In the new country, they cannot isolate themselves and refrain from exposure. They might not understand the "alien language" of the electronic systems, but it doesn't take long before they begin to grasp the concepts and identify the multitude of new idioms. The isolation is broken and new linkages with the external world are established. This explains why the assimilation process of new arrivals is considerably faster than it was for those who came to the United States at the turn of the century. The difference is often interpreted as consequence of education, and lessening of the family ties, though the answer is much simpler: the exposure and the drive to achieve greater benefits by establishing the external links prevents isolation, and by consequence generates need for interaction, which leads to assimilation and integration.

Gumilev (1973:p.471) acknowledges that the ethnos is a complex multi-level system and not a simple sum of individuals, but rather a system of relationships uniting those individuals. "These linkages extend not only through space, but through time, and are set off by a limited burst of innate drive that gives rise to the given ethnic whole." In expanding his argument, the behavior of the system of the Italian ethnic aggregate is affected by the ability to exchange information, influence, even goods, through the medium of the Italian language. The maintenance of the language becomes, therefore, an essential means of the system operation, and the preservation of such a language a vital integrative medium in the aggregate.

The use of the language and the conservation of cultural distinctiveness is therefore a response to the maximization of benefits which are obtained through the use of the language medium or the rewards which are obtained through the association with and within the group. When such benefits become marginal, the utilization of the language loses its vital importance, and the process of adoption of the second language goes underway, first with the biglossia (or bilingualism) and in a later stage by substitution of the original language with the new language of the larger society.

The isolation, and segregation, which as a culturally conditioned symbol, is in fact a functionally conditioned phenomenon of bounded space in which the communication medium, flowing through the network, provides the most significant element of identity. Sociological motives for language substitution (Alvar, 1972; Fishman, 1972; Bathes, 1973), in this light reflect the functional demand for maximization of benefits. As long as the communication is primarily face-to-face, the territorial clustering of people of the same linguistic group is beneficial. The electronic devices reduced the distance constraints and enabled the communication over longer distances. But even in the most modern technological society the significance of distance (separation) cannot be denied.

MacDonalds concentrated their analysis on the movement itself and the employment opportunities at destination. They state that "They had little desire to learn English and to become acquainted with the United States environment, except so far as it involved their employment" (MacDonald, 1962: 442). The reality of the immigrant's existence, nevertheless, points to the lack of perceived advantage in learning the language or gaining the acquaintance with the American environment. The "padrone" provided the function of the middle-man, isolating the immigrant within the restricted circle of his own countrymen and serving as the intermediary with the larger society (Iorizzo, 1970). The position of the padroni declined when the immigrants moved to the factory works and acquired the basic skills for which there was some demand in the newly expanded industries in the United States.

Even the padrone system, exploitive and discriminatory, in essence provided an employment opportunity and reasonable isolation form; the "exotic" exterior, with all the negative facets nevertheless served as a cushion, within which the new immigrant, not knowledgeable of the external world and not able to communicate directly, was nevertheless absorbed in a social group, which was also a production unit. The "padrone" served as the external link. He was able to communicate within and without the group, serve as the intermediary, and as such in a controling position over the group. The disbanding of the group, left the individual at the mercy of the outside world, while it did not equip him to cope alone with the demand, economic, social, or cultural of the American environment. It is clear, that many individuals returned to the "gang" fully aware of its exploitive nature, but the sense of belonging and the sense of protection outweigh the negative aspect of the arrangement.

The Italian immigrant community is not a passive entity which only responds to the outside forces, but an active system of interlinked components, which seeks internal adjustment to the internal and external demands, influenced by the perception of the world and the accepted individual and group values.

The identity of the Italian immigrant is therefore determined by his position in an interacting system, by the character of the communication network which he utilizes. The identity in this sense is functional, so is his network. The area within which he exists is characterized essentially by his activities. The traditional emphasis on territorial communities of immigrants acquires a new relevance with the assessment of the network linkages and their operations.

In this light, the ethnic community is not dead. The consequences of such newly established group identity is the further postponements of the complete merger and a further delay of societal homogenization. If such a process is beneficial or not for the society as a whole, is beyond the scope of this analysis.

The resurgence of the community identities, provides a new level of awareness for the Italian immigrants in the United States: the society as a whole is recognizing the value of grouping, and as such views the survival of the ethnic community as a model by which the non-ethnic groups could be patterned. The 'Little Italies' are becoming in this sense tested cases of complex adaptive system with confirmed identity and firmly established functional network within the American urban scene.

This system ceased to operate in its rigid form during the first decade of the century; the informal components, nevertheless, persisted for much longer: the Italian immigrant leaned on the support of his countrymen. They helped him to find shelter and employment, they provided the first social gratifications. They functioned as intermediaries with the external world. The sense of isolation, and related protectionism persisted into contemporary world, as is evident in the consequences of massive migration process in Toronto and Montreal (Boissevain, 1970; Velikonja, 1965; Baldacci, 1972). The principal change, however, is that in the past, the community system frequently presented more of a retained segment of the old world, and the effort for its maintenance was dominated with the conservative view of "keeping the good old ways" in contemporary world, as Gans (1962), Glazer and Moynihan (1963) stressed; the identifiable ethnic group is a present, contemporary, even forward looking community, which keeps together, strengthens its internal ties and formulating a defensive mechanism since it considers it valuable and "benefit yielding" regardless of its ties with the "old country." The community so interpreted, provides an identity to an aggregate within the generally alienated urbanized society.

In summary, the immigrant community is a personal contact system.

The interacting elements (objects) in this system are immigrants who receive, process, use and issue information. The relationship (links) in the system are the contacts between the elements, namely immigrants. Törnquist (1970) developed this approach in his study of regional development; it is applied here to the analysis of the immigrant's existence.

The interaction can occur when the recognizable symbols are adopted and used as the medium of information exchange. The language becomes the most significant medium without which the process of information exchange, the use of available opportunities, and the usufruct of existing potential benefits cannot be achieved. For an Italian immigrant-newcomer, the Italian language is such a medium, the consequence is therefore the spatial aggregation of the Italian newcomers in the predominantly Italian speaking communities. At a later stage and for the contacts with the outside world, the command of English (or French in Montreal) is essential for the utilization of the non-Italian surroundings, economic, social or cultural.

Recently, Glazer and Moynihan pointed to the new role of ethnicity as a symbol around which the immigrants rally and which enables them to be identified as an aggregate in the otherwise alienated society. The ethnic group itself is now behaving as an interest group and is becoming more salient "because it can combine an interest with an affective tie" (Glazer-Moynihan, 1974, p. 37). While Törnquist stresses the importance of contact at place of work for the interpretation of social existence of Swedish society, the contacts of the neighboring community dominate in the new-immigration society. The long process of adjustment gradually expands the contact field of the immigrant and dilutes the linguistic and cultural peculiarities by the process of substitution, which would eventually lead to total merger of the two cultures and total substitution of the foreign mother tongue with the complete adoption of the functional language of the new society.

REFERENCES

Manuel Alvar. "Motivaciones sociologicas en el cambio linguistico", *Ethnica* (Barcelona), No. 3 (1972), pp. 9-28.

Osvaldo Baldacci, "I'incidenza geografico-culturale del gruppo etnico italiano nel contesto urbano di Toronto." *Publicazioni dell' Istituto di Geografia*, Università di Roma, Facoltà di Lettere e Filosofia, Serie A (Antropica e Fisica), Roma, 1972.

Roland Barthes, "La Division des langages," pp. 343-366 in *Une Nouvelle Civilisation?* Hommage a Georges Friendmann. Paris, Gallimard, 1973, pp. vii + 494.

William S. Bernard, "New Direction in Integration and Ethnicity," *International Migration Review*, Vol. 5, No. 16 (Winter 1971), pp. 464-473.

Annemarie H. Bleiker. "The Proximity Model and Urban Social Relations," *Urban Sociology*, Vol. 1, No. 2 (Fall, 1972), pp. 151-175.

Jeremy Boissevain. The Italians of Montreal. Social Adjustment in a Plural Society. *Studies of the Royal Commission on Bilingualism and Biculturalism*. No. 7. Ottawa: Queen's Printer, 1970.

Anne Buttimer, "Social Space and the Planning of Residential Areas," *Environment and Behavior*, Vol. 4, No. 3 (September, 1972), pp. 279-318.

Constance Cronin. *The Sting of Change*. Chicago, The University of Chicago Press, 1970.

Joshua A. Fishman. *Language in Sociocultural Change*. Stanford: Stanford University Press, 1972, pp. xiv + 275.

Herbert Gans. *The Urban Villagers*, New York: The Free Press of Glencoe, 1962.

Nathan Glazer and Daniel P. Moynihan. *Beyond the Melting Pot*. Cambridge: The MIT Press, 1963.

Nathan Glazer and Daniel P. Moynihan, "Why Ethnicity"? *Commentary*, Vol. 58, No. 4 (October 1974), pp. 33-39.

Stephen M. Golant, "Adjustment Process in a System: A Behavioral Model of Human Movement," *Geographical Analysis*, Vol. 3 (July, 1971), pp. 203-220.

Feliks Gross. *Il Paese. Values and Social Change in an Italian Village*. New York-Rome: New York University Press and University of Rome, 1971.

L. N. Gumilev, "The Nature of Ethnic Wholeness" (English translation). *Soviet Geography*, September 1973, pp. 467-476.

Luciano J. Iorizzo, "The Padrone and Immigrant Distribution," pp. 43-75, in S. M. Tomasi—M. H. Engel. *The Italian Experience in the United States*.

Istituto di Studi Americani. Università degli Studi di Firenze. *Gli Italiani negli Stati Uniti*. Firenze, 1972.

Joseph Lopreato. *Italian Americans*. New York: Random House, 1970, pp. x + 205.

John S. and L. D. MacDonald, "Urbanization, Ethnic Groups, and Social Segmentation," *Social Research*, Vol. 29 (1962), pp. 433-448.

John S. and L. D. MacDonald, "Chain Migration, Ethnic Neighborhood Formation and Social Networks," *The Milbank Memorial Fund Quarterly*, Vol. 42, No. 1 (1964), pp. 82-97.

Vance O. Packard. *A Nation of Strangers*. New York: McKay, 1972, pp. xiv and 368.

Silvano M. Tomasi and Madeline H. Engel. *The Italian Experience in the United States*, Staten Island. N.Y.: Center for Migration Studies, 1970.

Silvano M. Tomasi. *Piety and Power. The Role of Italian Parishes in the New York Metropolitan Area (1880-1930)*. Staten Island: Center for Migration Studies, 1975.

Gunnar Törnquist. Contact Systems and Regional Development. *Lund Studies in Geography*. Ser. B. Human Geography No. 35. Lund, 1970, 148 p.

Rudolf J. Vecoli, "Contadini in Chicago: A Critique of the Uprooted," *The Journal of American History*, Vol. 51, No. 3 (Dec. 1964), pp. 404-417.

Joseph Velikonja. "Gli Italiani nelle città canadesi—Appunti geografici," *Atti,*

Congresso Geografico Italiano, Como, 1964. Como: Editrice Eseda, 1965, pp. 271-288.

Joseph Velikonja, "Contributi italiano al carattere geografico di Tontitown, Arkansas, e Rosati, Missouri," pp. 423-452 in *Gli Italiani Negli Stati Uniti,* Firenze, 1972.

Gerald Walker, "Social Transactions in Space: Conceptualizing the Behavioural Environment." York University, Department of Geography, *Discussion Paper No. 7.* Toronto, Canada, 1973.

Julian Wolpert, "Behavioral Aspects of the Decision to Migrate," *Papers, Regional Science Association,* Vol. 15 (1965), pp. 159-169.

Julian Wolpert, "Migration as Adjustment to Environmental Stress," *Journal of Social Issues.* Vol. 22 (1966), pp. 92-102.

VALENTINE ROSSILLI WINSEY

The Italian Immigrant Women Who Arrived in the United States Before World War I

Of an approximate total of fifteen-million Italian emigrants who left Italy between 1875 and 1915, the bulk of whom arrived in New York City, little more than 10%, at first, were women. After 1887 the percentage of women began slowly to increase. Why such a disproportionate ratio of one woman to every nine Italian males? How did this experience affect the Italian immigrant woman? What kind of life did she subsequently lead here?

Answer to the first question is rooted in the last four centuries of Italian history, when political turmoil combined with a series of devastating natural forces to produce such grim and unrelenting poverty, that the only merciful, life-sustaining measure for the Italian peasant appeared in the form of whatever seasonal wage-earning work he could find, and no matter where.

Beginning in the sixteenth century in the plains of the north, the male peasant left his native land alone, or accompanied by his wife and family, and returned home after each seasonal stint. Several centuries later the peasant of Southern Italy was constrained to follow suit. Through this practice of seasonal and temporary emigration the Italian developed, in time, a homing instinct not unlike the swallow. So much so, that he achieved, finally, a frequency of globe-trotting that only the rich could rival.

Small wonder that when need for unskilled labor arose in the United States in the last three decades of the nineteenth century, that such a disproportionate percentage of male over female migrants responded. Among these early arrivals, the female invariably came with a husband or father, either one of whom she was traditionally obliged to obey, and for whom she was expected to keep house. As an immigrant woman of that period told the writer:

"My mother say (to me), '*you* gotta do, an' *I* gotta do what your father say to do.' My father," she added, "want somebody t' keep house fa' him."

Keeping house in New York City during those years, however, presented a woman with no small challenge. In Italy, as Dr. L. Covello described in his classic study, *The Social Background of the Italian-American School Child,* family and family-life both physically and spiritually, were the focal point of a woman's concern and pleasure. Her family was likely to be large with many children, and extensive with many relatives. Since her town or village was geographically isolated, it had, of necessity, evolved into a self-contained organization structured on a simple, agrarian economy. The inhabitants spoke their own dialect, practiced their distinctive mode of cooking, their traditions and their memories. Their peasant dress and their fiesta garments were handed down from generation to generation. All of these factors nurtured an intense communal loyalty.

Despite her poverty, each woman developed a wholesome feeling of individuality. Her father, like all other male villagers, tilled his soil, or plied his trade, and looked after all family matters. Though carefully supervised, the Italian girl was, nevertheless, allowed to join with the rest of the community in the village square to barter, gossip or dance. Her church provided her with a traditional religious social life through innumerable annual fiestas, all of which were initiated by her village priest, and were almost always climaxed by a procession, the patron saint which every village had, leading the way. These fiestas would often last for a week, with one fiesta sometimes overlapping another.

Her religion, her extreme poverty combined with a continuous succession of such violent natural forces as volcanic eruptions, hot winds from the African Sirocco, etc., predisposed her to find comfort in the rich lore of communal superstitions. Her heritage of fatalism was inescapable— one's life was predetermined by one's "destino," a belief which, unbeknownst to her, was tacitly encouraged by the nobles and clergy whose welfare depended on submission of the peasant class.

The Italian girl knew that while her future roles were destined to be those of wife and mother, her husband's roles were also defined with equal clarity. He would be trained as her future breadwinner, and as head of their joint household. His childhood would include an apprenticeship to his father. As for formal schooling, like herself, he, too, was an unlikely candidate, since it was a luxury few could afford.

Once married, the market place, the public fountain where her children romped while she and other matrons procured the family drinking and cooking water, or washed clothes in the village stream, would constitute her social and workaday life. For the daily meals she could count on preparing breads and soups and, if the harvest permitted, wine. Meat was seasonal and there was little to be had. Such were the factors of traditions and customs which had influenced the personality and outlook on life of the Southern Italian immigrant woman.

By contrast, in the gloomy New York City flat to which her father or husband had taken her, the immigrant woman could no longer bake bread, mend or wash clothes outdoors in the warm sunshine, and in the pleasant company of her neighbors. She was confined, instead, to a congested tenement in which poor ventilation and defective drainage produced a sick, everpresent miasma from which there was no escape.

More than half a century later, an immigrant woman vividly recalled the place to which she had been brought upon arrival, and in which she had been obliged to live for a number of years.

"We had a sink in the hall with nothing else, and four families to share it. And one bathroom in the yard where garbage was also thrown. How could a body wash and have a bit of privacy that way? I died a little everytime I went there."

Housing units, water supply, street illumination, fire-protection measures, sewage, garbage disposal, etc., were on the same level that had been adequate to serve the city's needs of half a century earlier, while it was still a seaport town. With the completion in 1825 of the Erie Canal, however, New York City was transformed into the largest immigrant port in the world.

Problems of settlement and population distribution which had been created by immigrant groups that had preceded the Italian were exacerbated beyond all hope of solution. Rental demands for run-down shacks, or old warehouses which had been converted into dwellings that more closely resembled rabbit warrens were exorbitant. To meet these and other staggering expenses the early Italian couples developed, as an expedient solution, the practice of taking in boarders, thus ushering in the first, and most pernicious change for the Italian immigrant woman—the destruction of privacy in her home.

Whereas in Italy almost all the immigrant women with whom the writer spoke recalled being poor, they, nevertheless, harbored vivid recollections of their town of origin, its population, its altitude, its vacation spots, sulphur springs, churches, historic places and, above all, their own home, with its luxury of privacy.

". . . we had a house of four rooms, a kitchen and an oven for bread. (. . .) in my town there was a fountain with clear water which we took home to use, drink and wash. We had a few chickens which I helped to take care of. And when papa was alive, he'd bring home a lot of surprises from his hunting trips. There were rabbits, wild geese and other things".

Another woman described the house in Southern Italy in which she had been born three quarters of a century ago.

"Our little house was made of rocks. It had two floors, one room on the first floor and one on the second. The large floor on the top had our bedroom, and on the first floor mama had her bedroom. There was a kitchen and for water we had to go to the fountain. (. . .) in my family all had animals. In fact, before I was born my father went selling milk from the sheep. . . . the town I lived in had mountains all around. The air was fine. . . ."

In sum, home in Italy for the immigrant woman had been a place which accommodated members of the immediate family only, including, when necessary, aged parents or parents-in-law. Other family members comprising her relatives, among whom were numbered distant aunts, uncles and cousins, lived in their own homes. The presence, therefore, of paying boarders in her new York City home constituted an unprecedented intrusion that portended the destruction of family life for her in the United States.

As labor demands continued for several decades more to evoke a barometric-like response from the endless stream of male migrants which ebbed and flowed from Southern Italy to New York City, the intrusion of paying boarders in the Italian home persisted. These boarders were almost all fellow townsmen between the ages of fourteen and forty-five. Married or not, their relative indifference to the crowded and unsanitary living conditions in the flats in which they boarded was due to the temporary nature of their stay. So long as cheap and rapid transoceanic transportation was available, so long as inexpensive living accommodations in homes run by Italian housekeepers remained flexible, they continued, for the most part, their cultural practice of seasonal emigration. For example, of those who arrived between 1908 and 1915, three-fourths returned to Italy. In the previous decade 1897 to 1906, of the Italians returning from the United States, 41% were returning to Italy for the second time.

Year after year, decade after decade, up till the beginning of World War I, the number of arrivals from Southern Italy continued to dwarf those of any other country. However, as increasing awareness developed that economic opportunities in the United States were far better than in Italy, a growing number of migrants began to stake a permanent claim in the United States. Some by joining forces with union activists, others through the purchase of retail shops and wholesale houses, and a considerable number through real estate holdings which, in New York City alone, was estimated in 1909 to be in excess of twenty-million dollars.

Married men sent for their women and children. The majority, however, were bachelors. Eager to start their own families, they enlisted the help of a family member or townsman, here or abroad, in finding a bride. Countless girls from their own native villages were screened in a vigorous campaign of matchmaking. The Italian girl in Southern Italy who had seen the eligible males of her town leave one after the other for New York had little choice. All she could hope for was that the offer for marriage from a townsman in America, which came to her most often through a parent or close relative, portended her future happiness. Many among them, however, who underwent such an experience had a different story to tell.

"When my aunt and uncle, they wrote me to come to America, I did not know they had in mind the iceman. I wonder who they thought he was—somebody big? He was just a man, that's all"!

Just a man? The Italian girl of her generation had, indeed been trained for "just a man," and *one* man, alone. From birth her duties and responsibilities as future wife and mother had been so impressed upon her, that she obeyed almost instinctively the centuries-old rules of proper female behavior. Carefully supervised at all times, she knew that her success in marriage depended far more on a spotless reputation than on the size of her dowry. Courtship procedures were highly structured and marriage outside her village was a rarity. So, too, was separation or divorce, which her immigrant male counterpart disparaged as "the American invention." For the unhappily married immigrant woman the only refuge was a brooding resentment bordering on despair, as revealed by the following:

"It was 1906 when I married. I was seventeen-years-old, then. My husband came from my town in Italy. His sister and I had worked together."

The speaker, a seventy-seven-year-old, frail-looking woman paused to tuck a wisp of hair behind her ear, and with a sudden burst of anger exclaimed:

"I didn't want to marry. (But) in those days if you were married and you separated. . . ."

A gush of tears stemmed the flow of her protest. She smoothed her fine wavy hair which she had tied into a neat bun at the nape of her neck. This hairstyle and her simple black dress characterized the immigrant peasant woman who had come to New York half a century or more ago. She smiled easily, wistfully, trying vainly to disguise her embarassment, for an Italian-born woman seldom betrayed to a relative stranger such intimate negative sentiments about her husband.

A second matron in her middle seventies had the same note of despair in her tone as she recounted her experience.

"I was only thirteen when I came. After three months I got married. My father found the man for me. (. . .) My father said to my husband at that time, 'Hey, she's just a child, so go easy with her.' (. . .) I got white hair when

I was twenty-six. My life was finished. (. . .) my husband and I didn't get along."

Whether they got along or no, most of these unhappily married Italian-born, immigrant women remained with their husbands, partly through fear of being ostracized by the Italian community, partly for the sake of their children, but above all, for economic reasons.

Division of labor between the sexes in Italy had always been accepted as essential. Whenever necessary, women worked beside their husbands in the field, but their work, for the most part, was circumscribed to the home. Arrived in New York City, however, they were confronted with the second, unprecedented historic experience—wage-earning work outside the home The dire need for cheap labor in a variety of industries in the city was so great that it lured many Italian women not only out of their homes, but out of their homeland, as well, as indicated by an increase in their immigration.

The majority came with relatives or close friends and were carefully chaperoned from the moment of departure to the moment of embarkation. Closely guarded indoors for awhile, their sense of physical confinement was exacerbated further by the over-crowded, dark, ill-equipped quarters —conditions which bred considerable and widespread discontent. Most of them sought the only escape they knew was certain—marriage. Marriage to an Italian-born male, however, created little change, at first, in their lives here. The women simply continued to be confined in the home with the added responsibility, in most cases, of rearing children, and on an allowance which was not always forthcoming. This latter condition was particularly prevalent after World War I, and during an economic recession a decade earlier when immigrant women were forced to supplement their husband's incomes.

Although options for the kind of work open to them may have differed, the same economic necessity that spurred them over half a century or more ago, has since spurred the majority of modern women to seek employment outside the home. For the Italian immigrant woman of yester-year, however, work outside the home allowed for little or no leisure time. In addition to her full-time job and her responsibilities to her family, she was pressured further into bringing work home on consignment. Driven by exhaustion, she even allowed her youngsters to help with whatever her contractual tasks were, such as fastening buttons, baking bread, assembling artificial flowers, etc., all for a total earning which averaged forty-cents a night.

Kitchen kerosene lamps burned for hours in a fetid evening atmosphere of relentless toil. Tenement fires became a widespread menace, as did Tuberculosis, Anemia, Malaria and accidents, particularly in summers when bedding appeared on the roofs and fire-escapes, with the not-infrequent consequence of people falling to the ground. These were among the major changes in living, in family roles, and in the wage-earning patterns that recalled grim memories, such as the following:

"I worked hard. I worked very hard making bread. In one hour's time I made something like five loaves of bread—all by hand, kneading, kneading."

The speaker was a short, heavy-set woman in her mid-seventies who had arrived in the States at age seventeen. She moved slowly, stopping often to adjust her bandaged legs which were densely networked with varicose veins—mute testimony to a life of unrelieved drudgery.

Coarse-featured, with a mass of red hair streaked with white, and a mole like a giant lentil under her left eye, a seventy-nine-year-old immigrant woman remarked vigorously:

"Years ago, it was lousy, lousy. I made cigars for three to five dollars a week. I thought life (here) would be different." Pointing to the paper on which the writer had been jotting notes, she directed, "Write that I was poor in Italy, and that I'm poor here"!

The next speaker was dwarfish with no neck, and a large face that was like a rough chunk of bread-dough. Her two enormous dark eyes betrayed a quick intelligence and a volatile temperament. Soberly, she described her experience.

"I went to work when I first came, too. (It) was in a rag shop. I'm even 'shamed t' say. You know, there—there is old clothes. There is a 'pick-people.' They pick rags. In the shop they give everyone a box o' stuff, an' you gotta divide. They were clean rags, but you gotta divide silk, an' cotton, an' wool. They pay me six dollars a week."

A neat-looking, tiny woman who was also in her late seventies spoke softly and with some effort at recall.

"I worked almost all my life. Then one day I hurt my arms, and so I stayed home. But I became a superintendent. Later, I went to work again as a packer. Then I went to work making sleeves, putting buttons on blouses."

She catalogued her employment history tonelessly, like a child reciting in rote. There was about her, the air of a perplexed little girl, who had never been able to reconcile herself to the fast, inexplicable changes that life had wrought.

The next speaker, also in her late seventies, delivered each thought as if it were a final pronouncement.

"When I came here, I went to work in a laundry for four dollars a week. I wanted to go back right away—but—you know."

Statuesque and graceful, with soft white hair and merry blue eyes, she flicked the fingers of her right hand under her chin to dismiss the suggestion that her's was a story too long to tell. Struggling for the right words, she concluded ruefully:

"I would never have come here. I would never have made this life."

"This life" for her and all of her companions included yet another particularly painful experience through the depth of prejudice they encountered here. While they did not know, nor could they comprehend it, the Italian immigrants suffered the automatic reaction of one culture to the large presence of a different culture. A few exotics can be tolerated, perhaps, even enjoyed. A large quantity is both frightening and threatening.

So threatening was the large Italian presence that there came into existence such organizations as Boston's Immigration Restriction League. Vitriolic articles began to appear, and one commentator went so far as to warn that the Italian "invasion" threatened to cause the extermination of the American culture.

Although she could neither read nor write, nevertheless, ghetto-living provided the immigrant woman with the quick word-of-mouth access to the continuous series of anti-Italian incidents which occurred daily. The more sensational ones appeared in the local Italian newspapers of the time. Early in 1900, for example, *The Cronica d'America* reported that thirty Italians had been arrested and fined $10.00 each for rag-picking; that police killed two Italians who were having an argument; that thirty Italian workers in West Troy were burned as strikebreakers.

Adding to the prejudice was the fact that, in the beginning of union efforts to organize, Italian men and women did, indeed, act as strikebreakers. Quick to learn, however, that the major goal of these union efforts was to protect all immigrant workers from exploitation, they, too, not only joined the picket lines, but, on occasion, even exercised their own forms of justice. When, for example, an employer in Boston arbitrarily reduced by 10% the wages of his Italian workers, the workers, though indignant, said nothing. That same night, however, they worked busily and without letup. Next morning the Italian laborers reported for work, as usual, but with a single difference that was immediately apparent—the end of each worker's shovel had been cut by an inch. Their wordless resolution had been accomplished—less money, less dirt!

An additional aspect of prejudice against the Italian immigrant was reflected in the many instances of police brutality which became cause for serious concern. Basically religious, the Italians' attitude toward the Catholic church and its priests had become one of indifference bordering on suspicion. Part of the reason was the failure of the church and the clergy to support the peasant in the past, during unification attempts in Italy. Another reason stemmed from the fact that the Irish dominated not only New York City's Police Force, but the American Catholic hierarchy, as well. The Italian immigrants' indifference, therefore, to anything more religious than ceremonial observance so bewildered the Irish immigrants, whose own commitment to Catholicism was, by contrast, intense, that it aroused continuous antagonism between the two groups. This antagonism was intensified even further by underworld organizations from Sicily and Naples whose criminal activities were regarded as another hateful Italian trait. (Ironically, these organizations better known as the "Mafia," "Camorra," or "Black Hand" aimed their criminal activities against the Italian immigrant themselves in the United States.)

All of these cumulative injustices were vigorously deplored not only in Italian-language newspapers, but also in New York's English-language newspapers, as well. Anti-Italian prejudice, however continued to fester till it culminated, finally, in the tragic execution of Sacco and Vanzetti, several years after the first World War.

Its bitter fruit distilled in the memories of all the Italian immigrant women with whom the writer spoke, as expressed, for example by an aged widow.

"During the winter, it was the worst time. You could hardly go out. My mother used to wear those heavy, warm shawls. They turned out to be protection for more than just the cold. My mother would huddle into the shawl when she went out, and then the snowballs would start flying. Sometimes they hit her so hard, she was afraid to walk. And those who threw them shouted, 'guinea, guinea,' and followed her down the street. (. . .) My mother would pretend she had a knife in her pocket sometime, just to scare them off. They *were* scared, too, especially because they expected Italians to carry knives in those days."

Today it's the Negro or Puerto Rican who is expected to carry knives. Whom will it be tomorrow? The experiences may differ somewhat from one group to the next, but the expressed attitudes remain rooted in fear; a fear which has neither color nor ethnic identity, and remains ageless.

One woman poignantly described her first lesson in fear in the following words:

"Those were brute times, those years when I first came here. The Irish were terrible, and I remember lots of fights. I shall never forget to this day those awful fights and the police. They made fun of us, sometimes. There were good ones—Irish, I mean, but they were few. I learned to be afraid here. I never was afraid before."

Was it fear, born of prejudice, that drove her to hold fast to her own native values and customs? That served to isolate her psychologically, as she had isolated herself geographically by remaining for the rest of her life within the confines of the same, crowded, Italian colony in East Harlem. Over the years, as she watched her children grow, was it fear, born of prejudice, that weighed heavily on her mind, triggering one anxiety after another through such questions as: Why were her children being made to study only English in public school? Why were they learning nothing about Italy? Wouldn't it be better if they had less formal schooling and went to work in their early teens, just as their father had done? Why were they becoming so stubbornly opposed to every bit of parental advice? Why did so many of them make fun of their Italian heritage? These and other anxieties continued to gnaw at her spirit, as she struggled to combat the challenges and frustrations involved in transmitting old culture patterns to her children, while attempting to protect them against the pernicious effects of anti-Italian prejudice.

Memories of the efforts which these immigrant women had made to cope with their struggles are eclipsed partially by the present well-being of their offspring. One immigrant woman brightened visibly as she catalogued the accomplishments of each.

"I had good children—five. One is a bartender, and my daughter, she makes corsets in a factory. And I got a son, he clean inna shop—you know—repair. And another son, he works in the Post Office, and I got a married daughter. My daughter, she was forty-two when she got married. Her husband 'taliano. Only one of my children, I got, no marry Italiano—the smallest. His wife is half Irish, half German. They respect me, though."

More than one immigrant woman reported that an offspring of her's had married the son or daughter of an Irish immigrant. The matter-of-fact way in which they mentioned it revealed a wholesome absence of rancour from the early days when Irish immigrant hostility against them was rife.

The next speaker particularized with great facility and pride about her children.

"I am a mother of ten children. Seven boys and all of them finished public school. And one girl finished Junior High School. One boy works for the Sanitation Department, two own their own business—dry cleaning and a small flower shop. Another two work in business. Then there's a butcher, and still another is a mechanic in iron works—he's an airplane mechanic in business. Two (girls) stay at home with me. They don't marry, but the one, the other girl did. And I had three of my sons in the war. I gotta say they were very lucky and came through, alright."

Many immigrant women reported not only that their American-born sons had served in the United States armed forces during World War II, but that their Italian-born husbands had preceded their sons as U.S. soldiers in World War I. As peasants in Italy, both male and female immigrants had had no formal political experience in local or national government. During their first few years in this country there was no thought of citizenship status, simply because they had not intended to stay. However, no sooner did they crystallize their decision to remain, both men and women actively sought citizenship status; a sizeable percentage of men through enlisting in the United States' Army, and the women through examples of their husbands and friends.

One immigrant woman recalled her experience with considerable vehemence:

"I am a citizen, since my husband went to war, an' on accounta him, they let me pass. But I say to myself, I want my own. I vote under *his* name? What for? I wanna vote myself! So I went, an' ten years later, I became a citizen."

While only a small percentage of Italian women failed to obtain citizenship status, nevertheless, all had developed a greater political awareness of its importance and relevance to their family and its welfare. The following is a typical example:

"I never made myself a citizen. I don't know how to read and write, so what was the sense. My husband became a citizen. Through his club, it happened—you know—the Society. At election time he found himself there with people who knew how to make citizens, and so, I don't know how, I don't know why, but they used to call him all the time when elections were held. It helped the Italians, he told me—those elections. If it weren't for them, my husband couldn't be sure of a job all the time."

Particularly bewildering for these immigrant women is their present experience of finding themselves old and alone, a fate which they could never have anticipated from their native backgrounds in which grandparents, widowers and widows like themselves, would find a haven within the bosom of the beloved family.

Many continue to live as they have for the past half century in the same neighborhood in East Harlem. Their children have long since established families of their own and in geographical locations too far to allow for frequent contact. For daily companionship, the immigrant women find their way to La Guardia Settlement House where other Italian immigrants like themselves congregate.

Of their present situation of aloneness and loneliness, their time-honored belief in destiny sustains them; a belief which had long-ago taught them to expect little, and to expect to pay a high price for that "little." One immigrant woman might well have been speaking for all her companions as she concluded:

"Here you pay for everything, even a 'good morning.' Everything has a price, and the piece of bread you eat every day is hard to swallow because there is no smiling face to look at.

Now I am eighty. Look at my legs, these swollen veins. And still they hold me up, these legs of mine.

I am not complaining because I am old. To become old is according to God's will. But to be old, and alone—even dogs have their companions.

I don't even see my children anymore. 'Hello ma,' an' 'Goodby.'

You think they're happy? How can they be happy, running, running all the time like they do. 'Hello ma,' an' 'Goodby.'

My grandchildren run even faster. Bread rises only when its allowed to stand awhile. The soul, too, has its own yeast, but it cannot rise while its running.

It's certain that I got things here which in Italy, I never could have gotten.

But I had things in Italy which in America, still cannot find—yeast, yeast for the soul"!

Social Background and Educational Problems of the Italian Family in America

[Leonard Covello]

I. SOCIAL BACKGROUNDS IN RELATION TO THE PROBLEMS OF EDUCATION AND ASSIMILATION.
   A. *Minority Groups in the United States.*
      1—Problems of minorities.
      2—Their significance from the national standpoint.
   B. *Social Backgrounds of Italo-Americans and Problems of Assimilation Among Italo-Americans.*
      1—Status of the Italo-American minority group.
         a—Numerical aspects. Distribution.
         b—Homogeneity of Italian communities. (Little Italy)
         c—American attitudes towards Italians.
         d—Italian attitudes towards Americans.
         e—Retardation of assimilation among Italians.
      2—Essentials of the Italo-American Background.
         a—Persistence of the Italo-American background and its inherent problems.
      3—Factors affecting adjustment of Italo-Americans.
         a—Complexity of adjustment problems.
         b—Problems of Italian foreign-born people and continuing problems of the second generation.
         c—The language problem.
         d—Inter-action with older Americans.
         e—Inter-action with other foreign cultural groups.
         f—Psychic forces in the Italo-American community.
   C. *Need for Appraisal of Social Backgrounds.*
      1—Necessity for adjusting local problems.
      2—Assimilation an urgent problem.
      3—The school as a factor in assimilation.
      4—Study of Italo-American social backgrounds as a basis for an assimilation program.

II. PERSONAL EXPERIENCES AND OBJECTIVE DATA: THEIR SIGNIFICANCE IN EVALUATING THE SOCIAL BACKGROUND OF THE ITALIAN CHILD IN AMERICA.
   A. *Preliminary Statement.*
      1—Need for assembling personal observations and of relating them to objective data.

B. *Methods of studying social backgrounds.*
   1—Membership in Italian community.
   2—The "Participant Observer" and his function.
C. *Spheres of Participation.*
   1—Community activities.
   2—Membership in Italo-American organizations.
   3—Work with children, adolescents, and adults.
   4—Other contacts with Italian interests through
     a—Leadership in enterprises related to Italian life.
     b—Educational, social welfare, guidance, and community programs.
     c—Collecting and recording of data of various kinds.
       1c—Research studies as projected in the pamphlet, *Italians In America.*
       2c—Studies by the Participant Observer
         (1)—Statistical analyses and interpretations of available data
           (a)—From Questionnaires
             1a—Inter-racial attitudes
             2a—Motion Picture Study
             3a—Miscellaneous questionnaires
             4a—Teacher attitudes towards boys
             5a—Third Generation Italians
             6a—Mobility of families
             7a—Educational trends among Italians: based on graduate and college records
           (b)—Occupational Trends
           (c)—Delinquency Data.
           (d)—Mental Ability of Italian Boys.
         (2)—Descriptive material
           (a)—Italo-American organizational records and programs.
           (b)—Letters by Italians (Classified and analyzed).
           (c)—Italian cultural programs.
           (d)—Autobiographic material.
           (e)—Community Documents.
         (3)—Special material
           (a)—Case Studies (Family and Home Relations).
           (b)—Newspaper Clippings.
         (4)—Interpretative Material
           (a)—Lectures, articles, and books by a "Participating Observer."
D. *Illustrative Materials.*
   1—Forms.
   2—Schedules.
   3—Circulars.
   4—Miscellaneous material.

III. GEOGRAPHY, RACE, AND LANGUAGE

A. *Destiny of nations shaped by many forces.*
   1—Pressures in Italian national life.
B. *Geography and its Relation to Italian life and history.*
   1—Strategic position of the peninsula in the Mediterranean.
   2—Influence of geography on Italian history.

      3—The Mediterranean Sea.
        a—"Mare Nostrum" of ancient Rome and of modern Italy.
        b—Influence on Italian cultural patterns.
      4—Geography as a factor in the unification of Italian people.
  C. *Topography of Italy.*
      1—Mountain ranges.
      2—Lowlands and plains.
      3—Climatic variations.
      4—Watersheds and water supply.
  D. *Land Usage.*
      1—Agricultural aspects.
      2—Malarial marshes.
      3—Soil.
  E. *Geographic Divisions of the Peninsula.*
      1—Northern Italy.
      2—Central Italy.
      3—Southern Italy.
  F. *Southern Italy.*
      1—General characteristics.
      2—Differences between northern and southern Italy.
      3—Relation of geographic factors to emigration.
  G. *Racial origins of the Italian people.*
      1—Fusion of many ethnic elements.
        a—Invasions.
        b—Interpenetrations of cultural patterns.
        c—Distribution of racial stock.
      2—Development of a homogeneous people a long process.
        a—The race question.
        b—Racial differences among Italians of various localities.
      3—Early Rome and Latinization of Italians.
        a—Ethnographic origins obscure.
        b—The Mediterranean type.
        c—Tribal groups in the peninsula.
        d—Influence of Roman law in unifying the peoples of the peninsula.
  H. *The Italian Language.*
      1—Language as a social force.
      2—The Latin base of Italian.
      3—The dialects in Italy and in Italo-American life.
III. HISTORICAL RETROSPECT
  A. *Early Roman History.*
      1—Greek Colonies.
      2—Conquest of Magna Graecia.
      3—Expansion of Rome.
  B. *Republican Period.*
  C. *The Roman Empire.*
  D. *Decline of Rome.*
      1—Barbaric Invasions.
  E. *Christianity and Church power.*
  F. *Medieval Italy.*
      1—Independent Cities.

2—Foreign dominations.
3—Renaissance
G. *Southern Italy—from the Middle Ages to the Napoleonic Era.*
H. *The Risorgimento.*
   1—Mazzini and Garibaldi.
   2—Unification of Italy.
I. *Italy of the XXth Century.*

IV. ITALO-AMERICAN PROBLEMS IN THE LIGHT OF DIFFEREN-
TIATION BETWEEN NORTHERN AND SOUTHERN ITALIANS.
  A. *Discrimination between Northern and Southern Italians in the U.S.*
   1—"Inferiority" of Southern Italian immigrants.
   2—Preponderance of Southern Italians in the U.S.
  B. *"The Southern Question" in Italy.*
   1—North-South controversies.
   2—The South of Italy in the Italian popular opinion.
  C. *Adjustments of Southern Italian immigrants in the U.S. in the light of
their difference from North Italians.*
   1—Pertinency of Italo-American problems to immigrants from Southern
      Italy.
  D. *The Need to emphasize the social background of Southern Italians.*

V. ECONOMICS OF SOUTHERN ITALY. THE AGRICULTURAL
SYSTEM.
  A. *Economic factors affecting the diversity of the South from the North of
Italy.*
   1—Water power.
   2—Communications.
   3—Natural resources.
   4—Neglect of Southern economy by the Italian governments.
   5—Taxation in the South.
   6—Industrialization of Northern Italy.
  B. *The Agricultural System of the South.*
   1—Climatic conditions and its affect upon the character of southern
      agriculture.
   2—Deforestation and water scarcity.
   3—Deterioration of Southern Italian productivity of the soil.
     a—Obsoleteness of agricultural methods and implements.
   4—Ownership of land.
   5—Land contracts.
   6—Economic status of Southern Italian peasants.
     a—Income from land.

VI. THE SOUTHERN ITALIAN TOWN. THE SOCIAL CLASSES.
  A. *The town as rural habitat.*
  B. *Physical aspects of towns.*
   1—Housing and sanitation.
  C. *Social Classes. The caste system.*
  D. *The day laborer.*
   1—His status among the peasant society.
  E. *The contadino (the peasant).*

1—Barriers between peasant and other classes.
F. *The Artisans.*
1—Their function as a middle class.
G. *The "Galantuomo" (the gentleman).*
1—Landed gentry.
2—The officials.
3—The priest.
4—The professionals.

VII. CULTURAL PATTERNS OF THE SOUTHERN ITALIAN
COMMUNITY.
A. *Individualism of Southern Italians.*
1—The individual and the State.
2—The individual and his group.
3—Regionalism and "campanilismo".
4—Lack of cooperation.
B. *The Southern Italian family.*
1—Family solidarity and tradition.
a—The family as a social and economic unit.
2—Status of men.
a—Fathers and sons.
3—Status of women.
a—Economic role of women.
4—Role of children.
5—The family in relation to the community.
a—Clannishness.
b—Behavior in family life and community mores.
C. *Religious life among Southern Italians.*
1—The role of the Church and the priest.
2—Church ritual and religious practices.
a—Survival of ancient usages and concepts.
b—Superstitions.
D. *The Educational System.*
1—Southern Italian illiteracy.
2—The School in the South of Italy.
a—Distribution and type of schools.
b—School curricula and school attendance.
c—Segregation of sexes.
3—Attitudes towards education.
a—Social and economic significance of education.
b—Education of women.
4—Attitudes toward teacher.
a—Parent-Teacher relationship.
b—Role of teacher in the community.
E. *The Community at Work.*
1—Farming.
2—The artisan's shop.
3—Home industries.
4—Children at work.
a—In parental home.

    b—As apprentices.

    c—As paid workers.

  5—Southern Italian philosophy of work.

    a—Workmanship standards.

F. *The Community at play.*

  1—Recreation within family circle.

  2—Religious and Civic festivals.

  3—Contests.

  4—Music, song and dance.

    a—The marionette show.

G. *Health in the South of Italy.*

  1—Medical care.

    a—The physician and the midwife.

    b—The hospital.

  2—Health problems and cultural patterns.

    a—Concept of health and sickness.

    b—Superstitions and magic remedies.

  3—Care for aged and orphans.

H. *Basic community mores.*

  1—Sanctity of the family.

  2—Integrity of the individual.

  3—Friendship—a fundamental verity.

    a—Loyalty to friends (the Sicilian omertà).

  4—Ancestor cult.

    a—Respect for the old.

  5—Fatalism.

  6—Alcoholism and suicides.

  7—Violence in Southern Italian behaviour.

    a—Vendetta—the traditional code of honor.

    b—Brigandage—a product of a political education.

    c—Southern Italian crime and delinquency.

VIII. EMIGRATION FROM SOUTHERN ITALY.

A. *Dominant concepts in the U.S. as to causes of Italian emigration.*

B. *Tangible causes of emigration.*

  1—The validity of economic causes.

C. *Socio-political factors in emigration.*

  1—The revolutionary character of Southern Italian emigration.

D. *Incentives to emigration.*

  1—Tales of returning emigrants.

  2—Employment agencies.

E. *Numerical aspects of Italian emigration.*

  1—Northern and Southern emigrants.

  2—Continental and transoceanic emigration.

F. *Emigration to the U.S.*

  1—Distribution by provinces, sex, age, etc.

  2—Regulations and qualifications.

  3—The journey to the U.S.

    a—First contacts with America and first impressions

IX. THE ITALIAN IMMIGRANT COMMUNITY. ITS ORIGIN AND GROWTH.
   A. *Early Italian pioneers in the U.S.*
      1—Explorers, missionaries.
      2—Individual immigrants.
         a—Mazzei, Vigo, Garibaldi and others.
      3—Itinerant groups—colonists.
   B. *Beginnings of Italian Settlements in the U.S.*
      1—Factors that determined the location of Italian concentrations.
      2—Principles of aggregation.
      3—Occupational status of early Italian immigrants.
      4—Social aspects in the life of early settlers.

X. OUTSTANDING ASPECTS OF LIFE IN ITALO-AMERICAN COMMUNITIES TODAY.
   A. *Community cohesion.*
      1—Biological and cultural affinities.
      2—Uniformity of economic backgrounds and standards of living.
         a—Poverty.
         b—Unemployment.
      3—Geographical isolation of community.
         a—Segregation of community.
      4—Organizational aspects of community.
         a—Leadership and cooperation.
         b—Problems of social control.
         c—Ethnic conflicts within the community.
      5—Community of emotional patterns.
         a—Social isolation from the American milieu.
         b—Sense of inferiority.
         c—Estrangement of Second Generation.
      6—Oscillation of cultural attachment.
         a—The "call of the fatherland".
      7—Confusion in the philosophy of living.
   B. *Slum—the habitat of Italo-American communities.*
      1—Housing conditions.
      2—Health and sanitation.
      3—Recreational patterns.
      4—"Slum" as impetus for provincialism.
         a—Limitation of social horizons.
      5—Slum as breeder of pathological conditions.
         a—Personality demoralization.
         b—Lowering of family mores.
   C. *Delinquency and crime.*
      1—Delinquency in relation to cultural maladjustment.
      2—Street life.
      3—Susceptibility of Second generation to delinquency and crime.
      4—Survey of crime among Italo-Americans.
   D. *The Italo-Americans in the attitude of other Americans.*
      1—Misconceptions and prejudices.

a—Lack of knowledge of Italian cultural background.
b—The Italian and Italo-American as a stereotype.
2—Antagonisms.
a—Fear of impairment of American biological type.
b—Fear of "polluting" American culture.
3—Mental ability of Italo-Americans.
a—Mental deficiency or arrested personality.
E. *The Italo-American and the American environment.*
1—Basic cultural divergence.
2—Acculturation lag of Italo-Americans in comparison with some other immigrant group.

XI. THE ROLE OF ITALO-AMERICAN INSTITUTIONS IN THE PRESERVATION AND MODIFICATION OF THE ITALO-AMERICAN SOCIAL BACKGROUND.
A. *Italo-American Institution, definition of term.*
1—Cultural synthesis embodied in it.
B. *The Parish Church.*
1—Influence of Church and priest upon community life.
2—The Italo-American Church as agency of assimilation and "Italianization."
C. *The Italo-American newspaper.*
1—Types of publications.
2—Contents of publication.
3—The press as a stabilizing factor in Italo-American communities.
a—Educational values.
b—Means for political education.
4—The newspaper as an aid to assimilation.
5—The press as a factor alienating Italo-Americans from the American environment.
D. *The Italo-American Associations.*
1—Their programs, aims, membership and distribution.
a—Political clubs.
b—Labor organizations
c—Mutual Aid Societies.
d—Cultural organizations.
e—Professional associations.
f—Welfare organizations.
2—Italo-American Associations established on a nation-wide basis, such as:
a—Italian Chamber of Commerce.
b—Association of teachers of Italian origin.
c—Italo-American Lodges.
(1)—The Order Sons of Italy in America.
(2)—The National Italian American Union.
(3)—The Alpha Phi Delta Fraternity.
3—Influence of Italy-American banks upon the socio-economic patterns.
4—The Italian National Theatre in the U.S.
a—Travelling groups.
b—Spoken and musical drama.
c—Marionettes.

5—The Cultural significance of Italo-American Associations.
   a—Perpetuation of old world patterns.
   b—Initiation into democratic processes.
   c—The Italo-American association as amalgamation of two cultural heritages.

XII. INFLUENCE OF ITALIANS AND ITALO-AMERICANS IN THE DEVELOPMENT OF NATIONAL LIFE IN THE UNITED STATES.
  A. *The Roman tradition and the Renaissance in the American culture.*
  B. *Outstanding Italians and Italo-Americans in the life of the United States.*
    1—Their participation in the social, political and cultural life of this country.
    2—Contribution of individual Italians and Italo-Americans.
      a—In industry, commerce.
      b—In Military affairs.
      c—In politics.
      d—In science.
      e—In Arts.
      f—In education.
  C. *Diffusion of Italian and Italo-American cultural patterns among other groups in the United States.*
    1—Introduction of new fruit and vegetable cultures.
    2—Influence upon American food habits.
    3—Contribution in the building industries.
    4—Promotion of wine drinking habit.
  D. *Diffusion of crime patterns presumably of Southern Italian origin. The case for and against its probability.*
  E. *Prognosis of further Italo-American cultural contributions.*
    1—Conditions for optimum contributions.

XIII. AMERICANIZATION OF THE SECOND GENERATION ITALO-AMERICAN.
  A. *Environmental conflicts.*
    1—As members of family unit.
      a—Dual cultural heritage.
    2—As members of an Italo-American community.
      a—Inheritance of individualism—"living one's own life".
      b—Lack of community participation.
      c—Lack of personal prestige.
    3—As member of a large American community.
      a—Ethnocentric residues.
      b—Sense of inferiority.
      c—Social limitations.
        (1)—Discrimination.
    4—Within the school.
      a—Language and prejudice.
      b—Discrimination and prejudice.
      c—Disciplinary problems.
      d—Sense of inferiority.
  B. *State of assimilation.*

1—Educational phase.
  a—Availability of schooling.
  b—Influence of parental home.
  c—Attitude of Second Generation toward education.
    (1)—Emancipation of Italo-American girls.
2—Occupational phase.
  a—Vocational ambitions.
  b—Vocational patterns among second generation Italo-Americans.
    (1)—The professionals.
    (2)—The pull toward trades.
    (3)—In commerce and business.
    (4)—In manual crafts.
    (5)—Office work.
    (6)—In agriculture.
  c—Vocational status of women.
    (1)—Occupational changes.
    (2)—Tendency toward artistic trades.
  d—Occupational limitations.
    (1)—Lack of financial resources.
    (2)—Lack of enterprise and cooperation.
    (3)—Inadequacy of schooling.
  e—Unemployment among second generation Italo-Americans.
    (1)—Inaptitude for occupational adjustment.
3—Political phase.
  a—Utilitarian character of politics among Italo-Americans.
  b—Nature of allegiances.
  c—Participation in political life.
    (1)—Adherence to Italo-American group as a minority.
    (2)—Struggles for political domination within Italo-American community.
    (3)—Political leadership.
    (4)—Holding of office.
4—Social phase.
  a—Deviations from parental patterns.
  b—Interaction with groups of the "new immigration."
  c—Interaction with the older American group.
    (1)—Opportunities for interaction.
    (2)—Impediments for interaction.
    (3)—Intermarriage.
C. *Adaptation of American norms.*
  1—Diversity of degrees in cultural adaptation among individuals and Italo-American groups.
    a—Factors determining the diversity.
  2—Differentials of cultural adaptation-Types of Italo-Americans.
    a—The Italo-American adhering to his community standards.
    b—The "social distance" type.
    c—The oscillating type.
    d—The superior type.
    e—The bi-cultural leader type.

3—Outward Americanization.
    a—Conformity to American standards in dress, slang, mannerisms.
        (1)—Emulation of patterns.
    b—In leisure time patterns.
    c—The reach for higher economic levels.
        (1)—Pathology attendant upon it.
D. *What ails the second generation Italo-American?*
    1—Illusion of assimilation.
        a—"Broken moorings."
        b—Retention of cultural heritage of parents.
    2—Confusion of social values.
    3—Undeveloped personalities.

APPENDIX II

Outline for Study of Cultural Change in an Italian Community

[Leonard Covello]

I. Description of Community Previous to Appearance of Italians.
  A. Physical Aspects of Neighborhood.
  B. Cultural:
    1. Nationalities and Languages.
    2. Religions.
    3. Education.
    4. Family Life.
    5. Mores: modes of living, customs, traditions, etc.
  C. Economic:
    1. Occupations.
    2. Problems of Wealth and Poverty.
  D. Community Organizations:
    1. Social Functions.
    2. Inter-relationships of Cultural Patterns. (The influence of homogenous component groups of the area upon various phases of communal life: local government, political adherence, social traits peculiar to East Harlem, etc.).

II. Beginnings of the Italian Settlement: Italian Infiltration.
  A. Individual Pioneers (if any):
    1. Their social and Economic Status.
    2. Motives for Migration and Selection of the Particular Area.
  B. Embryonic Groups:
    1. Date of establishment.
    2. Circumstances leading to settlement: Did the group emigrate directly from Europe or was it remigration within the United States? A remigration within the city?
    3. Motives for migration and selection of particular area:
      a. Economic (media by which they came).
      b. Social.
      c. Specific reasons.
  C. Background of the members of the early Italian Community:
    1. From what provinces and villages did the majority of members come?
    2. Ecology of native habitat. Similarity between local Italian forms and those in the new settlement.

3. Detailed history of manners, customs, occupations (predominant gainful occupations: Agriculture—chief products of the soil; Industrial occupations; Home industries; Others—trades), and community life of the Italian village or province from which members of the community emigrated.

D. Early Days of the Italian Colony in East Harlem:
  1. Manner of Settling down. Segregation of Groups (by provinces, by Clans etc.).
  2. Approximate numerical strength of the groups, proportion of men, women; unattached persons, families with children, blood relationship.
  3. Illiteracy and status of schooling.
  4. Representation of intelligentsia within the group; professional and cultured individuals attached to the group—priests, physicians, lawyers etc.
  5. Somewhat detailed conditions under which the members of the original settlement lived.
      a. Occupational adjustment:
          (1) Labor gangs (Chief occupation).
          (2) Individual employment.
          (3) Modes of earning livelihood.
          (4) Wages—in relation to earnings of earlier settlers.
      b. Housing:
          (1) Types of houses.
          (2) Innovations introduced by newcomers.
      c. Family Life:
          (1) Form of households found among early settlers (association of individuals for purposes of housekeeping).
          (2) Boarding with families.
          (3) Early furnished rooming houses.
      d. Problems of migration occupying minds of early Italian settlers in regard to:
          (1) Duration of residence.
          (2) Anticipation of return.
          (3) Care for families abroad.
          (4) Attempts to bring families from abroad.
      c. Food Habits:
          (1) Types of food consumed; difficulties in obtaining certain articles.
          (2) Where food was purchased.
          (3) Restaurants.
      f. Financial aspects of early Italian settlement:
          (1) Credits.
          (2) Usury.
          (3) Immigrant banking—savings and money remittances abroad.
      g. Leisure Time Activities.
      h. Religion:
          (1) Practice of worship—what church?
          (2) First church for Italians.
          (3) Mission work among Italians.
      j. Social Functions:
          (1) First society (mutual aid, club etc.).

    (2) Places of gatherings; celebrations.

    (3) Relationship between Italian men and women of other nationalities.

  k. Attitudes and behavior in relation to early settlers.

  l. Early traces of problematical clashes with local mores.

  m. Evidences, if any, of early law violations.

III. Development of Italian Community.

  A. Additions to Colony:

    1. Did the additions to the original colony come from Europe directly or from other communities in the United States.

    2. Reasons for influx: social, economic, other.

    3. Pre-war and Post-war groups:

      a. Did the newcomers come in a constantly flowing stream up to 1914?

      b. Did any newcomers arrive after the war and under what circumstances.

      c. From what provinces did the newcomers of both groups come?

      d. Types represented: mentally, socially, economic, etc.

      e. How were they absorbed by the community:

        (1) By Provinces?

        (2) By educational status?

        (3) By Profession?

        (4) By military adherence?

  B. Geographical Changes—Maps indicating changes in geographical distribution. A series of maps marked 1910, if data for that period is available; similarly for 1915, 1925, 1930 indicating:

    1. Streets and areas where a high percentage of Italians resided.

    2. Churches of the Italians.

    3. Halls where lodges met.

    4. Theatres, restaurants, banks and steamship companies owned by or patronized by this nationality.

    5. Offices of newspapers and magazines.

    6. Italian physicians.

    7. Midwives.

    8. Lawyers.

    9. Prominent persons in other professions or in business.

   10. Stores owned or managed by individual Italians; also stores owned and patronized by Italians; those merely patronized or owned but not patronized.

   11. Social foci (meeting places, "hang outs").

   12. Italian furnished rooming houses.

   13. Distribution of homogenous non-Italian nationality groups within East Harlem.

  C. Changes in Numerical Strength.

    1. Statistics indicating population changes in the Italian community of East Harlem:

      a. In actual numbers in the community—Federal Census Data giving numbers of Italians by country of birth and by mother tongue over a period of years 1900, 1910, 1920, and 1930; estimates based on

information supplied by church or school records, and on opinions of informed observers over a period of years.
    b. In Composition of the Population by Sex and Age Groups.
    c. In Geographical Distribution as shown by:
       (1) Federal and state census returns by wards or by assembly districts.
       (2) School census, by school districts.
       (3) By Health Areas.
  2. Comment:
    a. Extent to which population groups within the area have changed.
    b. Succession of population groups:
       (1) Pre-Italian groups supplanted.
       (2) Migration in and out of the area on the part of Italians.
       (3) Newer groups that have moved in.
       (4) Effects of immigration legislation upon the growth of the Italian community.
       (5) Population changes as affected by shift of employment centers.
D. Development of Typical Institutions:
  1. In Institutions characteristic of the group:
    a. The Parish Church:
       (1) Date of founding.
       (2) Membership; fluctuation.
       (3) Nationality of the priest.
       (4) Activities of the church other than religious services:
         (a) Maintenance of Parochial school.
         (b) Late afternoon classes for religious instruction and instruction in the parents' mother tongue.
       (5) Changes within the constitution of the Church:
         (a) Appearance of sectarianism among Italians.
         (b) New forms of church organization.
       (6) The church as a social as well as a religious institution: the changing character of the social activities sponsored by the church:
         (a) Athletic equipment in parish halls.
         (b) Use of English and Italian in parish activities.
         (c) Influence in Americanization, Italianism.
       (7) Attitude of the first generation toward the church as a religious institution: as a social institution. Attitude of second generation.
    b. History of leading Mutual Aid Society:
       (1) Date of founding.
       (2) Number of members at various periods in the history of the society.
       (3) Persons eligible to membership.
       (4) Persons eligible to hold office.
       (5) Actual officers.
       (6) Dues.
       (7) Insurance features.
       (8) Money resources (assets).
       (9) Primary functions.
     (10) Social features.

(11) A comparison of the programs of the meetings held ten years ago and the meetings held now, noting:
  (a) Methods adopted in the hopes of holding the second generation such as:
    (1) Sponsoring trips to Europe to educate the second generation.
    (2) Greater use of English in programs.
    (3) Emphasis on athletics.
  (b) Subjects of interest to original members.
(12) Changes in by-laws and functions (political purposes).
c. Foreign Language Newspaper:
  (1) Date of founding of foreign language paper.
  (2) Personnel of the staff in terms of citizenship and political affiliations.
  (3) Circulation and localities served.
  (4) By whom read: first generation, second generation.
  (5) Subscriptions or sale from stands or home delivery.
  (6) Character of news:
    (a) Amount of general news.
    (b) Local happenings.
    (c) Methods of gathering information.
    (d) Character of advertising.
  (7) English language page (if any):
    (a) When introduced.
    (b) Character of news on this page.
    (c) To what extent is this page used by "second generation."
  (8) Editorial comment reflecting the attitude of the nationality community toward:
    (a) Language assimilation.
    (b) New freedom demanded by youth.
    (c) Forgetfulness of the "Old Country."
    (d) Americanization or glorification of the "Old Country."
  (9) Extent to which read in East Harlem.
  (10) Other Italian newspapers read in East Harlem.
  (11) Influence of Italian newspapers on mode of living in general.
d. The Local Nationality Theatre (if such ever existed).
2. Changes in economic and social conditions effecting Italian group life:
a. Occupational Changes:
  (1) In field of industry:
    (a) List major industries in which Italian men worked. Similarly, industries employing women, boys, girls, age at which boys and girls entered industry.
    (b) Classification and nature of their work at various stages in the history of the community:
      (1) Skilled.
      (2) Semi-Skilled.
      (3) Unskilled.
      (4) Correspondence, if any, to work in homeland.
    (c) Major industries in which they are at present employed, classification and nature of work.

(d) What are the wages received by the workers of Italian group?
  (1) Comparison of same with those of other nationalities as well as with the general standard.
  (2) Change in wage scales in relation to standards of living or purchasing power.
(e) Advancement in status of workers; foremen, superintendants, etc.
(f) Have girls changed from industrial work to other forms of employment:
  (1) Clerical, trades, others.
  (2) Relative wage scales.
(g) Labor Unions:
  (1) Composition of locals in regard to nationality.
  (2) Predominance of nationality in certain labor unions; plasterers, building trades, etc.
  (3) Adherence of nationalities to unionism (proportion of the nationality groups belonging to unions—open shops, industrial enterprise, contracting).
  (4) Into what types of unions are Italians likely to organize (U.S. labor movement, syndicalism, radicalism).
(h) Employment by local governments:
  (1) Type of nature of work.
  (2) Underlying political motives for employment.
(2) In commercial pursuits or trades:
  (a) Approximate number owning or employed in stores, banks, real estate, insurance, etc.
  (b) Changes in proportions so employed over a period of years.
  (c) Approximate yearly income.
  (d) Tendency of owners to employ people of their own nationality.
  (e) Dominance of the nationality in specific trade (barber-shops, produce).
  (f) Competition with other business groups.
(3) In the professions:
  (a) Which professions are represented in the Italian community?
  (b) How long have members of the profession lived in the community?
  (c) Which professions predominate?
  (d) Approximate number of physicians, lawyers, teachers, etc., in the community. Were they educated abroad? In the United States? Are they first generation or second generation.
  (e) What is the attitude of parents who were peasants, towards professional education for their sons? For their daughters?
  (f) Attitude of the Italian group toward professionals of their own nationality in terms of patronage.
  (g) Attitude of non-Italians toward Italian professionals.
b. Ownership of Real Estate:
  (1) To what extent do members of the Italian community own land in section where they originally settled in the city? In the outskirts? In a satellite community?

(2) How many giving full time to farming?

(3) Is there a tendency among Italians to utilize vacant city plots for gardening?

(4) Does hunger for land manifest itself? What forms does same take on? Do American born children sympathize with their parents' hunger for land?

(5) Is the land within the city owned by members of the nationality community largely used for business or residential purposes. Give an approximate idea of its assessed evaluation.

(6) Has there been an increase in land ownership by members of this group during the past decade?

(7) Describe changes in housing, including general character of tenements, number of persons per room, etc. . . . at various periods in the life of the community.

(8) In how far are changes in housing a reflection of economic status?

   (a) Ownership (trend to own homes).

   (b) Acquisition of property.

(9) In how far is the property clear of mortgages? To what extent have members of the community lost mortgaged real estate during the past two years.

(10) In how far due also to:

   (a) Increased familiarity with types of housing available?

   (b) Desire for social prestige?

   (c) Pressure from other members of the family?

   (d) Cheap transportation to less congested sections?

   (e) Forces outside the community working for better housing?

(11) Care and improvement of property motivated by nationality consciousness.

(12) Use of vacant spaces (backyard, house frontage).

(13) Physical aspects of houses characteristic of nationality neighborhood.

c. Other Changes in Economic Status:

   (1) Wealth and Poverty—General outline.

   (2) Investments—in real estate, bonds, cash savings.

   (3) Unemployment:

      (a) Which branches of industries and trade in which the Italian group is employed were affected.

      (b) Relief—Charity.

      (c) Efforts of the nationality group itself to alleviate poverty, (through societies, political agencies individual efforts).

   (4) How far did the local labor laws affect the earning capacity (limitation of working hours, child labor laws, denial of right to work overtime etc.).

3. Changes in education (i.e. A history of educational facilities offered at various stages in development of the community):

a. Adult Education for first generation:

   (1) Schools—English, citizenship, cultural subjects, technical training:

      (a) day schools for adults (for men and women).

      (b) Evening schools for adults (for men and women).

(c) Special classes for women.

(d) Parents-teachers association connected with the schools.

(2) Questions regarding the above educational facilities:

(a) What progress has been made in adult education for the first generation. List proportion of illiteracy among foreign born of this nationality by census periods?

(b) Give an account of the extent to which the nationality has attended night schools, home classes maintained by Board of Education; classes maintained by private agencies.

(c) If records are available indicate numbers in classes.

(d) Is night school attendance limited to persons preparing for naturalization or are there also advanced classes for persons already citizens?

(1) To what extent are such classes attended by Italians.

(2) To what extent are university extension courses attached.

b. Education of second generation:

(1) Indicate numbers of second generation in kindergartens, elementary schools, (public schools and parochial schools) High Schools, trade schools and college.

(2) How many are having special training in Art?

(3) Commercial, vocational schools and courses (their existence within the community, number of pupils from the nationality group).

(4) Financial backing of students (support by parents, self support, loans and scholarships).

(5) Attitude of parents toward their children's education and influence exerted by them in these matters. Attitude of parents toward American educational system in general. Is there overt desire to send children abroad for higher education?

(6) Is the home environment complimentary to the process of school education?

c. Reading habits:

(1) Give an account of the changing habits of the first generation, second generation.

(2) List newspapers and magazines read regularly, occasionally.

(3) What books are most popular. Are these books read by the first generation in native language only?

(4) In how far is the second generation able to read books in their parents' language?

(5) To what extent does this group use public libraries? How many books written in the language of the group are owned by the library?

(6) Circulating libraries within the community group. Type of books read and frequency of borrowing among the nationality group.

(7) Italian book stores, newspaper stands, etc., within the area. Scope of business.

E. Changes in Citizenship and participation in political life:

1. Naturalization:

a. Citizenship figures by sex for successive decades. Number of declarants, petitioners and citizens for successive periods. Records from the local naturalization court, giving statistics for Italians specifically.

      b. How many women of this nationality have become citizens since September 22, 1922.
2. Literacy Test for Voters: Statistics for Italians in East Harlem qualifying, if this figure is available.
3. Actual Voting: List of enrolled voters regarding the number of citizens of the nationality who have enrolled for voting, (if available).
4. Office Holding:
      a. List the public offices held by persons of this nationality, indicating whether these office holders are first or second generation.
      b. Has there been an appreciable change in the amount of political power attained by the nationality during the past decade? Trace changes.
5. Political clubs within the community (membership, functions, influence upon social life of the group).
F. Changes in provisions for recreation and social life:
   1. Analysis of Social Resources within the nationality community:
      a. Names and description of organizations: those within the group, and those outside the group but catering to the demands of the local community:
         (1) Organizations affiliated with the church: Missions, sectarian institutions.
         (2) Settlement houses.
         (3) Social clubs.
         (4) Others.
      b. Organizations functioning predominantly among men:
         (1) Political clubs.
         (2) Labor organizations.
         (3) Others.
         (4) Social focal points catering to men such as pool rooms, "hang-outs," barber shops, etc.
      c. Organizations exclusively for women:
         (1) Auxiliary Church Organizations for women only.
         (2) Womens clubs.
         (3) Various organizations affiliated with men's organizations.
      d. Organizations doing work with boys:
         (1) Along nationality lines.
         (2) Along cosmopolitan lines; clubs, boy scouts, etc.
         (3) So called boys clubs—independent organizations officially existing under the title of social and athletic clubs.
      e. Organizations dealing with girls.
      f. Forms of recreation and social functions sponsored by the community itself; festivals, block parties, bazaars, etc.
      g. Means of recreational and social interchange for youth as offered by:
         (1) School.
         (2) Movies.
         (3) Street.
      h. Influence of all these social resources upon either the preservation of Italianism or the development of a cosmopolitan attitude.
      i. This study on recreational resources is to be graphically represented if possible.

2. General description of any outside organization that stimulates the recreational and social life of the nationality group (formation of new organizations in Italy and elsewere).
3. Analysis of opportunities offered the Italians by the city:
   a. Social centers in schools.
   b. Parks, Playgrounds.
   c. Settlements.
   d. Choral and oratorio societies.
   e. Folk art societies.
   f. Little theatres or "Theatre of Nations."
   g. Concerts (free).
G. Changes in Mores:
   1. Prevalent standards for:
      a. Relations between husband and wife.
      b. Relations between parent and child.
      c. Relations toward other family members.
      d. Relations towards neighbors.
      e. Relations toward employers.
      f. Relations toward recognized authority. Description of conduct which brings social approval at time of birth, courtship, betrothal, marriage, baptism and death of a member of one's family.
   2. Evidences of break-down of old standards.
   3. Substitution of changed modes of behavior which neither conform to the old pattern of Italian Community Life nor to the general pattern of the established American Community.
   4. Evidence of substitution of the mores of the older Americans, partial? Complete?
   5. Survival of characteristic Italian customs.
H. Changes in personality patterns:
   1. Nationality Patterns:
      a. Do members of the community consider themselves Italians, Americans, or Italo-Americans? How do they react in times of emotional mass stirring?
      b. Participation in the World War; volunteers for Italian army, in the American army.
      c. Patriotism: Italian or American—The significance of the American Legion; especially posts with predominant Italian membership.
      d. To what extent do members of the community consider important the preservation of legends, traditions and folk art. Differences in this regard between first and second generation.
      e. Preservation of Italian localisms.
      f. Disintegration of the Italian language. (usage of English words).
   2. Occupational Patterns:
      a. Changes in ideology of industrial workers (acceptance, repulsion of American standards).
      b. Changes in professional ethics (as applied to Italian teachers, physicians, etc.).
   3. Religious Patterns: ethical, social ideals; superstitions.
I. Extent and nature of Social Contacts with older Americans and other Nationality groups:

1. With older Americans:
   a. Media of contact with older white American individuals within the community, also with groups outside.
   (1) Nature and opportunities for such contracts.
   (2) Character of social intercourse with them as neighbors in same apartment house, street, "hangouts," public places (mingling on street and shopping centers).
   (3) Opportunities for meeting older American groups; those of same economic status, those of different economic status. In how far do individuals of the two groups belong to the same clubs? Meet at social gatherings Serve on the same Boards of Directors? belong to the same Lodges? The same labor organizations? Boards of Social Agencies?
   (4) Attitude toward individual older Americans as compared with attitude toward members of other nationality groups. (Respect, Prestige? Is respect or prestige brought about by their economic status or political and social standing?).
   (5) Reactions against a concrete American Group.
   (6) Attitude of American toward Italians: as individuals, as a group —toward first generation, toward second generation. (American sense of superiority, Nordic problem).
2. With Other Nationality groups:
   a. Media and nature of contact with them: within same apartment house, street, neighborhood etc. . . .
   b. Community consciousness of the Italian group:
   (1) Attitude of members of the colony towards one another.
   (2) Attitude toward Italian new comers ("Green Horns") and those of other nationality groups.
   (3) Cooperation with other nationality groups in local and other affairs.
   (4) Rivalry and competition.
   (5) Migration and succession of population groups (causes and results ensuing therefrom).
   c. Cultural and racial conflicts with other groups:
   (1) Religious antagonism.
   (2) Racial incompatibilities. (Also attitudes that reveal innate sympathy or antipathy towards a specific group).
   (3) Social distance. Differences in economic status.
   (4) Clash of traditions, mores, etc. historical animosities.
   (5) Overt excesses.
   d. Propensities of various nationality groupings in creating an atmosphere of mutual understanding, sympathy, etc. . . .
   e. Social intercourse among youth. Role of School, street. Animosities, sympathies between "Child groups." How much are the relationships influenced by their respective parents?
3. Ethnic Fusion:
   a. Biological Fusion:
   (1) What is the attitude of the older Americans toward intermarriage with persons from the Italian community? Theirs toward the older Americans?

(2) What is the attitude toward intermarriage with persons of other nationality communities?

(3) What has been the extent of intermarriage in the community?

(4) The extent of intermarriages among young people at present. Are these marriages successful? How much family solidarity ensues? (Case histories showing successful and unsuccessful marriages might be of interest.)

   b. Cultural Diffusion:

(1) Adaptation of Italian standards and patterns by other nationality groups. (Art appreciation, music, home decoration, food, lingual variations, customs, etc. . . .)

(2) Disintegration of Italian Community in terms of social, political, economic, linguistic isolation.

K. Summary—Changes in an Italian Community against a background of a constantly changing "American Scene.":

1. Changes in family life:
   a. Effect on patriarchial mode:
     (1) The new position of the women.
     (2) Basis of marriage ties.
     (3) Responsibilities and control over children.
     (4) Parents—children conflict.
   b. Economic changes:
     (1) Earnings of members.
     (2) Sense of security.
     (3) Family budgeting and financial arrangements.
     (4) Standards of living and household organization.
   c. Social intercourse: (Relationships with other families, clannishness, boarders.)
   d. Eugenics:
     (1) Size of families (decline in births).
     (2) Marriages and divorces.
   e. Health and Housing.

2. Changes in Economic Life:
   a. Occupational trends.
   b. Trends in proprietorship and ownership.
   c. Wealth and poverty (economic factors in process of segregation).
   d. Cooperative movements.
   e. An acquired conception concerning the general economic milieu, the whole economic system of the country.

3. Changes in social life:
   a. Religious changes: sectarian, role of the church.
   b. Changes in use of leisure time and recreation (sport, games, theatre, radio, movies, etc. . . .).
   c. Language.
   d. Disappearance of demarcation lines between provincial groups.
   e. Changes in social ideals (radicalism, conservation).
   f. Intensity of ties with the "old country".
   g. A new Italian social pattern characteristic of East Harlem.
   h. Italo-American assimilation as manifested by changes in content of Italian newspapers.

APPENDIX III

A Handlist of Selected Writings by Leonard Covello

(With Annita Giacobbe) *First Book in Italian.* New York: Macmillan, 1927.
(With Annita Giacobbe) *First Reader in Italian.* New York: Macmillan, 1933.
The Casa Italiana Educational Bureau: Its Purpose and Program. New York: Casa Italiana Educational Bureau, Columbia University, 1933. (Bulletin No. 4).
The Italians in America: A Brief Survey of a Sociological Research Program of Italo-American Communities. (With Two Population Maps and a Table). New York: Casa Italiana Educational Bureau, Columbia University, 1934. (Bulletin No. 6).
"Language Usage in Italian Families," *Atlantica* (November, December, 1934). (Part I and II).
"A High School and Its Immigrant Community," *Journal of Educational Sociology,* Vol. 9 (February, 1936), pp. 331-346.
"The School as the Center of Community Life," in Samuel Everett, ed., *The Community School* (New York: Appleton-Century-Crofts, 1937), pp. 125-156.
"Italian Americans," in F. Brown and J. Roucek, *Our Racial and National Minorities* (New York: Prentice-Hall, 1937), pp. 357-387. Also, "Language as a Factor in Social Adjustment," *loc. cit.*, pp. 681-696.
"Neighborhood Growth and the Schools," *Progressive Education* (February, 1938).
"Language as a Factor in Integration and Assimilation," *Modern Language Journal* (February, 1939).
"A Neighborhood School in the World's Greatest Metropolis," *Interpreter Releases,* Vol. 16 (May 20, 1939).
"Building Democratic Ideals Through School Community Programs," *Library Journal,* Vol. 65 (February, 1940), pp. 106-109.
"School As a Factor in Community Life," *School Executive,* Vol. 59 (May, 1940), pp. 20-31.
"Adult Education at Benjamin Franklin High School," *Journal of Adult Education,* Vol. 12 (October, 1940).
"Development of the Community Centered School Idea," *Understanding the Child,* Vol. 11 (October, 1942).
"A Community Centered School and the Problem of Housing," *Educational Forum,* Vol. 7 (January, 1943), pp. 133-143.

"Cultural Minorities in the Present Crisis," *Bisophical Review*, Vol. 7 (1943).

"A Principal Speaks to His Community," *American Unity*, Vol. 2 (May, 1944).

"What Should We Tell Our Pupils About the Axis," *Educational Digest* (January, 1944).

"Cultural Assimilation and the Church," *Religíous Education*, Vol. 39 (July-August, 1944), pp. 229-235.

"Puerto Rican Pupils in New York City Public Schools," in *Report* (Mayor's Committee on Puerto Rican Affairs), 1951. (New York City).

"Puerto Rican Life in New York City as Seen by the Puerto Rican Press," *High Points* (December, 1953).

"Community Education in Metropolita," in Edward Olsen, ed., *The Modern Community School* (New York: Appleton-Century-Crofts, 1953).

"Americans of Italian Ancestry," in *Report of the Committee on the Role of Foreign Languages in American Life.* (Northeast Conference on the Teaching of Foreign Languages). 1955.

"The Community School in a Great Metropolis," in *Education for Better Living: The Role of the School in Community Improvement* (Washington: Government Printing Office, 1957), pp. 193-212. (With Simon Beagle and Leon Beck).

The Heart Is the Teacher. New York: McGraw-Hill, 1958. (With Guido D'Agostino). Reissued as *Teacher in the Urban Community: A Half Century in City Schools* (With an Introduction by Francesco Cordasco), Totowa, N.J.: Littlefield, Adams, 1970.

"Bilingualism: Our Untapped National Resource," *American Unity Magazine* (September-October, 1960); also in *La Prensa* (Spanish text), January 20, 1960.

(With Francesco Cordasco) *Educational Sociology: A Subject Index of Doctoral Dissertations Completed at American Universities, 1941-1963.* New York: Scarecrow Press, 1965.

The Social Background of the Italo-American School Child: A Study of the Southern Italian Family Mores and Their Effect on the School Situation in Italy and America. Edited and with an Introduction by Francesco Cordasco. Leiden, The Netherlands: E. J. Brill, 1967; Totowa, N.J.: Rowman and Littlefield, 1972. (Originally, Ph.D. dissertation, New York University, 1944).

BIBLIOGRAPHY OF
SELECTED REFERENCES

I. Bibliographies

The fullest bibliography is Francesco Cordasco, *Italians in the United States: A Bibliography of Reports, Texts, Critical Studies and Related Materials* (New York: Oriole Editions, 1972) which is a partially annotated bibliography of 1462 items on all aspects of the Italian experience in America (*i.e.*, Bibliographies; Emigration; Italian American History and Regional Studies; Sociology of Italian American Life; Italian American in the Politico-Economic Context; Belles-Lettres and the Arts). Considerable bibliography is found in many of the entries in the following classified list, and this is indicated for some of the entries. An excellent bibliographical essay on extant sources is Silvano M. Tomasi, *The Italians in America* (New York: Istituto Italiana di Cultura, Occasional Paper, July, 1971); and notices of recent works are in F. Cordasco, "The Children of Columbus: The New Italian-American Ethnic Historiography," *Phylon: The Atlanta University Review of Race & Culture* (September, 1973). Reference should also be made to:

Baden, Anne L. *Immigration in the United States: A Selected List of Recent References.* Washington, D.C.: Government Printing Office, 1943.

Cordasco, Francesco. *The Italian-American Experience: An Annotated and Classified Bibliographical Guide. With Selected Publications of the Casa Italiana Educational Bureau.* New York: Burt Franklin, 1974.

Dore, Grazia. *La Democrazia italiana e L'emigrazione in America.* Brescia: Morcelliana, 1964. (Bibliography, pp. 389-493). A major work.

Firkins, Ina Teneyck. "Italians in the United States," *Bulletin of Bibliography,* v. 8 (January, 1915), pp. 129-133.

New York Public Library. [The] *Italian People in the United States.* New York: the Library, 1936. 2 vols. [A collection of clippings and pamphlets.]

"A selected list of bibliographical references and records of the Italians in the United States," *Italian Library of Information* [New York]. Outline Series. Series 1, No. 5 (August, 1958), pp. 1-19.

Velikonja, Joseph. *Italians in the United States.* Occasional Papers, No. 1. Department of Geography, Southern Illinois University. Carbondale, Illinois: 1963. [See *Review* (corrections), Joseph G. Fucilla, *Italica* vol. 41 (June 1964), pp. 213-216.] Awkwardly arranged, but a valuable pioneer compilation and list on the Italian experience in the United

States. No annotations; includes an author index. Some copies of the mimeographed list are miscollated.

II. Italian Emigration to America

A. GENERAL STUDIES AND REPORTS

Beccherini, Francesco. *Il fenomeno dell'emigrazione italiani negli Stati Uniti.* San Sepoloro: Tip. Boncompagni, 1906.

[Centro Studi Emigrazione] *La Società Italiana di fronte alle prime migrazione di masse.* Roma: Centro Studi Emigrazione, 1968. [A special issue of the Center's *Studi Emigrazione* which studies Italian emigration with G. B. Scalabrini, Bishop of Piacenza, and his efforts in behalf of immigrants as central themes. Invaluable. Reissued, with a new foreword by F. Cordasco, New York: Arno Press, 1975.]

D'Ambrosio, Manlio. *Il Mezzogiorno d'Italia e l'emigrazione negli Stati Uniti.* Roma: Athenaeum, 1924.

Dore, Grazia. *La Democrazia italiana e L'emigrazione in America.* Brescia: Morcelliana, 1964. (Bibliography, pp. 389-493). A major work.

Foerster, Robert F. *The Italian Emigration of Our Times.* Cambridge: Harvard University Press, 1919. Reissued with an introductory note by F. Cordasco, New York: Russell & Russell, 1968.

Livi-Bacci, Massimo. *L'immigrazione e l'assimilazione degli italiani negli Stati Uniti secondo le statisiche demographiche Americane* (Milano: Giuffre, 1961). [Estimates that there were in 1950 in the U.S. no fewer than 7 million people, belonging to three generations, who had at least one Italian grandparent. Other estimates have run at least as high as 21 million and over.] See Giuseppe Lucrezio Monticelli, "Italian Emigration: Basic Characteristics and Trends," in S. M. Tomasi and M. H. Engel, eds., *The Italian Experience In The United States* (1970), pp. 3-22.

United States Immigration Commission. *Report of the Immigration Commission.* 41 vols. Washington Government Printing Office, 1911. *Index of Reports of the Immigration Commission,* S. Doc. No. 785, 61st Congress, 3rd Session, was never published. [Abstracts, vols. 1-2; includes statistical review of immigration; emigration conditions in Europe; dictionary of races or peoples; immigrants in industries; immigrants in cities; occupations of immigrants; fecundity of immigrant women; children of immigrants in schools; immigrants as charity seekers; immigration and crime; steerage conditions; bodily form of descendants of immigrants; federal immigration legislation; state immigration and alien laws; other countries; statements and recommendations.] The restrictive quotas derive from this work.

Villari, Luigi. *Gli Stati Uniti d'America e l'emigrazione italiana.* Milano: Fratelli Treves, 1912.

B. SPECIAL STUDIES

Bonacci, Giovanni. *Calabria e emigrazione.* Firenze: Ricci, 1908.

Cattapani, Carlo. "Gli emigranti italiani fra gli Anglo-Sassoni," *Atti, Congresso Geografico Italiano* [Palermo, 1911], pp. 143-162.

Cerase, Francesco P. "A Study of Italian Migrants Returning from the U.S.A.," *International Migration Review*, Vol. I. New Series (Summer, 1967), pp. 67-74.

"Character Of Italian Immigration." *New England Magazine*, n.s., 35 (1906), pp. 216-220.

Dore, Grazia. "Some Social and Historical Aspects of Italian Emigration to America," *Journal of Social History* (Winter 1968).

Dickinson, Joan Y. "Aspects of Italian Immigration to Philadelphia," *Pennsylvania Magazine of History and Biography*, vol. 40 (October 1966), pp. 445-465.

Foerster, Robert F. "A Statistical Survey of Italian Emigration," *Quarterly Journal of Economics*, v. 23 (November 1908), pp. 66-103.

Gans, Herbert J. "Some Comments on the History of Italian Migration and on the Nature of Historical Research," *International Migration Review*, Vol. I New Series (Summer 1967), pp. 5-9.

Gilkey, George R. "The United States and Italy: Migration and Repatriation," *Journal of Developing Areas* (1967), pp. 23-35.

Hall, Prescott F. "Italian Immigration," *North American Review*, v. 163 (August 1896), pp. 252-254.

Haughwont, Frank G. "Italian Emigration," *U.S. Consular Reports*, v. 11 (December, 1883), pp. 364-366.

Huntington, Henry G. "Italian Emigration to the United States," *U.S. Consular Reports*, v. 44 (February, 1894), pp. 308-309.

Monticelli, G. Lucrezio. "Italian Emigration: Basic Characteristics and Trends with Special Reference to the Last Twenty Years," *International Migration Review*, Vol. I, New Series (Summer 1967), pp. 10-24.

Senner, Joseph H. "Immigration from Italy," *North American Review*, v. 162 (May 1896), pp. 649-656. Reply by P. F. Hall, v. 163 (August 1896), pp. 252-254.

Speranza, Gino C. "Our Italian Immigration," *Nation*, v. 80 (1905), p. 304; also, "The Italian Emigration Department in 1904," *Charities*, v. 15 (October 21, 1905), pp. 114-116.

Stella, Antonio A. *Some Aspects of Italian Immigration to the United States; Statistical Data Based Chiefly Upon the U.S. Census and Other Official Publications.* New York: Putnam's Sons, 1924. Reprinted, San Francisco: R & E Research Associates, 1970.

C. MISCELLANEOUS

Barker, Folger. "What of the Italian Immigrant?" *Arena*, v. 34 (August 1905), pp. 174-176.

Bodio, Luigi. *Protection of Italian Immigrants in America.* U.S. Bureau of Education (1895), v. 2, pp. 1789-1793.

Corsi, Edward. *In The Shadow Of Liberty: The Chronicle of Ellis Island.* New York: Macmillan, 1935.

Lopreato, Joseph. *Peasants No More* (San Francisco: Chandler, 1967). [Social change in southern Italy as a consequence of emigration.]

Merlino, S. "Italian Immigrants and Their Enslavement," *Forum*, v. 15 (April, 1893), pp. 183-190.

Tomasi, Silvano M. *An Overview of Current Efforts and Studies in the Field of Italian Immigration.* Staten Island, New York: Center for Migration Studies [*circa* 1968].

Tosti, Gustavo. "Italy's Attitude Toward Her Emigrants," *North American Review*, v. 180 (May 1905), pp. 720-726.

Velikonja, Joseph. "Italian Immigrants in the United States in the Mid-Sixties," *International Migration Review*, Vol. I, New Series (Summer 1967), pp. 25-37.

Von Borosini, Victor. "Home-going Italians," *Survey*, v. 28 (September 28, 1912), pp. 791-793.

III. Italian American History and Regional Studies

A. GENERAL STUDIES

Amfitheatrof, Erik. *The Children of Columbus: An Informal History of the Italians in the New World.* Boston: Little, Brown, 1973.

Clark, Francis Edward. *Our Italian Fellow Citizens in Their Old Homes and Their New.* Boston: Small, Maynard, & Co., 1919.

Cordasco, Francesco, and Eugene Bucchioni. *The Italians: Social Backgrounds of an American Group.* Clifton, N.J.: Augustus M. Kelley, 1974. [Documentary sourcebook on Italians in the United States, largely between 1880-1940.]

DeConde, Alexander. *Half Bitter, Half Sweet: An Excursion into Italian-American History.* New York: Charles Scribner's Sons, 1971.

Green, Rose B. *The Italian-American Novel: A Document of the Interaction of Two Cultures.* Rutherford, N.J.: Fairleigh Dickinson University Press, 1974.

Grossman, Ronald P. *The Italians in America.* Minneapolis: Lerner Publications, 1966.

Iorizzo, Luciano J. and Salvatore Mondello. *The Italian Americans.* New York: Twayne, 1971.

[Istituto Di Studi Americani] *Gli Italiani negli Stati Uniti.* Firenze: Università degli Studi, 1972. [Texts of 21 papers presented at symposium on American studies, May 27-29, 1969.]

Lopreato, Joseph. *The Italian Americans.* New York: Random House, 1970.

Lord, Elliot, John D. Trenner, Samuel Barrows. *The Italian in America.* New York: B. F. Buck and Company, 1906. Reprinted, San Francisco: R & E Research Associates, 1970.

Moquin, Wayne, with Charles Van Doren. *A Documentary History of the Italian Americans.* New York: Praeger, 1974.

Musmanno, Michael A. *The Story of the Italians in America* (New York: Doubleday, 1965).

Pisani, Lawrence Frank. *The Italian in America. A Social Study and History.* New York: Exposition Press, 1957.

Rolle, Andrew F. *The Immigrant Upraised: Italian Adventurers and Colonists in an Expanding America.* (Norman, Oklahoma: University of Oklahoma Press, 1968). Bibliography, pp. 351-371.

Rolle, Andrew F. *The American Italians: Their History and Culture.* Belmont, California: Wadsworth, 1972.

Rose, Philip M. *The Italians in America.* New York: George H. Doran Co., 1922.

Schiavo, Giovanni E. *Italian-American History.* 2 vols. New York: Vigo Press, 1947-49.

Schiavo, Giovanni Ermenegildo. *Italians in America before the Civil War.* New York: G. P. Putnam's Sons, 1924. [1934]

Tomasi, Lydio F., ed. *The Italian in America: The Progressive View, 1891-1914.* New York: Center for Migration Studies, 1972. [Brings together out of the progressive journal, *Charities*, a significant corpus of materials.]

Tomasi, Silvano M. and M. H. Engel, eds. *The Italian Experience in the United States.* Staten Island, New York: Center for Migration Studies, 1970. [Includes extensive bibliographies.]

B. REMINISCENCES, BIOGRAPHIES AND NARRATIVES

Arrigioni, Leone Sante. *Un Viaggio in America.* Impressioni. Torino: Tipografia Salesiana, 1906.

Barzini, Luigi. *Americans Are Alone in the World.* New York: Random House, 1953. See also, *The Italians.* New York: Atheneum, 1964.

Biagi, Ernest L. *The Purple Aster, a History of the Order Sons of Italy in America.* New York: Veritas Publishing Co., 1961.

Conte, Gaetano. *Dieci anni in America. Impressioni e ricordi.* Palermo: G. Spinnato, 1903.

Covello, Leonard (with Guido D'Agostino). *The Heart is the Teacher.* New York: McGraw-Hill, 1958. Reprinted with *An Introduction* by F. Cordasco, New York: Littlefield & Adams, 1970 [*The Teacher in the Urban Community: A Half Century in City Schools.*]

Falbo, Ernest S., ed. [and Trans.]. Count Leonetto Cipriani, *California and Overland Diaries from 1853-1871.* Portland, Oregon: Champoeg Press, 1961.

Ferrari, Robert. *Days Pleasant and Unpleasant in the Order Sons of Italy; The Problem of Race and Racial Societies in the United States. Assimilation or Isolation?* New York: Mandy Press, 1926. Reprinted with a new Foreword by F. Cordasco, Clifton, N.J.: Augustus M. Kelley, 1973.

Gallenga, Antonio Carlo Napoleone. *Episodes of My Second Life. American and English Experiences.* Philadelphia: J. B. Lippincott, 1885.

Iamurri, Gabriel A. *The True Story of an Immigrant.* Rev. ed. Boston: Christopher Publishing House, 1951.

Mazzei, Philip. *Memoirs.* Trans. by H. R. Marraro. New York: Columbia University Press, 1942.

Neidle, Cecyle S. *The New Americans.* New York: Twayne, 1967. Includes notices of Leonard Covello, Angelo Pellegrini, Constantine Nunzio, Edward Corsi and Pascal d'Angelo.

Panunzio, Constantine M. *Immigrant Crossroads.* New York: The Macmillan Co., 1927.

Panunzio, Constantine M. *The Immigrant Portrayed in Biography and Story: A Selected List with Notes.* New York: Foreign Language Information Service, 1925.

Panunzio, Constantine M. *The Soul of an Immigrant.* New York: The Macmillan Co., 1922. [1924; 1934]

Peebles, Robert. *Leonard Covello: An Immigrant's Contribution to New York City.* Unpublished doctoral thesis, New York University, 1967.

Pellegrini, Angelo M. *Immigrant's Return.* New York: Macmillan, 1951.

Pellegrini, Angelo M. *American by Choice.* New York: Macmillan, 1956.

Speranza, Gino C. *The Diary of Gino Speranza, Italy, 1915-1919.* Edited by Florence Colgate Speranza. New York: Columbia University Press, 1941. 2 vols. [Gino Charles Speranza, 1872-1927].

Torielli, Andrew Joseph. *Italian Opinion on America as Revealed by Italian Travelers, 1850-1900.* Cambridge, Mass.: Harvard University Press, 1941.

C. REGIONAL STUDIES

a. Northeast

Adams, Charlotte. "Italian Life in New York," *Harper's Monthly,* v. 62, no. 371 (April, 1881), pp. 666-684.

Altarelli, Carlo C. *History and Present Conditions of the Italian Colony at Paterson, N.J.* New York: Columbia University Studies in Sociology, 1911.

Barrese, Pauline J. "Southern Italian Folklore in New York City," *New York Folklore Quarterly,* XXI (September 1965), pp. 181-193.

Betts, Lillian W. *The Italian in New York.* New York: University Settlement Studies, 1904-1905.

Bianco, Carla. *The Two Rosetos.* Bloomington: Indiana University Press, 1974. [Italian American community in Pennsylvania and "sister" village in southern Italy.]

Cordasco, F. and R. Galattioto. "Ethnic Displacement in the Interstitial Community: The East Harlem [New York City] Experience," *Phylon: The Atlanta University Review of Race & Culture,* vol. 31 (Fall 1970), pp. 302-312; also in *Journal of Negro Education,* vol. 40 (Winter 1971), pp. 56-65. [Notices of the Italian community.]

Cordasco, F. *Jacob Riis Revisited: Poverty and the Slum in Another Era.* New York: Doubleday, 1968. [Italians in New York. Riis' photographs of the Italian subcommunity in New York City (1890-1905?) are in the Jacob A. Riis Collection, Museum of the City of New York.]

Irwin, Grace. "Michelangelo in Newark," *Harper's Magazine,* v. 143 (September 1921), pp. 446-454.

Mangano, Antonio. *Italian Colonies in New York City.* New York: Columbia University Studies in Sociology, 1904.

Pileggi, Nicholas. "Little Italy: Study of an Italian Ghetto," *New York,* Vol. 1 (August 12, 1968), pp. 14-23.

Riis, Jacob A. "The Italian in New York," *How the Other Half Lives. Studies among the Tenements of New York.* New York: Charles Scribner's Sons, 1890.

Shedd, William B. "Italian Population in New York City," *The Casa Italiana Educational Bureau*, Bulletin No. 7 (1934); [Also published in *Atlantica*, September 1934].

U.S. Federal Writer's Project. New York City. *The Italians of New York.* A survey prepared by workers of the Federal Writer's Project. Work Progress Administration in the City of New York. New York: Random House, 1938. [Published also in Italian]

b. The South

"A Model Italian Colony in Arkansas," *Review of Reviews*, v. 34 (September 1906), pp. 361-362.

Brandfon, Robert L. "The End of Immigration to the Cotton Fields," *The Mississippi Valley Historical Review*, vol. 50 (March 1964), pp. 591-611. [On attempts to replace Negroes with Italian agricultural workers.]

Cunningham, G. E. "Italians: A Hindrance to White Solidarity in Louisiana, 1890-1898," *Journal of Negro History*, vol. 50 (January 1965), pp. 22-36.

Hewes, Leslie. "Tontitown: Ozark Vineyard Center [features of the predominantly Italian community and how it developed]," *Economic Geography*, vol. 29 (April 1953), pp. 125-143.

"Italians in the South;" "The South Wants Italians," *Outlook*, v. 87 (1907), pp. 556-558.

Langley, Lee J. "Italian as a Southern Farmer. Striking Characterization of Their Success and Value to the Community," *Manufacturers' Record* (August 1904).

Langley, Lee J. "Italians in Cotton Field. Their Superiority over Negroes Shown on an Arkansas Plantation," *Manufacturers' Record* (April 1904).

Phenis, Albert. "Italian Immigration to the South," *Manufacturers' Record* (May 1905).

Ramirez, M. D. "Italian Folklore from Tampa, Florida," *Southern Folklore Quarterly*, vol. 13 (June 1949), pp. 121-132; also, pp. 101-106.

c. Midwest

Boyer, Brian. "Chicago's Italians," *Midwest*, [Chicago Sun Times] (July 14, 1968), p. 6+.

La Piana, George. *The Italians in Milwaukee, Wisconsin: General survey, prepared under the direction of the Associated Charities.* Milwaukee, Wis.: 1915. Reprinted, San Francisco: R & E Research Associates, 1970.

Nelli, Humbert S. *The Italians in Chicago: A Study in Ethnic Mobility.* New York: Oxford University Press, 1970. [Considerable documentation and bibliographies.]

Schiavo, Giovanni. *The Italians in Chicago: A Study in Americanization.* Chicago: Italian American Publishing Company, 1928.

Schiavo, Giovanni. *The Italians in Missouri.* Chicago: Italian American Publishing Co., 1929.

U.S. Bureau of Labor. *The Italians in Chicago.* A social and economic study. Ninth Special Report of the Commissioner of Labor. Prepared under the direction of Caroll D. Wright. Washington, D.C.: Government Printing Office, 1897.

Vecoli, Rudolph J. *Chicago's Italians Prior to World War I: A Study of Their Social and Economic Adjustment.* [Unpublished doctoral thesis. University of Wisconsin, 1963.]

Vecoli, Rudolph J. "Contadini in Chicago: A Critique of *The Uprooted,*" *Journal of American History*, vol. 51 (December 1964), pp. 404-417.

Vismara, John C. "The Coming of the Italians to Detroit," *Michigan History Magazine*, v. 11 (January 1918), pp. 110-124.

Writers' Program [Nebraska]. *The Italians of Omaha.* Omaha: Independent Printing Co., 1941.

d. The West

Bohme, Frederick G. "The Italians in New Mexico," *New Mexico Historical Review* (April 1959), pp. 98-116.

Crespi, Cesare. *San Francisco e la sua catastrofe.* San Francisco, Tipografia internazionale, 1906.

La Voce Del Popolo [1868-1905]. Microfilm. San Francisco: R & E Research Associates, 1970. [The first Italian Newspaper in California.]

Radin, Paul. *The Italians of San Francisco: Their Adjustment and Acculturation.* California, Relief Administration. Cultural Anthropology Project. San Francisco, 1935. Reprinted, San Francisco: R & E Research Associates, 1970.

Rolle, Andrew F. "Italy in California," *Pacific Spectator*, v. 9 (Fall 1955), pp. 408-419.

Rolle, Andrew F. "Success in the Sun: Italians in California," *The Westerners.* Los Angeles Corral. Los Angeles: Brand Book, 1961.

Rolle, Andrew F. "The Italian Moves Westward: Jesuit Missionaries Formed the Vanguard of Italy's Many-sided Impact on the Frontier," *Montana* [the Magazine of Western History], Vol. 16 (January 1966), pp. 13-24.

Schiavo, Giovanni. "The Italian Fishermen in California," *Vigo Review* (December 1938).

Speroni, Charles. "The Development of the Columbus Day Pageant of San Francisco," *Western Folklore*, vol. 7 (1948), pp. 325-335; "California Fisherman's Festivals," *Ibid.*, vol. 14 (1955), pp. 77-91.

e. Miscellanea

Banfield, Edward C. *The Moral Basis of a Backward Society.* New York: Free Press, 1958. [On Southern Italian society.]

Carr, John Foster. "The Italian in the United States," *World's Work*, v. 8 (1904), pp. 5393-5404.

Carr, John Foster. "The Coming of the Italian," *Outlook*, v. 82 (February 29, 1906), pp. 419-431.

Covello, Leonard. "Italian Americans." Francis J. Brown and Joseph S. Roucek, eds. *Our Racial and National Minorities. Their History, Contributions, and Present Problems.* New York: Prentice Hall, 1937.

Covello, Leonard. *The Italians in America.* New York: Casa Italiana Education Bureau. Bulletin No. 6 [1932?]

David-Dubois, Rachel, ed. *Some of the Contributions of Italy and Her Sons to Civilization and American Life.* New York: Casa Italiana Educational Bureau, Bulletin No. 3 [1935?]

Fante, John. "The Odyssey of a Wop," *American Mercury,* v. 30 (September 1933), pp. 89-97.

Glanz, Rudolf. *Jew and Italian: Historic Group Relations and the New Immigration, 1881-1924.* New York: Ktav Publishing Co., 1971.

Jenkins, Hester. "And We Have Been Calling Them 'Dagoes,' " *World Outlook,* v. 3 (October 1907), p. 61.

Marinacci, Barbara. *They Came From Italy: The Story of Famous Italian-Americans.* New York: Dodd, 1967. [Text for Grades 8 and up.]

Mondello, Salvatore. "The Magazine *Charities* and the Italian Immigrants, 1903-14," *Journalism Quarterly,* vol. 44 (Spring 1967), pp. 91-98.

Pecorini, Alberto. "Our Italian Problem," *Review of Reviews,* v. 43 (1911), pp. 236-237.

Pecorini, Alberto. "The Italians in the United States," *The Forum,* v. 45 (January 1911), pp. 15-29.

Pileggi, Nicholas. "How We Italians Discovered America and Kept It Pure While Giving It Lots of Singers, Judges, and Other Swell People," *Esquire,* Vol. 69 (June 1968), pp. 80-82.

Pileggi, Nicholas. "The Risorgimento of Italian Power: The Red, White and Greening of New York," *New York,* vol. 4 (June 7, 1971), pp. 26-36.

Puzo, Mario. "The Italians, American Style," *New York Times Magazine* (August 6, 1967).

Sexton, Patricia. *Spanish Harlem.* New York: Harper & Row, 1965. [Italian community.] See also, F. Cordasco, "Spanish Harlem: The Anatomy of Poverty," *Phylon: The Atlanta Review of Race & Culture,* vol. 26 (Summer 1965), pp. 195-196.

Speranza, Gino. *Race or Nationality: A Conflict of Divided Loyalties.* Indianapolis. [1920?]

Tomasi, Lydio F., ed., *The Italian in America: The Progressive View, 1891-1914.* New York: Center for Migration Studies, 1972. Articles out of the progressive journal *Charities* (1894-1913) which deal with the Italian immigrant.

Velikonja, Joseph. "The Italian Born in the United States, 1950," *Annals of the Association of American Geographers,* Vol. 51 (December, 1961), p. 426.

IV. Sociology of Italian American Life

A. SOCIAL STRUCTURE: CONFLICT AND ACCULTURATION

Campisi, Paul J. "Ethnic Family Patterns: The Italian Family in the United States," *American Journal of Sociology,* v. 53 (May 1948), pp. 443-449. Also published as, "The Italian Family in the United States,"

Milton L. Barron, *American Minorities*. New York: Alfred Knopf, 1957.

Child, Irvin Long. *Italian or American? The Second Generation in Conflict*. New Haven: Published for the Institute of Human Relations by Yale University Press, 1943. Reissued with an introduction by F. Cordasco, New York: Russell & Russell, 1970 [originally, Ph.D. dissertation, Yale University, 1939].

Douglas, David W. *Influence of the Southern Italian in American Society*. (Columbia University Studies in Sociology), New York: Columbia University, 1915.

Gallo, Patrick J. *Ethnic Alienation: The Italian-Americans*. Rutherford, N.J.: Fairleigh Dickinson University Press, 1974.

Gans, Herbert J. *The Urban Villagers*. New York: Free Press, 1962. [Italian-American community of Boston].

Glazer, Nathan and Daniel P. Moynihan. *Beyond the Melting Pot: The Negroes, Puerto Ricans, Jews, Italians, and Irish of New York City*. 2nd ed. Cambridge: M.I.T. Press, 1970. [The section on Italians was written by Glazer].

Nelli, Humbert S. "Italians in Urban America: A Study in Ethnic Adjustment," *International Migration Review*, Vol. I. New Series (Summer 1967), pp. 38-55. [See entries for R. J. Vecoli for different view.]

Speranza, Gino C. "How It Feels to be a Problem: A Consideration of Certain Causes Which Prevent or Retard Assimilation," *Charities*, v. 12 (May 7, 1904), pp. 457-463.

Steiner, Edward A. "The Italian in America." *On the Trail of the Immigrant*. New York: Fleming H. Revell, 1906.

Wheeler, Thomas C. *The Immigrant Experience: The Anguish of Becoming an American*. New York: Dial, 1971. [Narrative by Mario Puzo].

Whyte, William F. *Street Corner Society: The Social Structure of an Italian Slum*. 2nd edition. Chicago: University of Chicago Press, 1955. [Revision of Ph.D. dissertation, University of Chicago, 1943].

Williams, Phyllis H. *South Italian Folkways in Europe and America: A Handbook for Social Workers, Visiting Nurses, School Teachers, and Physicians*. New Haven: Published for the Institute of Human Relations by Yale University Press, 1938. Reissued with An Introductory note by F. Cordasco, New York: Russell & Russell, 1969.

B. EDUCATION

Ayres, Leonard P. *Laggards in Our Schools*. New York: The Charities Publication Committee [of the Russell Sage Foundation]. 1909. [Useful data and information on Italian school children].

Children of Immigrants in Schools. vols. 29-33 of *Report of the Immigration Commission*. 41 vols. (Washington: Government Printing Office, 1911). Republished with *An Introductory Essay* by F. Cordasco, Metuchen, N.J.: Scarecrow Reprint Corp., 1970. [A vast repository of data on educational history of immigrant children in America. Detailed analysis of backgrounds, nativity, school progress and home environments of school children in 32 American cities.] See also, Morris

I. Berger, *The Settlement, the Immigrant and the Public School* (unpublished doctoral thesis, Columbia University, 1956); and F. Cordasco, "Educational Pelagianism: The Schools and the Poor," *Teachers College Record*, vol. 69 (April 1968), pp. 705-709.

Cordasco, F. "The Challenge of the non-English Speaking Child in American Schools," *School & Society* (March 30, 1968), pp. 198-201. [On the enactment of the bilingual amendments (Title VII) of the Elementary and Secondary Education Act.]

Cordasco, F. "The Children of Immigrants in the Schools: Historical Analogues of Educational Deprivation," *Kansas Journal of Sociology*, vol. 6 (Fall 1970), pp. 143-152. [Italian children in American schools.]

Cordasco, Francesco, ed. *The Italian Community and Its Language in the United States*. Totowa, N.J.: Rowman and Littlefield, 1974. [The *Reports* of the New York City Italian Teachers Association, 1921-1938.]

Covello, Leonard. "Language Usage in Italian Families," *Atlantica* (October-November 1934).

Covello, Leonard. "A High School and its Immigrant Community," *Journal of Educational Sociology*, vol. 9 (February 1936), pp. 333-346. [Benjamin Franklin High School, East Harlem.]

Covello, Leonard. *The Social Background of the Italo-American School Child. A Study of the Southern Italian Family Mores and Their Effect on the School Situation in Italy and America*. Edited and with an introduction by F. Cordasco. Leiden, The Netherlands: E. J. Brill, 1967. [Revision of doctoral thesis, New York University, 1944.]

Concestrè, Marie J. *Adult Education in a Local Area: A Study of a Decade in the Life and Education of the Adult Immigrant in East Harlem, New York City*. Unpublished doctoral thesis, New York University, 1944. [A major study of the Italian community].

Golden, Herbert H. "The Teaching of Italian: The 1962 Balance Sheet," *Italica*, vol. 39 (1962), pp. 275-288. [A significant statement on the decline in Italian language instruction in the U.S.]

Matthews, Sister Mary Fabian. *The Role of the Public School in the Assimilation of the Italian Immigrant Child in New York City 1900-1914*. Unpublished doctoral thesis, Fordham University, 1966.

May, Ellen. "Italian Education and Immigration," *Education*, v. 28 (March, 1908), pp. 450-453.

Patri, Angelo. *A School Master in the Great City*. New York: Macmillan, 1917.

Tait, Joseph W. *Some Aspects of the Effect of the Dominant American Culture Upon Children of Italian-Born Parents*. New York: Columbia University, 1942. (Teachers College Contributions to Education). [Reprinted with a Foreword by F. Cordasco, New York: Augustus M. Kelley, 1971.]

Thompson, Frank V. *Schooling of the Immigrant*. New York: Harper, 1920. See also Alan M. Thomas, "American Education and the Immigrant," *Teachers College Record*, vol. 55 (1953-54), pp. 253-267; also, F. Cordasco, "Summer Camp Education for Underprivileged Children," *School & Society*, vol. 93 (Summer 1965).

Wheaton, H. H. *Recent Progress in the Education of Immigrants*. Washington: Government Printing Office, 1915. See, in this connection, *Bibliography of Publications of the U.S. Office of Education 1867-1959*. With an Introductory Note by F. Cordasco. Totowa, N.J.: Rowman and Littlefield, 1971.

C. HEALTH AND RELATED CONCERNS

Breed, R. L. "Italians Fight Tuberculosis," *Survey*, v. 23 (February 12, 1910), pp. 702-703.

Bremner, Robert H., ed. *Children and Youth in America: A Documentary History*, vol. I (1600-1865); vol. II, 1866-1932: Parts 1-6; Parts 7-8. Cambridge: Harvard University Press, 1970-1971.

Dinwiddie, Emily W. "Some Aspects of Italian Housing and Social Conditions in Philadelphia," *Charities*, v. 12 (May 1904), pp. 490-494.

Gebhart, John C. *Growth and Development of Italian Children in New York*. New York: The Association for the Improvement of the Condition of the Poor, 1924.

Moseley, Daisy H. "The Catholic Social Worker in an Italian District," *Catholic World*, v. 114 (February 1922), pp. 618-628.

Stella, Antonio. *The Effects of Urban Congestion on Italian Women and Children*. New York: William Wood, 1908.

Stella, Antonio. "Tuberculosis and the Italians in the United States," *Charities*, v. 12 (May 7, 1904), pp. 486-489.

Stella, Antonio. "The Prevalence of Tuberculosis among Italians in the United States," *Transactions of the Sixth International Congress on Tuberculosis*. Washington, September 28-October 5, 1908, v. 1-5. Philadelphia: W. F. Fell, 1908.

Stella, Antonio. "[Tuberculosis] among the Italians," *Charities*, v. 21 (November 7, 1908), p. 248.

Stella, Antonio. *La lotta contro la tubercolosi fra gli Italiana nella città di New York ed effetti dell'urbanesimo*. Roma: Tip. Colombo, 1912.

D. RELIGION AND MISSIONARY WORK

Bandini, Albert. "Concerning the Italian Problem," *Ecclesiastic Review*, v. 62 (1920), pp. 278-285.

Browne, Henry J. "The 'Italian Problem' in the United States, 1880-1900," *U.S. Catholic Historical Society, Historical Records and Studies*, v. 35 (1946), pp. 46-72.

Felici, Icilio. *Father to the Immigrants. The Life of John Baptist Scalabrini*. New York: P. J. Kennedy & Sons, 1955.

Femminella, Francis X. "The Impact of Italian Migration and American Catholicism," *American Catholic Sociological Review*, vol. XXII (Fall 1961), pp. 233-241.

McLeod, Christian. [Anna C. Ruddy]. *The Heart of the Stranger. A Story of Little Italy*. New York: Fleming H. Revell Co., 1908. [The life of Italians in East Harlem, New York City, written by a social/religious reformer who founded the Home Garden (1901) later to become LaGuardia Memorial House.]

Mangano, Antonio. "The Associated Life of the Italians in New York City," *Charities*, v. 12 (May 7, 1904), pp. 476-482.

Mangano, Antonio. *Religious Work for Italians in America: A Handbook for Leaders in Missionary Work*. New York: Immigrant Work Committee of the Home Missions Council [c. 1915].

Mangano, Antonio. *Sons of Italy: A Social and Religious Study of the Italians in America*. New York: Missionary Education Movement of the United States and Canada, 1917. Reprinted with a Foreword by F. Cordasco, New York: Russell & Russell, 1972.

Mondello, Salvatore. "Protestant Proselytism among the Italians in the U.S.A. as Reported in American Magazines," *Social Sciences*, vol. 41 (April 1966), pp. 84-90.

Palmieri, Aurelio. *Il Grave Problema Religioso Italiano negli Stati Uniti*. Florence, 1921. [major work]

Sartorio, Enrico C. *Social and Religious Life of Italians in America*. Boston: The Christopher Publishing House, 1918. Reprinted with a Foreword by F. Cordasco, Clifton, N.J.: Augustus M. Kelley, 1973.

Tomasi, Silvano M. "The Ethnic Church and the Integration of Italian Immigrants in the United States," S. M. Tomasi and M. H. Engel, *The Italian Experience in the United States* (Staten Island, New York: Center for Migration Studies, 1970), pp. 163-193.

Vecoli, Rudolph J. "Prelates and Peasants: Italian Immigrants and the Catholic Church," *Journal of Social History*, vol. 2 (Spring 1969), pp. 217-268. [considerable bibliography]

E. CRIME, DELINQUENCY, AND SOCIAL DEVIANCE

Albini, Joseph L. *The American Mafia: Genesis of a Legend*. New York: Appleton-Century-Crofts, 1971. [Basic work]

Anderson, Robert T. "From Mafia to Cosa Nostra," *American Journal of Sociology*, vol. 71 (November 1965), pp. 302-310.

D'Amato, Gaetano. "The Black Hand Myth," *North American Review*, v. 187 (April 1908), pp. 543-549.

"Death of Joseph Petrosino," *Current Literature*, v. 46 (1909), pp. 478-480.

Howerth, I. A. "Are the Italians a Dangerous Class?" *Charities Review*, vol. 4 (November 1894).

Ianni, Francis A. J. *A Family Business: Kinship and Social Control in Organized Crime*. New York: Russell Sage Foundation, 1972. [Study of a "Mafia" family.]

Ianni, Francis A. J. "The Mafia and the Web of Kinship," *The Public Interest* (Winter 1971), pp. 78-100. [a major contribution]

Schiavo, Giovanni E. *The Truth about the Mafia and Organized Crime in America*. New York: Vigo Press, 1962.

Talese, Guy. "The Ethics of Frank Costello," *Esquire* (September 1961); also, "Joe Bonanno," *Ibid.* (Aug., Sept., Oct., 1971) ["Joe Bananas"]; also, *Honor Thy Father*. New York: World, 1971.

V. Italian American in the Politico-Economic Context

A. LABOR AND THE PADRONE SYSTEM

Baily, Samuel L. "The Italians and Organized Labor in the United States and Argentina: 1880-1910, *International Migration Review*, vol. I, New Series (Summer 1967), pp. 56-66.

Ciolli, Dominic T. "The 'Wop' in the Track Gang," *Immigrants in America Review*, v. 11 (July 1916), pp. 61-64.

D'Alessandre, John J. "Occupational Trends of Italians in New York City," *Italy-America Monthly*, v. 2 (February 25, 1935), pp. 11-21. *Casa Italiana Educational Bureau*, Bulletin No. 8, 1935.

Fenton, Edwin. "Italians in the Labor Movement," *Pennsylvania History*, v. 26, no. 2 (April 1959), pp. 133-148.

Iorizzo, Luciano J. "The Padrone and Immigrant Distribution," S. M. Tomasi and M. H. Engel, eds., *The Italian Experience in the United States* (Staten Island, N.Y.: Center for Migration Studies, 1970), pp. 43-75.

Lipari, Marie. "The Padrone System: An Aspect of American Economic History," *Italy-America Monthly*, vol. 2 (April 1935), pp. 4-10.

Nelli, Humbert. "The Italian Padrone System in the United States," *Labor History*, vol. 5 (Spring 1964), pp. 153-167.

Odencrantz, Louise C. *Italian Women in Industry: A Study of Conditions in New York City*. New York: Russell Sage Foundation, 1919.

Phipard, Charles B. "The Philanthropist Padrone," *Charities*, v. 12 (May 7, 1904), pp. 470-472.

Speranza, Gino C. "The Italian Foreman as a Social Agent," *Charities*, v. 11 (July 4, 1903), pp. 26-28.

B. POLITICS AND GOVERNMENT

Bone, Hugh A. "Political Parties in New York City," *The American Political Science Review*, April 1946. [Material on Italians in New York City politics.]

Coxe, John E. "The New Orleans Mafia Incident," *Louisiana Historical Quarterly*, v. 20 (1937), pp. 1066-1110. (Bibl. pp. 1109-1110).

Ehrmann, Herbert B. *The Case That Will Not Die: Commonwealth vs. Sacco-Vanzetti*. Boston: Little, Brown, 1969.

Felix, David. *Protest: Sacco-Vanzetti and the Intellectuals*. Bloomington, Indiana: Indiana University Press, 1965.

Karlin, Alexander J. "New Orleans Lynching of 1891 and the American Press," *Louisiana Historical Quarterly*, v. 24 (1941), pp. 187-204.

Mann, Arthur. *LaGuardia Comes to Power, 1933*. Philadelphia: Lippincott, 1965.

Mann, Arthur. *LaGuardia, A Fighter Against His Times, 1882-1933*. Chicago: University of Chicago Press, 1969.

Montgomery, Robert H. *Sacco-Vanzetti—The Murder and the Myth*. New York: Devin, 1960.

Parenti, Michael J. *Ethnic and Political Attitudes—A Depth Study of Italian Americans*. Unpublished doctoral thesis. Yale University, 1962.

Russell, Francis. *Tragedy in Dedham.* New York: McGraw-Hill, 1962. [Sacco-Vanzetti case]

[Sacco-Vanzetti Case] *Transcript of the Record of the Trial of Nicolà Sacco and Bartolomeo Vanzetti in the Courts of Massachusetts.* New York: Henry Holt, 1928-1929.

Schaffer, Alan. *Vito Marcantonio, Radical in Congress.* (Syracuse: Syracuse University Press, 1966). [Originally, Ph.D. dissertation, University of Virginia, 1962]

Speranza, Gino C. "Political Representation of Italo-American Colonies in the Italian Parliament," *Charities,* v. 15 (1906), pp. 521-522.

C. AGRICULTURE (RURAL SETTLEMENT)

Bennet, Alice. "Italians as Farmers and Fruit-Growers," *Outlook,* v. 90, no. 2 (September 12, 1908), pp. 87-88.

Bennet, Alice. "The Italian as a Farmer," *Charities,* v. 21 (October 3, 1908), pp. 57-60.

Meade, Emily F. "The Italian Immigrant on the Land," *Charities,* v. 13 (March 4, 1904), pp. 541-544.

Meade, Emily F. "Italians on the Land," *U.S. Labor Bureau. Bulletin.* No. 14 (May 1907), pp. 473-533. [Hammonton settlement]

Palmer, Hans C. *Italian Immigration and the Development of California Agriculture.* Unpublished doctoral thesis, University of California [Berkeley], 1965.

Pecorini, Alberto. "The Italian as an Agricultural Laborer," *Annals, American Academy of Political and Social Science,* v. 33 (1909), pp. 380-390.

[Rossi, Adolfo.] "Italian Farmers in the South" [An interview with Adolfo Rossi by Gino C. Speranza]. *Charities,* v. 15 (1905), pp. 307-308.

Scott, Charles. "Italian Farmers for Southern Agriculture," *Manufacturers' Record,* v. 48 (November 9, 1905), pp. 423-424.

"Tontitown: An Italian Farming Community," *Service Bureau for Intercultural Education* [New York], Publications (1937).

Tosti, Gustavo. "The Agricultural Possibilities of Italian Immigration," *Charities,* v. 12 (May 7, 1904), pp. 472-476.

Index